MULTIPLE PURPOSE RIVER DEVELOPMENT

MULTIPLE

PURPOSE

Studies in Applied

Published for RESOURCES FOR THE FUTURE, INC.

John V. Krutilla
&
Otto Eckstein

RIVER DEVELOPMENT

Economic Analysis

by THE JOHNS HOPKINS PRESS, *Baltimore*

Standard Book Number (clothbound edition) 8018-0351-9
Standard Book Number (paperback edition) 8018-1091-4

Originally published, 1958
Second printing, 1961
Third printing, 1964
Johns Hopkins Paperbacks edition, 1969

RESOURCES FOR THE FUTURE, INC.

1755 Massachusetts Avenue, N.W., Washington, D.C. 20036

Resources for the Future is a nonprofit corporation for research and education in the development, conservation, and use of natural resources. It was established in 1952 with the co-operation of The Ford Foundation and its activities have been financed by grants from the Foundation. Part of the work of Resources for the Future is carried out by its resident staff, part supported by grants to universities and other non-profit organizations. Unless otherwise stated, interpretations and conclusions in RFF publications are those of the authors; the organization takes responsibility for the selection of significant subjects for study, the competence of the researchers, and their freedom of inquiry.

John V. Krutilla is senior research associate on the RFF staff. Otto Eckstein, Professor of Economics at Harvard University, was a temporary staff member during his collaboration in the study.

The figures were drawn by Clare Ford.

RFF staff editors, Henry Jarrett, Vera W. Dodds, Nora E. Roots, Sheila M. Ekers.

Preface

The problems of multiple purpose river development cut across many disciplines—not only economics with various special fields such as production and value theory, public finance, and welfare economics; but also a number of other major areas, including engineering, geography, and public administration. This study is exclusively economic in viewpoint, although the authors have sought to avoid doing violence to the other disciplines that have a place in analysis of the development of water resources. Also, the authors hope that the application of economic analysis will illuminate the broader aspects of multipurpose development. One of the persistent difficulties in assessing the economic efficiency of particular river basin programs has been the fairly general absence of a meaningful framework for economic analysis of river system development. The first part of this study attempts to sketch out a suitable framework for this purpose, which is then used for analysis of actual cases in the second part of the study.

Our effort has been to select and analyze significant issues against a combined background of experience in the water resources field and professional training in the field of economic analysis. In such an effort, many things will not seem new to the professional economist, and others will be familiar to those experienced in the field of water resources development. At the same time, it is hoped that this combination of experience and training will result in much which is new—or presented in a new perspective—not only to economists and other professionals engaged in the field of water resources, but also to all serious students of issues in this area. In addition, one particular aim has been to prepare useful working material for upper-division or first-year graduate students in applied economics or conservation curricula sponsored by numerous universities for education in the field of natural resources.

John Krutilla is responsible for the outline and general content of the study and primarily responsible for Chapters I through III and Chapters V through IX. Otto Eckstein is principally responsible for Chapter IV, prepared during the summer of 1956 while he was a temporary member of the staff of Resources for the Future. He has also provided helpful comments and assistance on much of the remainder of the manuscript.

The study owes much to Edward A. Ackerman, under whose general direction it was undertaken; to other colleagues in Resources for the Future, principally Irving Fox, Paul Cootner, Henry Jarrett, and Marion Clawson; and to former colleagues and friends of the principal author, John M. Peterson, Rufus B. Hughes, and Vernon Ruttan, for their review and many perceptive comments on an earlier draft of the manuscript. Acknowledgment is also due Professor Arthur Smithies and Professor James Duesenberry for their comments on an earlier draft of Chapter IV.

We are grateful, too, for the assistance of the Project Planning Branch of Tennessee Valley Authority, the Bonneville Power Administration, and the Bureau of Reclamation in connection with material included in Chapter III; to the U. S. Corps of Engineers, the Federal Power Commission, and the Alabama Power Company in connection with material presented in Chapter VI; and to the U. S. Corps of Engineers for the material on which the illustrations in Chapters V through VII were based. For these illustrations as well as the preparation of all the graphical material we are indebted to Miss Clare M. O'Gorman.

Finally, a large measure of gratitude is due Miss Mildred Murphy and Mrs. Nina Brown of the Office of Public Reference, Federal Power Commission, for their cheerful co-operation in providing materials from the public record on the projects serving as cases for study in this volume.

Needless to say, while assistance has been rendered by numerous individuals and organizations, the responsibility for the material included and the conclusions remains exclusively with the authors.

J. V. K.

O. E.

Contents

PART II. APPLYING THE ANALYSIS:
SELECTED CASE STUDIES

LIST OF TABLES

LIST OF FIGURES

Part 1

CONCEPTS AND METHODS

I   Statement of the Problem

The purpose of this study is to help clarify some of the complex problems involved in river basin development. The popular bases for careful analyses have been inadequate; this study seeks to fill, at least partially, the need for more adequate bases. Moreover, on no important issue of natural resources has the discussion been more confused by preconceptions and emotionalism. On the one hand, one hears the epigram: "While the Tennessee River drains the seven Tennessee Valley states, the Tennessee Valley Authority drains the remaining forty-one states of the Union." On the other hand, co-operative arrangements involving private development of the nation's river basins have been likened to "a partnership, wherein the government operates the escalators, drinking fountains, and other such unprofitable appurtenances, while the private partners man the sales counters and cash registers." Neither statement is distinguished for its objective content. Both derive from only one significant issue in the problem of developing the nation's river basins. That issue is the equity considerations involved whenever income is redistributed, as a result either of the raising and spending of governmental funds or the dispensation of privileges for the use of the public's natural resource assets.

A second issue which is not reflected in these statements, and may in fact be relatively neglected, involves the matter of efficiency in developing the nation's water resources as well as the efficient use of public funds. Often these two matters are not clearly distinguished in public debate. Since, theoretically, only the second can be handled with objectivity, the controversy over some aspects of water resources development, even though couched in "efficiency" terms, has often involved a conflict of interests—a conflict on equity considerations, whose relative merits are not technically susceptible of objective evaluation.

There is then a need to spell out quite clearly, as a separate question, the efficiency considerations involved in the development of river basins. In attempting this, we recognize that wherever there is a possibility of governmental intervention to achieve efficiency objectives, or failure to exercise governmental prerogatives in achieving such objectives, there will also be different income distributive consequences, depending upon which course of action has been adopted. Economic analysis can describe the probable income redistributive consequences of each alternative, but it is not equipped to demonstrate objectively which alternative is preferable. Rather, the task of economic analysis is to demonstrate which course of action is the more efficient or economic. These are the two responsibilities which we are willing to assume in this study of multiple purpose river development.

To restate: We will attempt, first, to demonstrate which among several alternatives for development, in any particular case, is the more efficient, that is, which will contribute the most to national income and product. We then will compare the income redistributive consequences of alternatives in a particular situation. In neither instance will we be equipped, as economic analysts, to judge which is the "best" alternative from a "public" standpoint. While our discipline equips us for expertise in the analysis of economic problems, it does not provide us with any expertise in making value judgments or prescribing ethical values.

Characteristics of River Basin Development Programs

The development of water resources has involved a combination of efforts by both public and private enterprise. It is thus traditionally distinguished from the bulk of economic activities in a free enterprise economy. An understanding of the reasons for the mixture of private and public activity in the development of our rivers is a necessary forerunner to a critical examination of the ways by which such development can be undertaken. A variety of approaches has been used and, more recently, proposed in response to different and changing conditions. And in understanding what combination of circumstances characterize river basin development, a more dispassionate attitude, or even a more inventive approach, may commend itself for meeting the essential problems involved.

Basic to an understanding of the elements involved in the development of our streams is a clear perception of the nature and forms of the development itself, the raw materials with which a development program has to work, and the purposes to be met.

Water is required directly for human consumption. It is used indirectly when it enters agricultural produce as an element of growth and maturation, or in processing foods and making beverages. Water enters into many processes in the manufacture of commodities which are employed as productive factors in a variety of economic activities.

But direct and indirect requirements for human consumption do not exhaust the productive uses which the water resource may serve. Historically, water has served as a low-resistance medium on which to transport cargoes. It has served man as a means of disposing wastes from towns and cities. It has served as a habitat for wildlife on which man has fed and, more recently, hunted for sport. Water has provided the setting, in many cases for gratification of aesthetic and recreational needs.

Water resources have also served as a form of mechanical power: first, to liberate man from reliance on human and animal energy in early industrialization; later, as an input in operation of mechanical steam engines; and, finally, at the present stage of the industrial arts, either as mechanical power or steam to move turbines in the production of electricity.

Water's influence on human life has not always been beneficial; the uncontrolled river has potentialities of great destructive power. Nature is impervious to the ephemeral needs of man. In her grand design, the delicate balance—if indeed one is achieved—works out majestically in units of time and distance which afford cold comfort to the tillers of the soil in alluvial deltas, and the tenders of the shops on mainstreets in the flood plains, during the periods of extended drought or destructive floods which make up the pattern of the grand design. Even if nature had programmed her activities to conform more nearly to the schedule required by residents of flood plains, the water resources with which she had endowed them would not have been in the form needed for beneficial uses. This becomes apparent when we examine more closely some of the physical elements of a river basin and its resources.

Consider as a hypothetical example, Grand Basin, envisaged as a large valley encompassing thousands of square miles and inhabited by several million people. It is an elongated basin bordered on all sides by mountainous terrain, rising to elevations of several thousand feet. Rainfall and melting snow in the many mountain coves and valleys provide the runoff which becomes small brooks initially; these join to form creeks, and finally become tributary streams of the two main stems of rivers rising at each end of the valley. The rivers meander from each end of the valley floor toward a low area in the middle where they join, forming a substantial alluvial delta. Eventually, they escape to the sea through a gap in the coastal range. Precipitation on the outer side of the coastal ranges collects into substantial streams draining the watershed outside the rim of Grand Basin, but these, moving directly toward the sea, are beyond the immediate reach of the residents of the valley.

Precipitation on the valley floor at one end of the basin is moderate, increasing to very heavy in the mountains. At the other end of the basin, average precipitation shades off to very little on the valley floor, but increases to moderate in the mountains. This geographic distribution is especially ungenerous from the standpoint of valley residents, as the humid area having most of the water has but a small fraction of the arable land, whereas the arid section—where nearly all agricultural production requires irrigation—contains the preponderant share of the arable land and the majority of the population.

Moreover, the seasonal distribution of precipitation does not coincide with seasonal requirements. While little precipitation occurs in the summer months when crops are growing, heavy runoff from mountain areas during the winter and early spring often produces disastrous floods. Irregularity in the precipitation on the basin's watersheds is not only seasonal, but also cyclical. Average runoff during years of abnormally high precipitation is more than double that during dry phases. Thus the inhabitants of Grand Basin, with a regular need for water from year to year and seasonal peak requirements, are plagued by maldistribution of water resources—seasonally, annually, and geographically.

Given natural conditions of this kind, the original settlers of Grand Basin attempted to adapt the undeveloped water resources to their particular needs. As settlement progressed, successive generations relied on the conservational and developmental techniques appropriate to the time. In the early period of settlement, this took the form of stream diversions to irrigate fertile land within reach and appropriately located with respect to stream elevation. Such undertakings in many, if not all, cases could be achieved by settlers individually. Investment in these activities did not employ the financial markets. Diversion structures represented essentially an investment of time and labor, and of materials available with the expenditure also of time and effort. This does not imply that the undertakings were without cost, for the investments were made at the expense of current consumption which would have been possible in greater degree had time, effort, and materials been applied directly toward ministering to immediate wants.

The settlement of the basin continued; growing communities required water for domestic needs, industrial purposes, and disposal of community wastes; the demand for energy expanded. Increasing volumes of agricultural produce and timber rafted down the rivers suggested to enterprising elements in the valley the potential feasibility of power-driven river craft. The contrivances that had transformed a small portion of the productive potential of the basin's streams to beneficial uses during the previous generations proved inadequate. Central water supplies, developed by impounding surplus flows in retention basins for release during seasonally deficit periods, supplanted the cruder diversion structures. Larger reservoirs located in the more distant mountains, and canals to convey the increased regular supplies of water, were built to extend the distribution of water to areas previously having no access to surface sources of supply.

A proliferation of new institutional devices developed in response to the needs of the valley residents. New enterprises—private irrigation, canal, power, and water companies and public irrigation, water improvement, and conservancy districts—were launched during this period, either to develop sources of supply, or to distribute to local consumers the supplies developed by others. The capital markets were employed to raise necessary funds for these ventures; stock companies issued equity securities as well as debt instruments. Mutual companies were tried, found to be inflexible, and abandoned. Most speculative stock companies failed; few survived bankruptcy and reorganization. The public district device, enjoying quasi-governmental powers to levy assessments against district residents for repayment of financial obligations, emerged as the more stable institutional arrangement for the purpose. Extensive use of the district form of organization, with general obligation bonds, supplied the major part of the developmental capital during this phase of development.

Yet, while the practicable limit of such localized development was approaching, no evidence suggested that requirements for water would cease to grow. Residents at the arid end of the basin were becoming acutely aware of their deficient sources of supply and conscious of the large and often destructive surpluses from the other end which escaped to the sea unused.

The basin entered a dry phase at this point of its development. Even in the upper basin, where seasonal surpluses accrued, stream-bank pumping during the dry season for supplemental irrigation and diversions reduced downstream flows measurably. Pollution concentrations became high as stream flows declined. In the delta area, saline waters from the sea began intruding many miles upstream, reaching concentrations high enough to destroy the productive potential of many acres of agricultural lands and to threaten even larger areas. Pumping from subsurface aquifers reduced water tables in some areas at an alarming rate. In some localities, aquifers more than a thousand feet below the surface had to be tapped to supply water required to sustain the production on which a large portion of the population depended.

Local development programs proved inadequate for meeting problems arising under these circumstances. There was recognition that an integrated approach transcending local levels of jurisdiction was necessary to redress the imbalance. Equilibrium in the basin's supplies and requirements might require long-distance transfers of water from surplus to deficit areas; the capture of flood flows during the wet phase to replenish subsurface storage depleted during the dry phases; and co-ordinated releases from surface storage to generate power and to maintain flows in established stream beds for abating pollution, providing minimum channel depths for waterway transport, and repelling the intrusion of salinity at the river mouth. A water resources development plan equal to such a task might require extensive multiple purpose reservoirs in mountainous terrain where adequate storage could be developed at minimum costs. Power installations might be included to utilize mechanical energy coincident with water releases to serve other joint purposes. Moreover, the plan might conceivably include an interconnected canal system, as well as storage pools to permit water exchanges among different sections of the basin and to exploit non-coincident peak requirements seasonally and geographically. Complementary facilities would have to be used to distribute the projects' output to ultimate users. Existing local distribution systems could be utilized to distribute project outputs—whether irrigation water to supplement existing inadequate sources, or power to service increased consumption of existing but growing communities. A host of new distribution systems, however, might have to be organized, financed, and launched to serve the new areas brought into productive uses and settled over time. Reservoir areas might be exploited feasibly to provide recreational facilities for the urban areas of the basin; and programs in the tributary watersheds might be needed to prevent soil erosion, and thus protect reservoirs against sedimentation.

An integrated plan of these dimensions would differ radically, in a number of significant respects, from previous locally sponsored efforts. Technically, it represented a higher order of interdependent system. Local supply and distribution systems, up to this point, had restricted themselves to exploiting the possibilities in single segments of the basin's total water potential. Pooling the network of streams into an integrated system, and combining ground and surface water management as an integral part of the plan for water development, would add enormously to the technical possibilities for development and exploitation.

Large-scale economies are suggested by integration into a single system. Storage facilities required to accomplish any one of a number of separate purposes can be used to achieve equally well other common purposes. Capacity to impound water for agricultural, industrial, and residential requirements during seasonal surpluses can protect agricultural lands, industrial sites, and residential areas in the flood plain. Water released for navigation purposes during seasonally dry periods also can abate pollution and salinity intrusion.

Although technically and economically the integrated water development plan for Grand Basin represented an advance in conception, the institutional machinery for carrying it out was not readily at hand. Given the physical, economic, and institutional factors involved, the reasons for the difficulty in implementation are not difficult to understand. First, none of the public enterprises established for developing water resources was empowered by its charter, nor equipped by its organizational structure, to undertake a development task which would be sufficiently comprehensive to serve the residents in territories other than the one for which its charter was granted. No well-defined channels of communication, nor machinery for reaching and executing decisions, existed through which local groups, individuals, or communities could reach agreement and act upon it. Second, and perhaps equally significant, much of the benefit from the development of such water supplies would be freely available to both private and public groups unless the agency entrusted with the development enjoyed the coercive powers of government to levy assessments against the beneficiaries. Unless such powers were available, or machinery existed for transfer of income from general tax revenues to defray developmental expenses, development probably would not be financially feasible.

The advantages of the private corporate structure in reaching and implementing decisions would be largely irrelevant, principally for the second of the two reasons just mentioned. The feasibility of the private undertaking would depend on the ability to control access to its services—that is, to make enjoyment of the benefits from any private undertaking contingent on payment of some price. No privately organized venture intending to remain solvent could undertake the integrated development foreseen for the basin without concluding agreements in advance with potential beneficiaries to obtain compensation for the developmental costs. Since many of these beneficiaries would not materialize until further settlement occurred following development, the bargaining position of the developer would be hopelessly compromised. (There are other basic difficulties, but their demonstration will be part of the larger effort to which the study is addressed.)

The features of the developmental programs outlined for Grand Basin, of course, are not representative of every river basin in the country. But neither are they unique. A number of the fundamental problems involving efficiency that are implied in our hypothetical example will recur in much the same forms wherever multiple purpose development is involved. And where the solution of problems in the most efficient manner will require the intervention of a public body, the issues of equity as well as efficiency in the use of public funds—or in the distribution of program benefits —will reappear as equally vital considerations.

Objectives of the Study

Implicit in what we have said so far is the notion that the development of multiple purpose and integrated systems is dictated by efficiency considerations. In fact, this is commonly alleged and we have based our description of the characteristics of river basin development on this assumption. We have not demonstrated this to be the case, however; nor have we, as yet, defined in any precise way our understanding of what is meant by economic efficiency.

A preliminary task, therefore, must be to define the concept analytically. After this is done, we can reconsider the nature of a development program in the light of a more precise understanding of the concept of efficiency. We should then be able to satisfy ourselves by means of analysis as to whether or not efficiency considerations in river basin development require a different approach from that generally encountered in other sectors of a free market economy. If by taking this route we can come to conclusions dispassionately, we may succeed in reducing the emotional content of the reaction to the equity considerations posed in river basin development. At least, we can make explicit what is involved by way of efficiency. An unlimited range of possibilities may be open if no restraints are imposed. If we value efficiency highly, however, a decidedly narrower range of possible alternatives may remain. We may be able to isolate the obstacles to efficient river basin development and the changes in the institutional environment which would open additional opportunities for efficient development. Once this is done, the range of choice among alternatives of equal efficiency may be widened. Our first general objective, accordingly, is to spell out what we mean by efficiency, to define the special problems that arise in this connection in the field of river basin development, and to touch upon the conditions that must be satisfied, or criteria that must be met, to ensure our attaining the desired efficiency goals.

We hope to do all this without becoming involved, at the time, in equity considerations, even though we recognize that different ways of doing things may well involve a different distribution of the benefits and incidence of costs. After we have addressed the efficiency problems, the substance of the equity issue can command our explicit attention. We shall want to analyze objectively the differences involved in the distribution of income, depending on which of several alternatives is employed in obtaining efficient water resource development. We leave to the political process in our representative government the problem of distilling a consensus as to which among the several income distributive consequences is most consistent with the prevailing set of ethical values.

There are some self-imposed limitations on the scope of this study. First, we have confined ourselves to only a limited set of the total gamut of problems involved in water resources development. Since some of the major problems and the most significant issues arise in connection with multiple purpose river basin projects, we have concentrated on them. In doing so, we have neglected many other significant topics—as, for example, land-treatment programs in tributary watersheds or, somewhat further removed, the problems arising out of weather modification or utilization of saline waters.

In still another sense have we restricted the scope of the study. Equally as important as the efficiency and equity considerations involved, no doubt, are those concerning the most appropriate form of organization or instrumentality for the achievement of goals of water resources development. In many ways, prescribing the form of organization most appropriate for achieving efficiency goals, within restraints imposed by equity considerations, may be a less analytical task; but, also in many ways, it is beyond the grasp of a single discipline. It is for others—the experienced public administrators, the political scientists, the practitioners of the art of politics, and the electorate; in short, the architects of our social institutions—to design the institutional arrangements most appropriate for river basin development needs. We trust, however, that our effort will have utility in pointing up possibilities for institutional modifications which may serve efficiency as well as other values.

While it should become quite apparent what this study intends to do, it may not be as evident what it is not equipped to do. We recognize that in our society efficiency is a value to which a great deal of importance attaches. We also recognize that efficiency is not the only, and perhaps not the dominant, value; in a study of comparative efficiency among alternative courses of action, considerations of equity are also involved. But in a broader sense still, we recognize that there may be higher criteria than efficiency criteria. That is, river basin programs may be undertaken to increase the national product (consistent with efficiency considerations), but also may be undertaken for strategic, social, and perhaps other objectives, which may not be compatible with maximum efficiency in terms of the relatively narrow definition of efficiency employed in this study. Where projects are undertaken for the latter type of goals, there will be a smaller net economic gain than otherwise would be possible—national income will be smaller than if conditions of maximum efficiency were to prevail. This is not meant to imply that such objectives are unworthy, and that our efficiency considerations provide the preferable course of action. Social, strategic, and other objectives may be preferred, and may be undertaken with the sanction of collective choice expressed through the political process in a representative government. Even so, it does not follow that our efficiency criteria will be of no practical value for determining a course of action when higher criteria prevail. Efficiency criteria, even here, have a relevance in their ability to demonstrate the economic costs which society will incur—something which we feel is not always made explicit—when it decides upon a course of action based on such higher criteria.

Plan of the Study

A major portion of our effort is devoted to defining the conditions for achieving economic efficiency, isolating the circumstances which make water resources a "special case" among sectors of the free market economy, and determining, on the basis of this analysis, what general alternatives are open for achieving efficiency within our institutional environment. This task is undertaken principally in Chapter II, where we present the analytical framework used to define the conditions required for economic efficiency, and Chapter III, where we take another look at the river basin development problem, with the added perspective obtained from the efficiency concepts developed in the process. At this point, we conclude that to achieve efficiency through exclusive reliance on the market mechanism would require an unacceptable degree of concentration of economic power, whether public or private. This is a value judgment, of course; but it represents a distillation of a national consensus as indicated by public policy with respect to private monopoly and a tradition of antipathy to the concentration of such powers in a political institution. We then decide that the alternative is to rely on the intervention of representative government in a democracy, a decision which mirrors the tradition in this country's water resource development activities. A public body, however, has access to revenues arising out of its coercive powers to tax. Therefore, in Chapter IV, we analyze the social cost of tax-raised revenue to round out our efficiency criteria.

Chapters II through IV, dealing predominantly with the nature of the economic gains and costs of multiple purpose river basin development, provide the basis for analyzing a number of cases which add to our understanding of efficient ways of developing multiple purpose projects. Chapter V considers some significant problems which arise from circumstances akin to those represented by the development alternatives for Hells Canyon on the Snake River. In Chapter VI, we take up the Alabama-Coosa River development—where problems of the sort arising in the Hells Canyon case are not present owing to certain differences in economic magnitudes, but where issues of equity intrude strongly in spite of our main preoccupation with questions of efficiency.

Next, we look into the income redistributive consequences when different approaches promising relatively equal efficiency are considered. That is, we take the case of a hypothetical site in the Willamette River Basin where the amount of economic gains and costs will be approximately equal as among alternative approaches to the development of the site. The distribution of the gains and costs, however, will differ significantly depending upon which of several alternatives is assumed to be adopted. In Chapter VII, we describe the distribution of costs in a particular case wherein differences in economic efficiency appear to be of negligible significance. In Chapter VIII, we treat similarly the distribution of gains.

Finally, in the concluding chapter, we present the principal points established in the course of our investigation, and suggest their implications for policy in the water resources field.

II The Concept of

Economic Efficiency:

A THEORY OF EFFICIENT

RESOURCE ALLOCATION

This study is rooted in the belief that a large measure of objective analysis is possible, even in those areas of the water development field where controversy has eroded the common ground for fruitful discussion. But if a more dispassionate approach is to be accepted, its rationale must be presented clearly and precisely. Therefore, although this study is primarily concerned with specific problems of evaluating alternative approaches to multiple purpose river development, it must begin with a set of fundamental concepts of a fairly general nature. The most important of these, for the purpose of this book, is the concept of efficiency.

Efficiency may be regarded as the relationship between the quantity of input and the amount of resulting output. The larger the output per unit of input, the greater the efficiency of a process. This simple proposition, however, may not tell much in a practical situation. For example, a garden plot may support peach trees, rows of poppies, garden vegetables, guinea fowl, thistles, or an environment to inspire poets. Output from the garden plot, accordingly, may be defined in a number of ways: a ton of thistle per unit of plant nutrient, the number of vases of peach blossoms per acre of land, and so on. Any other one or combination of items of output per unit of any one or combination of inputs could be used to define *technical* efficiency relationships. As another example, consider a steam electric plant where the output in a physical sense consists of a certain volume of stack gasses, some smoke, ashes, exhaust heat, steam, and, of course, some electricity. In speaking of thermal efficiency of steam electric stations, the relationship is conventionally expressed as the heat rate (such as 9,000 Btu's per kilowatt-hour of electricity), and the proportion of heat output (3,413 Btu's per kilowatt-hour) to total heat input, as the per cent thermal efficiency. But there are other technical relationships. Under certain circumstances, it might be the better part of economic wisdom to maximize output of exhaust steam (thereby reducing the input of cooling water); then the desired efficiency relationship would be expressed differently. Other technical relationships—as, for example, between output of electricity and input of labor or capital—would have perfectly reasonable efficiency measures involving inputs other than fuel. In short, given the output to be maximized per unit of input (also given), the input-output relationship for measuring technical efficiency can be specified. Now this kind of relationship may be very useful as a means of defining technical performance levels for analysis of numerous engineering problems, but it does not convey directly the concept of efficiency with which this study is concerned.

The concept of economic efficiency for a free society must include some notion of maximizing the output of those items most preferred by the members of the community per unit of input of those resources which are relatively the more scarce. That is, beginning with the preferences of individuals making up a free society, our concept of economic efficiency will require for any given resource endowment and state of technological knowledge, the maximum level of the preferred composition of output. The concept of *economic* efficiency, therefore, does not ignore the problem of *technical* efficiency. But it does require that an element of rationality be employed in specifying what technical relationships are most relevant for the purpose of providing those goods and services relatively the more preferred by the community.

Economic efficiency, accordingly, is defined as a situation in which productive resources are so allocated among alternative uses that any reshuffling from the pattern cannot improve any individual's position and still leave all other individuals as well off as before. Of course, any change in the pattern of resource employment may improve the conditions of some people, but if this is done at the expense of others it may be only a redistribution of income. Income redistribution may be justified on various ethical grounds. But the reorganization can be regarded as more efficient only when those whose positions have been improved by the changes have gained more than enough to compensate the losses suffered by others. Economic efficiency implies that, given his income, every individual will allocate his expenditures in such a way as to maximize his satisfaction. It implies also that, given the demand for the resulting goods and services, productive resources will be so employed that no reallocation could achieve the same level and composition of output with a smaller expenditure of resources. When these conditions are fulfilled, the economy is operating with maximum efficiency.

The economy is a very complex organism, whose general efficiency must be inferred from conditions which exist throughout its various sectors. Our first task is to review the conditions required if efficiency is to prevail in each sector; this will provide the set of criteria needed later. We shall present in this chapter an overly simplified analog of the market economy, so that we can specify the necessary conditions as a matter of first approximation. This will provide a frame of reference which, while unrealistic standing alone, can be modified later in more detailed examination of applications in the instances relevant to this study. Next some of the fundamental qualifications of the model are reviewed to provide the basis for modifying the first approximation of efficiency criteria in order to achieve economic efficiency under actual conditions. We shall select from among the numerous qualifications of our theory of resource allocation those which appear most significant for the questions posed by analysis of multiple purpose river basin development.

Market Mechanics and Efficiency Criteria in a Perfectly Competitive Economy [1]

Economists from the time of Adam Smith have worked with an analog of the economic system which suppresses many details in presenting a first impression of the principles involved in "economizing." This analog is referred to as the economists' competitive model, and it represents a convenient starting point in understanding the forces at work in a competitive market economy.[2] Use of the model as an expository device does not imply that it faithfully represents the workings of the economic system. It helps, however, in understanding the conditions which represent economic efficiency, economic utilization of society's resources, etc., and thereby provides a basis for finally defining more realistic criteria for evaluating the efficiency of alternative undertakings.

Central to the framework of the model is the underlying belief that in democratic societies the economy and its institutions should serve the needs of its members, and that the members are themselves best qualified to determine their needs and desires. This is the rationale behind the phrase "consumer sovereignty." The efficiency with which an economy operates in a democratic society, in fact, is evaluated partly in terms of how well the system permits the organization of production and distribution to conform with individual preferences. This assumes that individuals have consistent preferences, and behave rationally in indulging them. That is, given a choice, the alternative yielding the greater satisfaction for consumers or profits for producers will be consistently preferred over the alternative yielding lesser satisfaction or profit. For example, if two market baskets contained the same number of all items except one, an individual is assumed to select the basket with the larger number of the single item. This, of course, might not be true if his rate of consumption of the item had reached a point of satiety. And this possibility suggests an empirical element of the model: that consumption of successive units of any item during a specified consumption period yield a diminishing marginal satisfaction.

Finally, in this model, markets are assumed to be perfectly com-

resource allocation and others who may be impatient with detail, the presentation is summarized even more briefly at the end of this section (pages 40-41). The body of the section, therefore, may be skipped without loss of continuity by those who prefer to do so.

[2] Our schematic presentation of the competitive model is an overly simple summary of the detail in which the model can be elaborated. For one of the best elaborated treatments of the competitive model, see Tibor Scitovsky, *Welfare and Competition* (Chicago: Richard D. Irwin, Inc., 1951), pp. 3-188.

petitive. That is, there is a relatively large number of buyers and sellers on each side of every market. The exact number is not relevant so long as no buyer or seller is so large that his purchase or sale will effect the price of the product or factor which he exchanges. Hence, every buyer or seller is a "price taker"; he accepts the price which prevails in the market and organizes his economic activities in response to market prices.

THE PRODUCT MARKET

It is a basic postulate that institutions in a democratic community exist for the individual. Beginning with the individual then, how do we define maximum satisfaction for the consumer? There are three elements to the problem: (a) the consumer's preferences, (b) his consumption budget, and (c) the prices which prevail in the product market.

To simplify the exposition of consumer preferences, consider a case where there are only two commodities on which the consumer will spend his entire budget. In this instance, his preference is measured in terms of his relative valuation of two commodities. Take, for example, a given combination of commodities A and B which will provide a level of satisfaction shown by point h on the line I_0 of Figure 1. Line I_0 is so drawn as to reveal all of the possible combinations of A and B which would provide the same level of satisfaction, and is therefore referred to as an "indifference curve." So far as his satisfaction is concerned, the consumer will be indifferent as to which of the possible alternative combinations is provided. This curve, in effect, represents the consumer's valuation of one commodity in terms of the other, and reflects varying amounts of one commodity which must be substituted for the other at different points along the curve to maintain the same level of satisfaction. The rate at which a consumer can substitute small quantities of one commodity for another while maintaining the same level of satisfaction is referred to as his marginal rate of substitution between the commodities.

Corresponding to I_0 there will be other indifference curves, such as I_1, I_2, and so on, each depicting combinations of the two commodities which would leave the consumer at a constant level of satisfaction. These successive curves represent higher levels of satisfaction, consistent with the proposition that a greater quantity

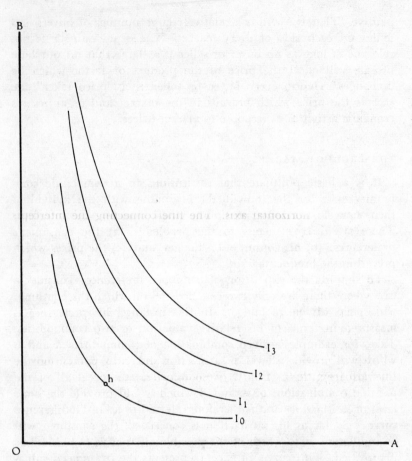

FIGURE 1. *The Consumer's Preference Map*

of a desired commodity is to be preferred over a smaller quantity.[3]
Such a set of indifference curves for two commodities represents a
consumer's preference map that can be inferred from his market
behavior. Doubtless, each consumer will have many commodities

---

[3] For a more detailed description of the properties and construction of indifference curves, the interested reader may consult a standard economics text. Two
excellent texts of this kind are Scitovsky's *Welfare and Competition, ibid.;* and
Erich Schneider's *Pricing and Equilibrium* (T. W. Hutchison translation; New
York: The Macmillan Company, 1952).

from which he will choose, and a preference map involving the larger number, in principle, could also be inferred.[4]

The second element of the problem involves the amount which the consumer budgets for consumption items. This can be shown on a diagram similar to Figure 1, but including a third element— the prices of the two commodities. For example, assume a price for commodity B of P_b and an expenditure budget of M. If the consumer were to spend his entire budget on B, the amount of the commodity which could be purchased would be represented by a distance along the vertical scale, shown on Figure 2 as M/P_b. Similarly the amount of commodity A which could be bought, were the entire budget allocated to A, would be represented by M/P_a, shown on the horizontal axis. The line connecting the intercepts on the two axes can be called the budget line. It reveals all the various combinations of A and B which can be obtained with a given expenditure, M, given the prices of A, P_a and B, P_b. The slope of the line is determined by the relative prices of A and B, i.e, b/a is equal to P_a/P_b.

Given his preferences (Figure 1), and his expenditure budget and the prices ruling in the market (Figure 2), how will the consumer allocate expenditures between the two commodities so as to maximize his satisfaction? Since indifference curves moving outward from the origin (0) of Figure 3 represent higher levels of satisfaction, the most efficient combination of A and B that can be obtained with a given expenditure is one in which the budget line just reaches an indifference curve as shown by J on I_1. A position on higher indifference curves (I_2, and I_3) is unattainable, given the budget, whereas it would be irrational for the consumer to select a position on lower indifference curves, such as I_0.

A line tangent to a curve expresses the slope of the curve at that point. It follows then that the slope of the budget line, expressed as the ratio of the prices of A and B (P_a/P_b), is equal to the slope of the indifference curve at the point of tangency—and the slope of the indifference curve, in turn, is expressed as the marginal rate

[4] For a generalized statement involving *n* commodities, a mathematical demonstration can be found in Paul Samuelson's *Foundations of Economic Analysis* (Cambridge: Harvard University Press, 1953), Chapter v; and Herman Wold and Lars Jureen's *Demand Analysis*, (New York: John Wiley and Sons, Inc., 1953), Chapter iv.

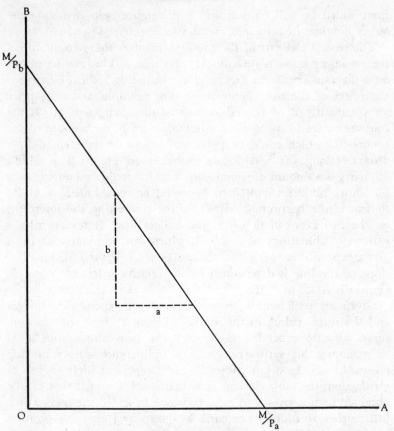

FIGURE 2. *The Consumer's Budget Line*

of substitution between A and B. An efficient allocation of the consumer's budget, then, will require that the marginal rate of substitution between two commodities used by the consumer is equal to the ratio of their prices.

In perfectly competitive markets, with only one price for any commodity,[5] it follows that the marginal rate of substitution between any two commodities must be the same for all consumers using both. This distribution by the competitive pricing system,

[5] Unless all units of a commodity are exchanged for the same price, purchases at below-equilibrium prices for resale at higher prices will bring all sales prices to an equilibrium. See Eugene V. Bohm-Bawerk, *The Positive Theory of Capital* (William Smart translation; New York: G. E. Stredhert & Co.), Book IV, Chapter IV.

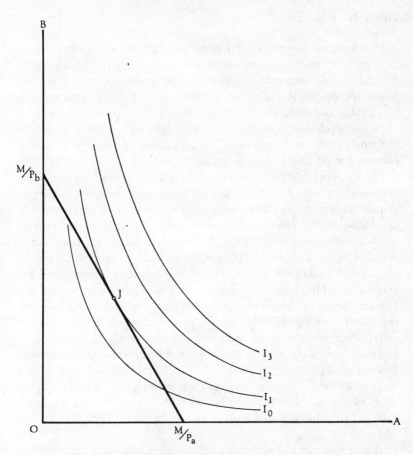

FIGURE 3. *The Consumer's Preferred Combination of Goods*

therefore, is regarded as the most efficient one since no exchanges among consumers could improve any individual's position and still permit others to remain as well off as before.

Thus far, both the expenditure budget and the total output to be distributed have been taken as given. How these are determined are legitimate questions. Let us begin with the consumer's budget. How much a consumer will spend for consumption purposes will depend partly on the amount of his income and partly on his time preference—on whether his expenditures are strongly influenced by current consumption needs or by his anticipated future requirements.

THE LABOR MARKET

Inheritances, possession of income-earning assets acquired out of past income, and other sources account for part of the aggregate income of consumers, but such problems as these can be taken up more appropriately later in the treatment of the capital market. It can be assumed, at this stage, that the consumer's income is obtained exclusively in the form of wages and salaries in return for work performed, and that the allocation of work in a market economy is performed by the labor market.

From a worker's point of view, the market provides given wage rates for any occupation. A worker is assumed to be at liberty to choose among occupations, balancing the costs and gains of each, according to his personal circumstances. The size of his income will depend on the number of hours he elects to work. The number of hours worked, in turn, is assumed to be determined by the worker's marginal valuation of his productive services and the wage rate. The longer the hours worked during any period, the greater becomes his marginal valuation of leisure. Thus, the individual worker will be in his preferred work-leisure position only when his marginal valuation of his productive services is equal to the wage rate prevailing in the market. Hours worked beyond that point are valued higher as leisure than the prevailing wage rate, and therefore will not be undertaken. Hours worked short of the equality between his marginal valuation and the wage rate provide leisure which does not compensate him for the loss of income.

While the rates of hire in alternative occupations are given to the individual, they are not fixed from the community's viewpoint. That is, the productive services which the community of consumers prefer to have performed, as revealed through their expenditures for commodities, must be reconciled with the job preferences of workers. These preferences in the aggregate, *at some structure of relative wages among occupations,* may not correspond to the requirements of the community. From the community point of view, however, there would be a constellation of wage rates for the various occupations which would elicit exactly the amount of each type of work that is preferred. This appears likely since, for any worker with a given order of occupational preferences, there would be a rate of hire for each alternative which would just induce him to change occupations. Within any occupation, there would be workers with different transfer prices, and the wage rate would have to equal the transfer price of the marginal worker to retain in the occupation the number the community prefers.

In summary, in a perfectly competitive labor market there is only one wage rate for any particular kind of work, and individual workers do not influence the rate. The individual worker is assumed to vary the amount of work offered at given wage rates to determine the amount of his income. Being free to do this, taking account of his marginal valuation of income and leisure, he can reach his preferred position. If there is a wage rate that will elicit precisely the amount of work of a particular kind preferred by the community, such a single rate will distribute work efficiently among workers in that particular occupation. Furthermore, if there is freedom of occupational choice, workers will specialize at tasks which reflect their preferences as given by relative earnings and the burdens of work in the alternatives open to them. And finally, competitive market forces establish the relationship of earnings among occupations by adjustments in the relative rates of hire in order to allocate the total work among occupations consistent with the consumers' preferences.

MARKET ADJUSTMENTS BY ENTERPRISES

Our explanation of the distribution of products and allocation of work by the market mechanism took the individual as the focal point, because to meet conditions consistent with individuals' preferences is a requirement of economic efficiency. In modern industrial societies, however, there are many stages in the process of transforming resources into final goods. At these, action is taken by enterprises that occupy a place between the individual in his role of seller of personal services and his role as buyer of consumer goods. The conditions which define efficiency in such enterprises, however, are considerably more complex than in the case of allocating work among individuals or distributing final products. Efficiency in this section involves two considerations—given the resources at the disposal of the community, output must be at a maximum, subject to conformance with consumers' preferences.

To describe the efficiency conditions that must be met by enterprises, we begin with some simplifying assumptions. First, we assume that the capital stock is fixed—that is, the plant and equipment with which the enterprises have to work cannot be altered during the time period under consideration. The main reason for this is to facilitate exposition, although it is noteworthy that changes in the capital stock are basically investment phenomena, which are taken up more systematically in our discussion of the market for investment capital. Second, as a counterpart of the assumption that consumers rationally seek maximum satisfaction, we assume that producers seek maximum profits. Finally, since we are employing the economists' competitive model, we assume that every producer is a price taker in the market, both when he buys his factors and sells his product.

As a groundwork for understanding the conditions of efficient factor allocation, it is necessary to examine some purely physical relationships. The first of these is what the economists call the producer's "production function." The term "function" in this context has a specialized meaning, being used in its mathematical sense. That is, the producer's output is a function of (varies with) the input of factors. Consider, for example, the operation of a farm which under natural conditions is handicapped by infertile soil and less than adequate moisture. Given the acreage, the soil cultivation, and seed, a given output can be assumed to be attainable, either by employing additional fertilizer or more water— physical inadequacies being limiting factors in both cases. Let us assume that by addition of an acre-foot of water the physical yield can be increased from 40 to 60 bushels of corn per year. Alternatively, the 20 additional bushels could have been achieved by increasing the input of fertilizer by a ton per acre. Of course, increasing both water and fertilizer by the stated amounts would probably increase output by a good deal more than 20 bushels. But the assumption here is that if a given yield is sought, it can be achieved by employing more water alone, more fertilizer alone, or some combination of the two.

There are, thus, two characteristics of the production function which we wish to develop somewhat more precisely—the substitutability of factors, or the different proportions in which factors can combine to achieve a given output; and the characteristics of scale, or variation in the level of output related to changes in total inputs. This, perhaps, can be illustrated better by use of diagrams.

In Figure 4, the input of two factors, X and Y, is measured along the horizontal and vertical axes. The output produced by employing the two factors in some combination is represented by the contour lines Z_0, Z_1, Z_2, and Z_3. Any point along a given contour represents a constant level of output and, in this sense, these constant product curves are not unlike the indifference curves of Figures 1 and 3. For example, an input of Ox_0 of factor X and Oy_0 of factor Y would produce an output equivalent to Z_0 in the vicinity of point J. Now an addition of one unit of X, the input of Y remaining as before, would increase output to the level of Z_1 in the vicinity of K. Alternatively, decreasing X to the original amount (Ox_0) and increasing the input of Y by a unit would increase output to Z_1 in the vicinity of L. In short, a substitution between a unit of X and Y would produce the same level of output using the two factors combined in different proportions. However, unless the two factors were perfect substitutes (a condition incompatible with their being "different" factors), the marginal rate of substitution at any point necessary to maintain total product constant would vary with changes in the proportions in which the two factors were used. This phenomenon of diminishing marginal rate of substitution between factors accounts for the convexity of the constant product curves.

The second characteristic of the production function also can be shown in Figure 4. Although the output can be increased from Z_0 in the vicinity of J to Z_1 by the increment of a unit input of either X or Y, it can be increased beyond Z_1 by a unit increase in both factors—that is, from Z_0 at J to Z_1 at K by a unit increase in factor X, and from Z_1 at K to Z_2' at M by an increase of a unit of Y. If we assume, however, that factor Y happens to be fixed and that all additions to output must be achieved by changes in the input of X alone, output can be increased from Z_0 in the vicinity of J to Z_1 at K and Z_2 at N, etc., only by more than proportional increases in the input of factor X.

This can be observed better perhaps in a diagram commonly used to illustrate the "law of diminishing returns." In Figure 5, factor X and output Z are measured, respectively, along the horizontal and vertical axes. Diagonal movements from the origin upward and to the right correspond to the movement from positions such as J, K, and N, on the constant product curves Z_0, Z_1, and Z_2 of Figure 4, when the input of Y is held constant at Oy_0 while the inputs of factor X are increased. The change in total output per unit increase in factor X is defined as the marginal physical product of X, or its marginal productivity. Conversely, the amount of X which is required to increase output by one unit

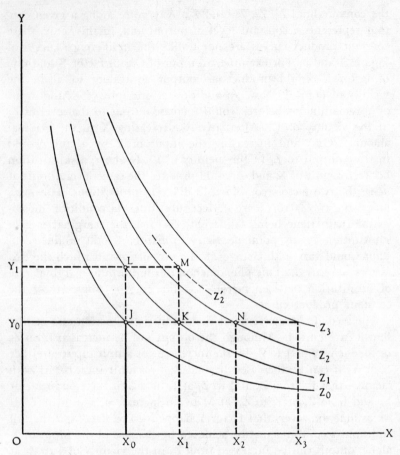

FIGURE 4. *The Production Function*

is called the marginal input, and this is seen to be the reciprocal of the input-output relationship which defines marginal productivity.

It is apparent from Figure 5 that, if the input of factor Y is held constant, beyond a certain point within the range of diminishing marginal productivity, increasingly larger marginal inputs of X are required to raise output by an additional unit. The concept of the diminishing marginal productivity of a factor can perhaps be made clearer by a concrete example. Let us employ the farm enterprise again, but this time assume that all factors other than water are held constant and increase in production is sought solely by means of water application. A total absence of water would prevent the seed from germinating and the inorganic salts in the fertilizer from dissolving. A minimum rate of application of water would be required for germination and plant nutrition. A higher rate would affect the rate of plant nutrient assimilation, increasing the physical yield. At some rate, a unit increase in the water input would be attended by a maximum incremental response in physical yield. Beyond that rate of application, higher rates of water input would be attended by successively smaller increments in output, until at some rate of application the soil fertility, seed, or physical structure of the plants would provide the technical restraint to any further increases in yields in response to increased rates of

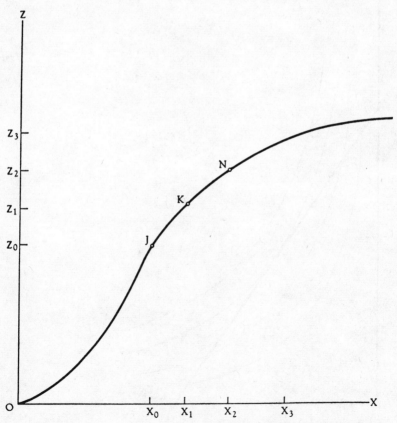

FIGURE 5. *The Production Function with One Factor Constant*

water input. Heavier rates of water use would be superfluous and would begin to reduce total output.

Thus far, we have dealt with purely physical relationships in which different technical means were considered for producing a given quantity of output. The particular choice of means—in our illustration, the choice of factor proportions in achieving a given output—is an economic problem. Given the prices of the two factors, just used in the illustration, the most efficient combination would be one which produced the maximum output for a given outlay. The conditions which would have to be met to achieve

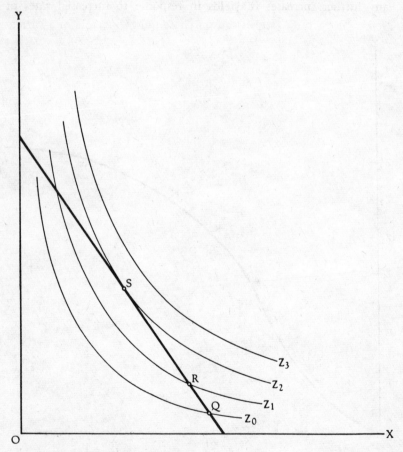

FIGURE 6. *The Producer's Choice of Efficient Factor Proportions*

this objective can be illustrated in a manner similar to the demonstration of efficient combination of consumers' products.

Figure 6 is comparable to Figure 4 in all respects except that an outlay line reflecting the prices of X and Y is included. This diagonal line represents all the different combinations of X and Y which can be obtained for the same outlay. The intercept on the Y axis represents the amount of factor Y which could be purchased if a given outlay were expended entirely for the purchase of Y. The X intercept correspondingly represents the amount of X available if the same outlay were used to purchase X alone. The slope of the line is determined by the ratio of the prices of X and Y, that is, P_x/P_y.

Since the outlay budget can purchase the two factors in a variety of combinations and the output also can be achieved by various combinations of factors, the most economically efficient means will involve selecting a combination which will maximize output for the specified outlay. The obvious choice will be the one in which the constant outlay line reaches the highest product curve, at S. The point of tangency (as in the case of commodity substitution in the problem involving the consumer) is the point at which the marginal rate of substitution between the factors is equal to the ratio of their prices. At any other point of contact between product curves and the outlay line—for example, Q or R—it will be possible to obtain output, but the quantity produced with those factor proportions will be less than that available when the marginal rate of substitution and the price ratios are equal.

The problem of choosing the most efficient scale of operation corresponds to the choice of the most efficient proportions. The rate of return will depend not only on the cost of factors, but on the rate of output and on product prices. Thus, profit maximization will involve determination of the rate of output given factor costs and product prices.

In the short run (defined as a period insufficiently long to permit changes in plant and equipment), expansion of output by increasing all factors save capital will encounter diminishing marginal productivity. Increasing marginal inputs per unit of output at constant factor prices will result in rising marginal costs. The efficient level of output is thus determined by the point at which the *cost of marginal inputs equals the value to the producer of the additional unit of output,* namely, the market price. Short of this point, increasing output would add more to revenues than to costs. At a level of output where price and marginal costs are equated, all possibilities for increasing profits by any adjustments would be realized. Beyond that point, every additional unit of output valued at market prices would provide less in revenue than it added in cost.

The proposition that equilibrium of a producer is determined by the level of output at which his marginal costs equal product prices, and that the marginal rates of substitution among factors are equal to the ratios of their prices, holds for any firm producing any product. Furthermore, granted the assumptions of the competitive model, these are necessary conditions for general economic efficiency, and can be rationalized as follows.

If there is perfect competition in product markets, the established prices reflect the marginal valuations of consumers in the aggregate, given their preferences, the distribution of income, and the amount and composition of total output. The resulting constellation of prices guides producers in their decisions regarding the production rate for any line. Output is expanded (or contracted) in every line of production so long as the cost incurred for the marginal unit is below (or above) the community's valuation at the margin (the price) of the additional unit of product. If perfect competition exists in factor markets also, the price of factors reflects their opportunity costs, or the returns at the margin in alternative uses. Marginal costs thus reflect the opportunities the community must forego to ensure the marginal unit of any particular product. Where marginal costs are all equal to the respective product prices, and marginal rates of substitution equal to the ratio of factor prices, *the value of every factor is the same at the margin in every application.* Therefore, no possibility remains that, by any changed combination of factors or reallocation of resources, any consumer or producer can improve his position without adversely affecting another's. In short, there is no further possibility of achieving a net gain from any reorganization, given the distribution of income, the preferences of consumers, and the resources at the disposal of the community.

FACTOR ALLOCATION OVER TIME: THE CAPITAL MARKET

Up to this point, the question of efficient allocation of resources has been treated as though the resources at the disposal of society were fixed. In the case of some resources and in a purely physical sense, this is doubtless true. In an economic sense, however, this will almost never be so. In progressive economies, total income and output have risen almost continuously through time. Yet growth in output requires either additional productive resources or advances in the state of the industrial arts. Both have occurred, and both have been accompanied by additional investment. In short, through development and with the employment of capital, productive resources of most kinds are being increased. For understanding of our competitive model, this raises several questions: What is the origin of capital? What determines the amount for use in new investment? And, given the quantity of investment funds, what represents an efficient allocation among investment alternatives?

The term "capital" has been given many meanings; we must first make clear the sense in which it is used here. Capital is simply the stock of goods produced in the past and available to assist in the present and future production of additional goods. Of the total national output produced in any period, a part is consumed and the remainder is added to the community's stock of capital. The change in capital stock over any period is called the net investment (positive or negative) in that period.

Since the total output of which an economy is capable depends among other things on its capital stock, the rate of investment helps to determine the rate of output. The amount of investment depends on the willingness of consumers, through savings, to release part of the output for investment purposes; thus the rate of growth in output depends on consumers' willingness to save.

Let us begin our examination of the competitive capital market by analyzing the supply side, that is, the willingness of consumers to save. In Figure 7, we assume that the consumer has a certain income, OY, and that he is free to save as much as he chooses at an interest rate of i per cent a year. The slope of the line XY is equal to the interest rate and indicates how large a future stream of income in the form of interest payments the consumer will receive per dollar saved. Whether a consumer will desire to save much or little depends on his preferences, as reflected by the indifference curves. He will be indifferent at all points on the same curve. At point a he will enjoy a high rate of current consumption, but will hold a relatively small stock of wealth and receive but little interest income. At point b his present consumption will be

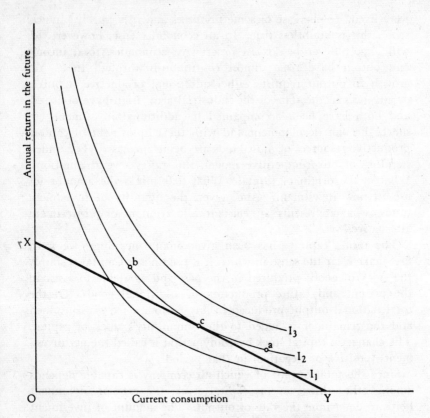

FIGURE 7. *The Consumer's Preferred Combination of Current Consumption and Increase in Future Annual Income*

low, but his future income and wealth will be much greater. A higher indifference curve, such as I_3, represents a higher state of satisfaction, and is preferred. If OY is his present income, through different amounts of saving, he can attain any of the points on the line XY, where each point represents some combination of consumption in the present plus the annual addition to future income of the specified interest payments. The consumer will attain his preferred position at the point of tangency c, where his willingness to substitute future interest income for present consumption is exactly equal to the interest rate. Should he select some other point, such as a, he would be sacrificing needlessly some of the possible satisfaction which his level of income permits.

The indifference curve must have the kind of curvature shown on our diagram. For as the consumer surrenders more of his present income for the sake of future returns, he will feel the loss more keenly, and as he adds more and more to the future income he will find that further additions will be worth successively less to him. Thus, the incentive to save must become increasingly larger in order to induce the consumer to save larger amounts.

Figure 8 shows the effects of an increase in the interest rate from i_1 to i_2. This permits the consumer to attain a higher set of combinations of present consumption and future interest receipts. He will thus select a new equilibrium point d. It is generally assumed that the new point will represent more saving.[6]

With an interest rate of i_1 our consumer will save YC; at a rate of i_2 his saving will rise to YD. Similarly, we can derive the rate of saving which corresponds to every interest rate. This enables us to derive the supply curve of saving for this individual. The curve is illustrated in Figure 9. Similar curves can be derived for all other individuals, and added horizontally to derive an aggregate curve of savings for the economy as a whole.

On the other side of the market, the demand for capital in the competitive model is governed by the profit motive. It is assumed that each entrepreneur is aware of a set of investment opportunities. They may be of many varieties: development of new products, new markets, new technological processes, etc. There is only one common denominator among them. Each opportunity holds the promise of producing an income stream in the future. This stream may come from an increase of sales revenue larger than the added operating costs, or it may result from reductions in operating costs made possible by the investment.

Suppose a perpetual investment of $1,000 will yield an income stream of $130. Its rate of return, or as it is sometimes called, its marginal efficiency of investment, would be 13 per cent. This assumes that, if the investment is subject to deterioration with use or to obsolescence, maintenance outlays and modernization expenditures have been made to keep intact the value of the lender's investment. Thus, the investment represents a commitment of a bundle of economic resources. If the investment is successful, it

---

[6] It is not inconceivable, however, that in the case of some individuals with a specific future income goal in mind, the situation may be reversed.

produces a revenue sufficient to cover the operating costs as well as expenditures required to maintain the value of the investment and, additionally, to provide a rate of return.

Different investment opportunities offer different rates of return. The enterprise seeking maximum profits will estimate the expected revenues and costs, will compute the rates of return, and will rank the possibilities according to this criterion. Granting the assumptions of the competitive model, the enterprise will then undertake all those possibilities which would add to its profits by yielding a

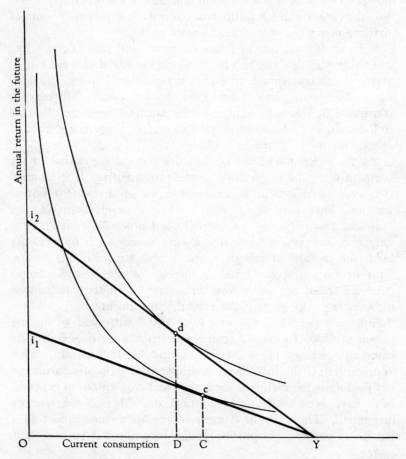

FIGURE 8. *Effects of Change in Interest Rate on Consumer's Consumption–Saving Decision*

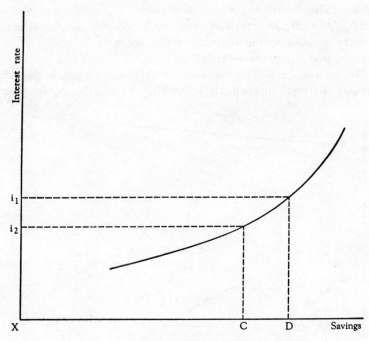

FIGURE 9.   *The Supply Curve of Savings*

rate of return greater than what it must pay for the use of capital. Thus, the level of investment of each enterprise is determined, given a rate of interest.

There will be instances when decisions will be made on alternative investment opportunities. For example, construction of a new plant may preclude modernization of an old one. The rate of return on the new plant may be lower, but the investment is much larger, and so the total return may be greater. Whether the new plant is the preferred investment will depend on the interest rate. If the rate is sufficiently low, the total return above borrowing costs may justify the larger investment.

Interdependence among investment opportunities within the enterprise complicates the decision-making process, insofar as projects cannot be considered as alternatives but only in reasonable combinations. This consideration does not affect the essential principle, however. Each enterprise, to maximize profits, will invest in the set of possibilities which yields the highest total profit above borrowing costs. And since total profit increases so long as the rate of return exceeds the borrowing cost, investment will be pushed to the point at which the rate of return at the margin will equal the interest rate.

An increase in the rate of interest disqualifies some of the previously marginal investment possibilities. Accordingly, for every

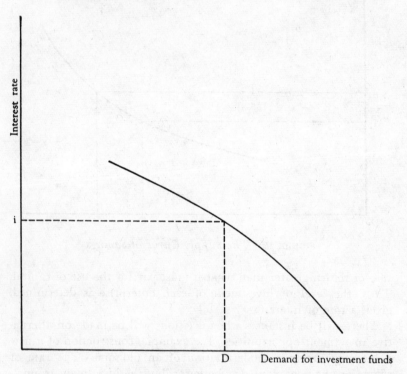

FIGURE 10. *The Enterprise's Demand for Investment Funds*

conceivable rate of interest, the total investment which an enterprise will make can be discovered, and a curve indicating the enterprise's demand for investment funds can be plotted, as in Figure 10. By adding the demand curves of all the enterprises in the economy horizontally, a schedule of the total demand for investment funds can be derived.

Combining the supply and demand schedules as in Figure 11, we obtain a picture of the capital market and how it determines the amount of investment for the total economy. If there is an increase in investment opportunities, the demand for funds will increase. This will be represented by a shift to the right of the schedule of the marginal efficiency of investment, accompanied by an increase in the rate of interest. An increase in the propensity

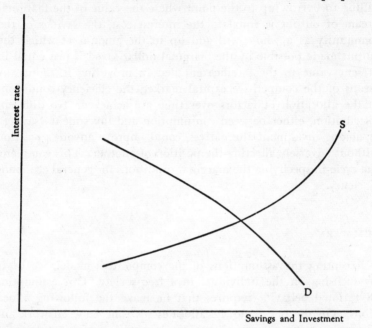

FIGURE 11. *Supply and Demand Curves in the Market for Investment Funds*

to save, on the other hand, will lower the saving schedule and will result in a decline in the rate of interest.

The competitive capital market assures that the community's savings are made available to those enterprises which have the most attractive investment opportunities, by permitting them to bid up the price of capital and thus to command the use of it. Accordingly, the capital is channeled into those areas where it will produce the highest return. In this manner, the capital market so allocates investment funds that no further gain can be achieved through any reallocation.

From the saver's point of view, a return is received on his savings equal to the return at the margin which is earned by the resources released for investment purposes. Each individual, given his preferences, will save out of his income up to the point where the sacrifice of current consumption is just compensated by the annual interest earned on the marginal dollar of saving. With producers willing to borrow up to the point where the value of the marginal stream of output is equal to the interest cost, the savings of the community as a whole will add up to the amount at which the output made possible by the marginal dollar saved is just equal in present value to the sacrifice entailed in providing it. Thus, by means of the competitive capital market, the efficiency conditions in the allocation of factors over time are achieved. No different distribution, either between consumption and investment (saving), or among investment alternatives, could improve anyone's position without adversely affecting the position of another. This completes the cycle in specifying the marginal conditions for general economic efficiency.

SUMMARY

Accepting the assumptions of the competitive model, we begin by focusing on the individual in a free society. Our assumption of rational behavior requires that he make the following allocations: On the one hand, he allocates his time between work and leisure so as to equate his marginal valuation of his productive services to the market rate of remuneration in the occupation of his choice. On the other hand, he allocates his income between consumption and saving so as to equate the market rate of interest on his savings to the sacrifice of current satisfaction entailed by the marginal dollar of saving. The portion of income left after savings becomes his consumption budget. His purchases of alternative goods and services are so budgeted as to equate his marginal valuation of each to its market price. Since this is done by all individuals in the economy and there is only one rate of remuneration for each occupation, one rate of interest, and one price for each kind of product or consumer service—the marginal valuations of the sacrifices and gains are the same to all the individuals in the market economy. No possibility remains for any improvement in the total gains by any reallocations.

Enterprises allocate their expenditures so that the marginal rates of substitution among factors is equal to the ratio of their prices. Accordingly, no factor substitutions can take place to increase output for a given outlay. Moreover, they make outlays for productive resources up to the point at which the cost of the marginal inputs is equal to the price of the product for which they are employed. Marginal costs in each line of production are then equal to the product prices—or, abstracting from prices, to the marginal valuation of the products or consumer services by the individuals in the community. In the competitive model, of course, marginal costs reflect ultimately the marginal sacrifice of current consumption and leisure, and thus reflect real costs. Hence, the marginal valuation of the sacrifices are just equal to the marginal valuation of the gains. No reorganization of any sort can achieve any net gain. Accordingly, any reallocation which would improve anyone's position could be done only at the expense of another, and hence would represent a redistribution of income rather than any gain in economic efficiency. The marginal conditions required for economic efficiency are met, and the economy is in a state of competitive equilibrium.

Critical Review of Some Fundamental Assumptions of the Competitive Model

Everyone knows that the economy in real life departs significantly in a number of respects from the competitive model. However, the model provides a beginning point for understanding the economizing principles in a market economy and the nature of the solutions to problems of economic efficiency. Having a formal apparatus that provides a set of efficiency criteria, we next go behind the criteria to examine the realism of some of the assumptions for treating comparative efficiency in the water development field.

In abstracting from much of the detail found in the actual economy, the competitive model leaves out of consideration two sorts of information which could compromise its general utility. Some of the relevant excluded information might qualify the utility of the model for guiding efficiency decisions. Conceivable departures from competitive conditions in actual markets may result in a constellation of costs and prices not directly useful in specifying efficiency criteria. Before examining the comparative efficiency of alternatives in actual cases in the water field, account must be taken of some of these weaknesses in our first approximation of the efficiency conditions.

UNSTATED ASSUMPTIONS OF THE MODEL

Although we made explicit some of the assumptions of the competitive model, we purposely left some implicit, in order to describe a framework of analysis without introducing complications at that point. Broadly speaking, we implied that the market mechanism was sufficiently comprehensive to allocate resources which would satisfy the community's demand for goods and services of every economic variety. Moreover, such goods and services were implicitly assumed to be available only through the intermediary of the market. Finally, granted the assumptions explicitly made, market prices were demonstrated to reflect commodity costs accurately and completely. And costs, in this case, were measured in terms of human effort and sacrifice, as appraised by individuals on their personal scale of values.

Satisfaction of Group Wants. The competitive model does not take explicit account of the fact that no markets exist to serve as intermediaries for the satisfaction of some economic wants. If participation in the enjoyment (consumption) of some types of goods or services cannot be made contingent on the payment of a price, once an investment decision for their provision had been made, the conditions for a market are lacking. If the enjoyment of a commodity cannot be denied any member of the community without simultaneously denying access to all consumers in the community, the pricing mechanism is not adequate for allocating resources to it. For no private party would undertake to provide such commodities if he could not recover costs. Examples of items of consumption that cannot be supplied separately to individual members of the community include such services as street lighting, police protection, protection for occupants of a flood plain, etc., which tend to blanket individuals who are members of a group or residents of a locality. Thus, there is no incentive to volunteer payment for the enjoyment of such services; failure to pay cannot result in restricting access to the enjoyment of the collective good.[7] The ideal of consumer sovereignty is compromised to the extent that there is no market to serve an important segment of human wants.

Direct Interdependence. The marginal conditions that define efficiency require that satisfaction in consumption derives exclusively from an individual's personal consumption of a commodity and is, therefore, independent of the consumption behavior of others. In cases where consumer satisfactions are interrelated, the efficiency conditions we have specified are somewhat ambiguous.[8] This problem is not peculiar to the pricing and investment criteria in the water resources field, however,[9] and is doubtless of a lower order of significance for this study than its counterpart in the area of production. On the production side, direct interdependence of the production functions of two or more fiscally independent producers could have significant consequences for our efficiency criteria. Hitherto, we have assumed that the output of any firm was exclusively a function of its inputs, and that variable factors would be employed up to the point at which the value of marginal products was equal to the respective factor costs. Under these conditions, costs and gains to the community would be balanced at the margin and no more efficient allocation would be possible. If the production functions of two or more fiscally independent enterprises are interdependent, however, the output of a given enterprise may vary not only with its own use of factors, but also with the way in which the productive resources of another enterprise are employed.[10] Under these conditions, therefore, the value

[7] For an elaboration of the notion of "collective or group wants," see Theo Suranyi-Unger, "Individual and Collective Wants," *Journal of Political Economy,* February 1948; and William J. Baumol, *Welfare Economics and the Theory of the State* (Cambridge: Harvard University Press, 1952).

[8] For a discussion of questions arising out of interdependence of utility functions, see Baumol, *ibid.,* Chapter VI; and H. Leibenstein, "Bandwagon, Snob and Veblen Effects in the Theory of Consumers' Demand," *Quarterly Journal of Economics,* May 1950.

[9] To the extent that we discuss drawing on the private capital market for investment funds for the water field, we must appreciate the effects of direct dependence among consumers' satisfaction on the savings schedule. For a discussion of this "Duesenberry Effect," see James Duesenberry, *Income, Savings, and the Theory of Consumer Behavior* (Cambridge: Harvard University Press, 1949).

[10] J. E. Meade, "External Economies and Diseconomies in a Competitive Situation," *Economic Journal,* March 1952.

of output of an enterprise, to an extent, may vary, independently of the cost it incurs in factor markets. Equating its marginal costs to the product price leaves out of account the positive or negative contribution of the factor services incidentally supplied by interdependent enterprises.

In some respects, the conditions which would give rise to costs or gains reflected outside the intermediary of the market are not unlike those giving rise to collective goods. For example, precipitation induced by means of artificial weather modification is not likely to be confined to the farm of the operator who paid for cloud seeding. The output of adjacent tracts of land will be affected (assuming the cloud seeding was successful), not only by the resource inputs of their operators, but also by the expenditure for factor services of the farmer who assumed the initiative. Compensation for the water cannot be exacted, so long as its use by benefited parties cannot be made contingent on payment of a fee. Similarly, an oil refinery can provide incidental services to other firms, say operators of orange groves, by reducing the hazards from frost through refinery smoke emission. However, compensation for these services to orange growers cannot be obtained so long as the supply cannot be controlled without interfering with the primary objectives for which the refinery is established. Of course, the emission of smoke, stack gasses, etc., is generally thought to inflict losses for which victims are not normally indemnified, and doubtless this is the more usual case.[11] In short, direct interdependence may have either a positive or negative effect. This, appearing as uncompensated costs or gains, vitiates the accuracy of market indicators for the efficient allocation of resources.

Direct interdependence is regarded by many economists as quite limited in the actual economy.[12] While this may be true as a general rule, it is a pervasive phenomenon in the water resources field.

Indivisibility in Production. Implicit in the discussion of the production function and marginal adjustments in the competitive

---

[11] See William Kapp, *The Social Cost of Private Enterprise* (Cambridge: Harvard University Press, 1950).

[12] For example, see Tibor Scitovsky, "Two Concepts of External Economies," *Journal of Political Economy*, April 1954.

model was an assumption that factors could be varied by small amounts. In some instances, however, there are technical reasons why factors can be employed, or some activity performed, only in large, indivisible doses; [13] it may not be feasible to vary output by small marginal adjustments.[14] If the minimum increment to output that would be feasible is large in relation to the market, a reduction in price per unit on all units of output may be required to clear the market of the total. For example, in some industries, production involves thermal processes in which vast quantities of coal are consumed. The sulfur content of coal, drawn from some sources, is quite high, and it is liberated in combustion. The sulfur can be recaptured, however, in the form of ammonium sulfate, which has value as a fertilizer. But the material is bulky (low plant nutrient per unit weight) and cannot be transported long distances without incurring prohibitive transport costs. The minimum amount which can be produced, therefore, from the standpoint of a reasonable cost per unit, is very large in relation to the market. The production of a technically efficient amount of ammonium sulfate under these circumstances accordingly results in a substantial effect on the price of plant nutrients in order to clear the market.

Conditions of this kind are incompatible with assumptions of the competitive model, for the producer cannot consider the market price as given, but must appreciate that it will be affected by his output. He will appraise the market value of his output as a decreasing function of the quantity supplied. Marketing a larger amount requires a reduction in revenue per unit on total sales, in addition to the change in costs associated with the expanded output. Unless the revenue from the additional units sold is enough to compensate for the reduction in revenue per unit on all of his output and the change in marginal costs, there is no incentive for the producer to increase output. The determining consideration,

---

[13] For a recent summary and extension of the developments in regard to this aspect of the production function, see Harvey Leibenstein, "The Proportionality Controversy and the Theory of Production," *Quarterly Journal of Economics*, November 1955.

[14] If the technically most efficient scale of plant is large, although the rate of output can be varied marginally, the rate which permits the minimum average cost of production may be very large.

if we assume profit maximization governs his decisions, is marginal revenue equal to marginal costs, and the former will always be below market price.[15] Accordingly, the condition that marginal costs be equal to the corresponding product price will not be met under such conditions. Moreover, if prices are used as guides to production and investment, the price under these conditions will not represent an invariant scale with which to weigh the value of the resulting output.

Viewed from a different perspective, when the minimum cost factor proportions require a scale of plant and rate of output that are large in relation to the market served, it is possible that the producers will be operating under conditions of declining average costs.[16] That is, the larger the output within the relevant range, the lower becomes the average unit cost because of the internal economies of scale. Within this range, marginal cost will be lower than average cost, since increments to output must be produced below the cost of preceding units in the sequence to cause the average to decline. Yet, if efficiency requires that output be pushed up to the point at which the cost of an additional unit is just equal to its market valuation, the block of output priced at marginal cost will not return full cost.

Conditions of this sort result in what is termed technical monopoly. Where the decreasing-cost nature of an industry is recognized, one solution is to grant legal sanction for exclusive access to a market territory in exchange for the assumption of a public utility responsibility. A companion solution involves providing the service as a public venture in adjacent marketing territories, as a form of countervailing power to assist in social regulation of franchised private monopoly. Whatever the solution in a pragmatic sense, it is not contained within the framework of the competitive model.

---

[15] See Kenneth E. Boulding, *Economic Analysis* (New York: Harper, 1948), p. 528; or for a more detailed graphical exposition of the identical phenomenon, see Joan Robinson, *The Economics of Imperfect Competition* (London: Macmillan and Co., 1933), Book I, Chapter II.

[16] For an empirically demonstrated example, see Leslie Cookenboo, Jr., *Crude Oil Pipe Lines and Competition in the Oil Industry* (Cambridge: Harvard University Press, 1955), Chapter I.

DEPARTURES FROM COMPETITIVE ASSUMPTIONS
IN THE CAPITAL MARKET

Two assumptions regarding the efficiency of the supply and
allocation of capital in the competitive model are subject to qualification. In the discussion of the supply of investment funds, it
was assumed that savers would be willing to lend an amount identical to what they would save at any rate of interest. Furthermore,
it was assumed that the enterprise would avail itself of an unrestricted access to the capital market at the prevailing market rate
so long as its anticipated returns exceeded the market rate of
interest.

From an individual saver's point of view, investing or lending
funds involves the risk of failing to recoup his investment or have
his loan repaid. Furthermore, in an uncertain world, the individual sacrifices security when he surrenders the liquidity which
cash or bank balances represent. The risk of losses, and the value
of remaining liquid when one's personal fortunes must remain
uncertain, require a premium to induce an individual to part with
his savings. Consequently, at any rate of interest, a smaller amount
of investment funds than savings would be provided. The market
rate of interest will depart from the rate inferred from the competitive model by an amount equal to the risk premium required.

The profit-maximizing behavior of the enterprise in the competitive model also assumed that investment would be carried to the
point where the rate of return at the margin equaled the interest
rate. This was a necessary condition for maximum economic
efficiency. In actual practice, however, the uncertainty of realizing
anticipations with respect to an investment opportunity means that
the future income stream is discounted significantly. Enterprises
do not knowingly invest in activities in which the prospective
returns at the margin only equal the borrowing cost. Expectations
are not always realized and returns may fall short of the *ex ante*
expectation. This is evidence of "imperfect foresight," a qualification of the competitive model rather than evidence that investment
is carried to the margin.

Enterprises, thus, may be reluctant to avail themselves of investment funds even though prospective returns exceed borrowing
costs. To elaborate this point: the higher the ratio of borrowed

to venture capital in an enterprise's financial structure, the greater the risk for any investor who lends it money. This is true because the nature of the bond contract entitles lenders to a prior lien on the earnings of the firm. If a high proportion of the financing is to be achieved by borrowing, there remains a correspondingly smaller residual risk-bearing component in the firm's capitalization to absorb any fluctuations in returns. An additional feature of debt financing is the claim of the lender to the assets of the borrowing enterprise should it fail to meet its interest obligation. This is a form of security, however, which decreases as the ratio of debt to risk capital increases, other factors remaining equal. For example, if financing were arranged so that all capital was raised by borrowing and the enterprise failed to meet its interest costs, the market value of the enterprise's assets would decline. An enterprise's market value is expressed as the capitalized value of its earnings, and if these were insufficient to meet interest obligations, the value of the assets would decline below the amount of the originally borrowed capital. From the lender's standpoint, this is tantamount to loss of a part of his principal. Hence, the security which access to an enterprise's assets affords will be limited unless the proportion of debt to venture capital is kept sufficiently low. Investors, correspondingly, will be reluctant to purchase an unlimited quantity of an enterprise's bonds, and the firm's access to investment funds at the prevailing rate in the bond market will be dependent on the amount of risk-bearing equity capital available to it.

Equity capital raised in the securities market may be substituted for borrwing to provide the risk component in the financial structure. Here, however, the volume of capital that an enterprise's management is willing to employ may be governed by its own share of the equity capital, for additional amounts of risk-bearing capital will dilute management's control over the policies of the enterprise and reduce the possible rate of return to the equity capital.

Thus, reluctance of investors to lend except at increasingly greater risk premiums, and reluctance of management to risk dilution of control by employing more equity capital, qualify the assumption of unrestricted access to the capital market at the prevailing market rate of interest and willingness to push investment to the point where the promised returns at the margin only equal the interest cost.

Income Distribution and Full Employment

By taking account of qualifications relevant to the water field, our model can be modified to serve as an appropriate frame of reference for appraising the comparative efficiency of alternatives among approaches to the development of multiple purpose river projects. A few loose ends must be gathered in, however, before we turn to specific problems.

One of the questions we have avoided, in specifying the conditions for economic efficiency, concerns income distribution. Income in the model originated as remuneration for factor services. Changes in relative rewards to factors among alternative uses were the means by which resources would be constantly rechanneled into the most productive alternative employments consistent with dynamic changes over time in consumers' preferences, improvement in technology, and the growth and distribution of income. In the competitive model, in short, factor remunerations allocated resources efficiently, and these rewards for factor services resulted in some unspecified distribution of income which was also implicitly "efficient."

In a somewhat different perspective, the distribution of ownership of resources could result in great extremes in the distribution of income and wealth. Where these extremes exist, it has been difficult to give expression to some of the fundamental tenets of a democratic society. Among these are equal opportunity for influencing political decisions, equal treatment before the law, and similar ideals of our society. Since the market mechanism does not allocate resources and distribute products with uniform impartiality, irrespective of the distribution of income, individuals with unequal personal fortunes have unequal influence on the allocation of resources. Conceivably, a conflict between efficiency—given the prevailing distribution of resource ownership—and "higher criteria" may result.

While we do not ignore the reality of this problem, it does not lie within the scope of the present study. We take for granted that the political, judicial, and other social processes in a democracy tend to adjudicate disputes involving the distribution of the national income.[17] How adequately this is being accomplished in

---

[17] For an analysis along different lines, see Anthony Downs, *An Economic Theory of Government Decision-Making in a Democracy*. Technical Report No. 32 (Stanford: Department of Economics, Stanford University, 1956).

our form of representative government may be the proper subject for a study in social justice, but it lies outside our immediate purview.

In a purely analytical sense, however, the issue of the distribution of income may arise to plague us unless it is clarified. Our efficiency criteria were derived analytically by taking as given the prevailing distribution of income. Changes in the distribution of income will affect the efficiency of a given allocation of resources. Since the decision to invest or not to invest—or a decision to employ untraditional approaches to water resources development—may result in a redistribution of income, it is necessary to contend with both the distribution existing before the event and that reflecting its consequences. It is conceivable that what would be an efficient solution in terms of the prevailing income distribution may be less efficient following a reshuffling of costs and gains among the members of the community. While this is a valid theoretical objection to carrying out studies of comparative efficiency, its practical significance will be negligible for the problems encountered in this study. The income redistribution would affect our efficiency criteria only through the influence on the constellation of relative prices.[18] This structure of prices arises out of the distribution of total income among individuals of differing preferences. (We take technology and resource endowment as given for this purpose.) The effect on the distribution of income of the magnitudes we will be treating, however, can be inferred from a numerical illustration. Assume a proposed river basin development program would involve a total investment of a billion dollars over a twenty-year period. The income redistributive consequences of alternative means of undertaking the development may approximate half the total.[19] If we assume an average annual national income of $500 billion, this will aggregate to ten trillion dollars over the time span considered. A redistribution of income amounting to as much as half the total investment funds committed to the program would represent only five-thousandths of one per cent of total national income. As a

[18] We postpone the discussion of a somewhat related problem until Chapter III.

[19] Some insight into the quantitative relationships may be inferred from the material presented in Chapters VII and VIII, where we treat income redistributive consequences explicitly.

practical consideration, the effects which this could have on the constellation of prices (and imputed prices) employed for evaluating comparative efficiency of alternatives can be ignored.

Finally, even if all of the required adjustments in the competitive model are made appropriately, there will be economic conditions under which our balancing of costs and gains at the margin, using market (or imputed) prices, will have no relevance for evaluating economic efficiency. In times of economic distress, when there is a substantial amount of involuntary unemployment, conditions of general economic efficiency cannot be specified by reference to market prices. However closely the marginal conditions are met in all other sectors, if there is a vast body of unemployed workers and idle productive capacity, it will not follow that the maximum amount of the preferred composition of output is being produced, given the resources available to society. Hence, we recognize that the empirical data in the efficiency criteria used in this study apply only to economic conditions of relatively full employment, such as have characterized the years in the postwar period. They are not relevant for evaluation of projects in periods of depressed economic conditions—nor for projects undertaken during past periods of economic depression. Furthermore, these criteria will be applicable only to new undertakings, as other criteria are required to evaluate the efficiency of operations for which economic resources already have been irrevocably committed.

III Market Mechanics,
River Basin Development,
and Efficiency

Under perfectly competitive conditions, the total output of an enterprise, valued at market prices, would reflect accurately the total returns from employing productive resources in a line of activity. In equilibrium, the opportunity cost of the factors employed at the margin of any line of activity would equal the returns, thus delimiting the possibilities for productive investment in that application. If similar conditions prevailed in every other productive application, there would be no further possibility—by allocating a little more of society's resources for producing more of one good and a little less for another—that any individual's gains would be more than sufficient to compensate the loss incurred by others.

In qualifying comments, we have indicated that these results would obtain only if market organization were sufficiently comprehensive to satisfy every variety of economic want. Furthermore, it also would be necessary that goods or services produced by the expenditure of scarce resources be available only through the intermediary of the market in return for a price. In the actual economy, there is evidence of conditions to the contrary; furthermore, these conditions are especially common in regard to water-derived commodities and services.[1] To become fully aware of the divergence

---

[1] The term water-derived commodity, or for the sake of brevity, water derivative, will be used to represent the group of heterogeneous commodities, services, or "benefits" from water resources development such as hydroelectricity, flood protection, services rendered by an inland waterway, etc.

between market and economic returns, these departures from specified conditions that arise in the water resources field need more
detailed examination. The problem is to understand the divergence between private returns from the sale of marketable goods
and services and economic returns—including those whose value
may not be susceptible of appropriation by an enterprise through
pricing.

We begin this chapter, then, by discussing the departures from
the competitive conditions that are inherent in some of the major
purposes of multiple purpose river programs. This discussion,
largely by way of illustration, will be confined primarily to flood
control, irrigation, navigation, and power. Next, we shall point
out the direct interdependence of some of the interrelated functions of a multiple purpose river project. Traditionally, a number
of the water derivatives from a multiple purpose river operation
have been made available without cost and have been commonly
accepted as "non-marketable." We not only shall treat these, but
also shall focus attention on some of the deficiencies of the competitive model, especially as they bear on analysis of hydroelectric
power, which traditionally has been accepted as a marketable
service. In many instances, problems of indivisibility and direct
interdependence in hydroelectric production make power markets
a special case among the commodity and service markets. This
requires at least brief treatment. In the concluding section, we
shall synthesize our conclusions, based on analysis of actual circumstances in the area of river basin development, and assess their
implications for efficiency in the allocation of resources within the
context of market mechanics. If efficiency in the development of
water resources is to be achieved, devices for extra-market allocation must be used to supplement the market. This requires
efficiency criteria which take account of the relevant social gains
and costs, to be used as an aid in budgeting public revenues for
development of water resources.

Interdependence and Indivisibility in Production
of Water Derivatives

A number of characteristics distinguish the production and
distribution of water derivatives from conditions assumed in the

competitive model. To a certain degree a water-derived commodity
or service provided to satisfy the want of one individual will also
render simultaneous satisfaction to other individuals, irrespective
of how exclusive the intent might have been. The reason for this
has been neatly summarized:

> Evidently there are not many common wants whose individual
> gratification is absolutely impossible, which can be satisfied
> *eo ipso* only for a group of individuals and which consequently
> may be called absolute group wants. . . . Likewise, the great
> majority of common wants can be gratified, discretely and sepa-
> rately, for the individual members of the community. . . . As a
> rule, the only essential question is the difficulty or ease—and on
> the basis of virtually the same consideration, the expensiveness
> or cheapness—of such an individual satisfaction.[2]

FLOOD CONTROL

Perhaps the most common example of collective or group
demand for a water derivative appears in the case of flood protection. A system of levees, if undertaken to provide protection to
any member of a community, will provide protection to all who
inhabit the protected area.[3] Or, to extend the example, any system
of tributary storage reservoirs required to control runoff and
protect one community at some point along the main stem will
incidentally and automatically afford some degree of protection
to other communities along the same reach of the river.[4] Usually,
it is prohibitively costly to provide such protection to an individual
or a single community, when compared with the value to them
alone; but in many cases, the cost becomes economically justified

---

[2] Theo Suranyi-Unger "Individual and Collective Wants," *Journal of Political
Economy,* February 1948, p. 17.

[3] There always remains the relatively expensive possibility that each occupant
of the flood plain will construct protective works around his property, as did
Samuel Colt, the manufacturer of the Colt revolver. See W. G. Hoyt and Walter
B. Langbein, *Floods* (Princeton: Princeton University Press, 1955), p. 202.

[4] A side issue, representing a qualification of the assumptions of our model, is
the case of channel straightening, dredging, and levee construction, which—
while facilitating the flow past a given point on a river—may contribute to the
flood stage at another. This will represent an external diseconomy resulting
from direct interdependence, of which there are many examples in the water
field.

in terms of the aggregate value to all beneficiaries considered collectively.[5]

In order to provide protection economically for a single occupant of an exposed reach of the flood plain, a given irreducible dose of investment—which may at times be very large—is required. If a project is undertaken at all, it will also gratify the needs of the remaining occupants. In the case of the system of tributary reservoirs, in addition to the indivisibility attending the construction of dams,[6] there is a functional interdependence among the several storage units for achieving a given objective. For example:

> Regulation of floods by the TVA system can be considered as a four-pronged effort: First, the acceleration of flood-threatening flows through the system; second, the impounding of the bulk of the contributing flow from tributary streams; third, a flattening of flood crests by impoundage at projects close to the point of flood hazard; and last, the gradual release of stored water following the flood crest to regain storage capacity. The first of these functions is accomplished largely by the chain of main stem projects. The second is accomplished by tributary projects having substantial reservoir capacity, while the third makes use of both tributary and main-river storage.[7]

This interdependence among units of the flood control system contributes to an investment indivisibility, since the system functions as a set of complementary facilities.

The combination of collective demand and large initial investment militates against satisfying this group want by means of private marketing arrangements. Even if the large original outlay would be small if divided equally among all beneficiaries, each individual might decide that it would be in his interest to avoid a commitment to pay on the chance that the contribution of others would make it unnecessary. Simultaneously, each might also

[5] Hoyt and Langbein, *op. cit.*, pp. 229-30.

[6] The average cost per acre-foot of storage at any given site tends to decrease, within a range, as the capacity of reservoir storage increases. This results from the fact that costs of spillways, as an example, remain constant (and in some cases may diminish) with increases in the storage to be provided. See Luna B. Leopold and Thomas Maddock, Jr., *The Flood Control Controversy* (New York: Ronald Press, 1955), pp. 34, 54.

[7] Reed A. Elliott, "TVA Experience in Multiple Purpose River Development," paper presented at the National Convention of the American Society of Civil Engineers, Knoxville, Tennessee, June 1956, p. 12.

be reluctant to commit himself to payment for fear others might fail to contribute, making the cost to him greater. On the other hand, the system of water control structures would not be provided by a profit-maximizing enterprise in the absence of previously concluded contracts for the service. The service accordingly would be nonmarketable. Pricing mechanics are not equal to the collection of payment so long as protection cannot be denied one who is delinquent without simultaneously denying protection to those who willingly meet their obligations. In the absence of extra-market incentives, no private enterprise has an incentive to provide the requisite services. Conventional market channels, therefore, are inadequate to assure economically efficient resource allocation for the provision of the water derivative.

IRRIGATION

Flood protection is perhaps the clearest illustration of the impossibility of gratifying every variety of human want in the field of river development through the intermediary of the market. But there are a number of instances in which neither satisfactions nor employment of productive services having their origin in water derivatives can be made contingent on the payment of a price. Physical interdependence in resource use, or what has been referred to as "technological external economies," [8] represents the primary source of this difficulty. An example concerns the use of Millerton Lake storage (Central Valley Project, California) for gravity-flow irrigation in Tulare and Kern counties. Aquifers, underlying much of the irrigated land, are recharged in the process of gravity-flow irrigation using surface sources. A significant part of the irrigation farming in Kern County, however, consists in use of water pumped from subsurface aquifers. Recharging these aquifers stabilizes the ground water tables and, thereby, reduces costs of pumping ground water. The recharging occurs as an interrelated result of gravity-flow irrigation. Accordingly, compensation cannot be exacted (by threat of discontinuing the service) without interfering with the success of the irrigation activities requiring the surface sources. The irrigators using ground water adjacent to the irrigation district

[8] Tibor Scitovsky, "Two Concepts of External Economics," *Journal of Political Economy*, April 1954.

thereby become beneficiaries of uncompensated factor services.[9]

Many technical and economic factors in the reclamation of arid land are at variance with the assumptions of competitive equilibrium theory. Perhaps Teele has summarized these most succinctly:

> . . . both physically and economically desert land must be reclaimed in large units. . . . Except for small areas here and there, it is not physically possible to build irrigation ditches to water single farms. Most irrigation farms are miles from the streams from which the water for their irrigation is taken. A stream of water only large enough for a single farm of 160 acres would be lost by evaporation into the desert air or by seepage into the desert soil long before it reached a farm only a few miles from the source, while the cost of an independent ditch for each farm would be prohibitive. Only by the use of large canals watering many farms, is it possible to carry water through the long distances necessary to reach the land far back from the stream at an expense that is justified by the returns from the land.
>
> Thus from the very nature of things, agricultural expansion into desert cannot be accomplished in that gradual way that is possible in other sections where single farms can be cut out of forests or plains and developed gradually as there is demand for their products.[10]

Of less significance, perhaps, is the interrelation of resource uses combined with indivisibility in production encountered by some types of agricultural processing industries. Indivisibility contributes to internal economies of large scale, and where the market for output, or the supply area, is not big enough to accommodate a large number of such enterprises, competition may suffer. Under certain circumstances, only one enterprise for processing agricultural output can be supported, and monopsony in the market at the farm level results. For example, the processing of dairy products and sugar beets and some types of fruit and vegetable

[9] For similar examples of direct interdependence in the water field, see Hoyt and Langbein, *op. cit.*, p. 154; William J. Baumol, *Welfare Economics and the Theory of the State* (Cambridge: Harvard University Press, 1952), Chapter 6; and The Presidents Materials Policy Commission, *Resources For Freedom,* Vol. 5, 1952, p. 88.

[10] R. P. Teele, "The Financing of Non-Governmental Irrigation Enterprises," *The Journal of Land and Public Utility Economics,* October 1926, p. 227.

dehydration exhibit substantial economies of scale.[11] The most efficient size of plant, in terms of unit processing costs, is often difficult to achieve because of a second characteristic. The conversion of raw materials into processed output is accompanied by substantial weight losses. This requires that the supply area serving each plant be confined to a relatively short radius about the plant, for material assembling costs rise proportionately with the distance from which supplies are drawn. It is not uncommon for assembly costs of raw materials to become prohibitive before a scale of output that represents the lowest processing cost per unit is reached. Any supply area, accordingly, can support economically only one processor.

Since physical yields per acre are substantially larger under irrigation agriculture, a given amount of raw materials can be supplied at a reduced average cost of material assembly, or else a larger scale of plant can operate at reduced average costs of production. The realizable reduction in costs at the processing level could be reflected in higher returns to irrigation farmers producing for the processing industries. If dairy products, sugar beets, or fruit and vegetables destined for dehydrating are exchanged in monopsonistic markets in the project areas, however, what might have been a higher return to irrigation farming, and an imputed higher value for water, may become a processor's surplus rather than a higher financial return to the water enterprise providing the advantage.[12]

Somewhat similar circumstances prevail in the case of utilities

[11] U. S. Department of Interior, Bureau of Reclamation, *Columbia Basin Joint Investigations—Agricultural Processing Industries,* Problem 24, 1945, and J. A. Guthrie, "Economies of Scale and Regional Development," *Papers and Proceedings of the Regional Science Association,* 1955.

[12] It can be argued that the bargaining position of farmers may not be compromised if the processor in reality bids for the services of the land, rather than being the sole buyer of a particular crop. To the extent that specialized resources, e.g., dairy herds, milkhouses and machinery, orchards, etc., represent sunk capital, production in these lines may be less sensitive to changes in relative prices and the bargaining strength of suppliers and processors may be sufficiently unequal to permit substantial monopsonistic rents for the processor. Under such conditions, if the incidence of the benefits associated with the irrigation water supply is shifted outside the market in which the irrigation water enterprise deals, pricing mechanics may fail to compensate the water enterprise for the cost it incurs and the factor services it renders.

which service irrigation projects. By virtue of the indivisibility present in utility enterprises, their decreasing-cost nature is recognized by legal arrangements granting them monopoly status in the areas which they serve. Profits of railroad enterprises, particularly, are affected favorably by the increase in load factor attending irrigation development.[13] Since freight rates are generally set for wide areas and are unlikely to be altered by the regulatory bodies as a result of an increased volume of freight from one relative small area, the "pecuniary external economies" to railroads serving farmers become significant.[14] This doubtless accounts for the support given reclamation projects by western railroads—but also accounts in part for the divergence between financial and economic returns to irrigation enterprises.

Perhaps of greater practical importance, however, is the superior bargaining position enjoyed by the irrigation farmers vis-à-vis the irrigation enterprise. Teele has recounted the difficulties arising from the ability of water users to wait out the water supplier in some cases and to buy out the bankrupt facilities on their own terms.[15] Reliance, during agricultural depressions, on the political process to scale down repayment obligation and water charges on federal reclamation projects has further affected the financial returns to investment for the provision of irrigation water. Improved incomes during prosperous periods, however, are capitalized in the value of the land and associated investments when ownerships are transferred. As a consequence, the returns associated with employment of water on reclamation farms tend to be

[13] Decreasing costs in the case of utilities and processing industries undoubtedly account for the interest taken in irrigation development. The Northern Pacific Railroad and the Holly Sugar Corporation, for example, were instrumental in importing irrigation farmers to the Yellowstone irrigation project. The sugar company, in fact, advanced loans to farmers to facilitate the settlement preparatory to establishing a sugar refinery. See H. C. Hoje, R. E. Huffman, and C. F. Kraenzel, *Indirect Benefits of Irrigation Development*, Bulletin 517 (Bozeman: Montana State College, 1956), p. 51.

[14] Pecuniary external economies are distinguished from technological external economies by the fact that they arise out of market, rather than physical, interdependence. Such external economies have been represented as the increase in profits which accrue to an enterprise as a result of the manner in which other independent parties engage their resources. See Tibor Scitovsky, *op. cit.*

[15] R. P. Teele, *op. cit.*, pp. 430-31.

distributed to other factors, and they escape appropriation, through user charges, as a return to reclamation investment.[16]

INLAND WATER NAVIGATION

Indivisibility and interdependence have been long recognized in connection with transportation facilities.[17] A particular dam which provides a slack-water channel making navigable a certain reach of the river will be of limited usefulness unless related reaches are developed in a continuum between principal trade centers. Indivisibility of this kind, as in the case of railroads, effectively precludes marginal doses of investment in opening up a new channel of commercial intercourse. Under the circumstances, financial returns to investment in developing portions of a navigation system would compare unfavorably with returns to alternative investment possibilities. If such investment is motivated by national long-run developmental objectives, uncompensated gains to third parties may justify subsidies of various forms, such as the land grants to achieve transcontinental railroad expansion. However, in the absence of incentives obtained outside the market, the market mechanism will fail to allocate resources for providing facilities where a large part of the value which accrues to individuals cannot be appropriated from recipients by means of pricing.

Provision of a minimum channel depth—or stream regulation to achieve this result—will also provide minimum stream flow, which mitigates pollution concentrations that frequently reach critical proportions.[18] Incidental pollution abatement achieved through regulating stream flows to meet the navigation objective, by reducing water treatment costs, represents an uncompensated service to those employing the stream as a source of water supply. Similarly, there is no compensation from those who, in the absence of the pollution abatement, would be required by legal measures to incur

[16] See *Federal Reclamation by Irrigation*, Senate Document No. 92, 68th Congress, 1st Session (Washington: Superintendent of Documents, 1924), pp. 118 ff.; also, H. E. Selby, "A Method of Determining Feasibly Irrigation Payments," *Journal of Farm Economics*, August 1942.

[17] See, for example, K. William Kapp, *The Social Cost of Private Enterprise* (Cambridge: Harvard University Press, 1950), Chapter 14.

[18] The flow of an extremely variable river such as the Tennessee would fluctuate between 5,000 and 500,000 feet per second under unregulated conditions.

costs for treatment of effluents discharged into the river. Since financial returns to investment which provide uncompensated returns to third parties understate economic returns, profits of such enterprises would not be the relevant guide to investment decisions if efficiency criteria were to govern.

HYDROELECTRIC POWER

One of the most significant departures from the divisibility and independence assumptions appears in the case of hydroelectricity. An excellent dam site in some cases will provide for more than a million kilowatts of power; Grand Coulee on the Columbia provides roughly two million. Until very recently, an increment to generating capacity of this magnitude would have exceeded the total generating capacity of all but the very largest power systems in the country.[19] The Shasta and Keswick sites of the Central Valley projects, along with the thermal station to firm up the hydroelectric generation, with but 600,000 kilowatts, would have represented approximately a third of the total generating capacity of the Pacific Gas and Electric system, one of the nation's largest systems at that time, and practically the sole supplier of the Northern California power market.[20] For the more sparsely populated areas with small power systems, excellent hydroelectric sites might represent an embarrassment of riches. The Hells Canyon site on the Snake River, for example, with a power potential of close to a million kilowatts, represents an increment to capacity of about three times the amount of the Idaho Power Company's total system capability.[21]

Since transmission losses restrict the size of an area in which power can be marketed economically, the inability to expand capacity by increments which are relatively small in relation to the market to be served is likely to depress rates at which the total block of energy can be marketed. Moreover, power markets differ from markets of the competitive model where spot transactions

[19] Until about 1950, even the largest power systems in the country had generating capacity of less than three million kilowatts.

[20] U. S. Department of Interior, Bureau of Reclamation, *Central Valley Project Studies; Economic Effects Problem 24,* 1949, p. 42.

[21] Federal Power Commission, *In the Matters of Idaho Power Company;* Project No. 1971, No. 2132, and No. 2133—*Decision,* pp. 23, 46.

are assumed to prevail. A short-term power surplus—of say five years or so—will normally be disposed of under conditions of bargaining where bilateral monopoly is the more appropriate theoretical model to explain the setting of rates and disposition of output. While a short-term surplus may prevail, the only bidder for the surplus power may be a bargain-hunting member of the electro-process industry, interested in an assured supply over the economic life of its production facilities. Long-term contracts at dump-power prices may have to be negotiated in order to dispose of a relatively short-term or intermediate-term surplus. This may be of substantial advantage to the attracted buyer,[22] but cold comfort to the investor in the hydroelectric development.

TABLE 1. *Technological External Economies of Hungry Horse Project*

Plants	Kilowatts	Plant owners
Hungry Horse, at-site	212,000	U. S. government
Downstream installations:		
Kerr	78,000	Montana Power Company
Thompson Falls	12,000	Montana Power Company
Cabinet Gorge	50,000	Washington Water Power Co.
Albeni Falls	7,000	U. S. government
Box Canyon	14,000	Pend Oreille County Public Utility District
Waneta	70,000	West Kootenay Power & Light Co. (British Columbia, Canada)
Grand Coulee	163,000	U. S. government
Chief Joseph	83,000	U. S. government
Rock Island	16,000	Chelan Public Utility District
McNary	49,000	U. S. government
The Dalles	52,000	U. S. government
Bonneville	34,000	U. S. government
Total downstream	628,000	
Total prime power from Hungry Horse	840,000	

Source: Bonneville Power Administration.

[22] It does not follow that electro-process industries obtaining power at dump-power rates find a substantial net advantage in purchasing such power, however. They may have to incur greater costs—particularly transport costs if the power is provided in a region remote from their markets—for other factor inputs to take advantage of the lower-cost power. This problem is treated in our discussion of the income redistribution consequences of a given project in Chapter VIII.

Hydroelectric sites of such magnitude, however, are restricted to a few of the nation's rivers. Of more general significance is the high degree of physical interdependence between headwater storage and downstream generating capacity. Storage provided at upstream reservoir sites will often do double, and in some cases greater, duty

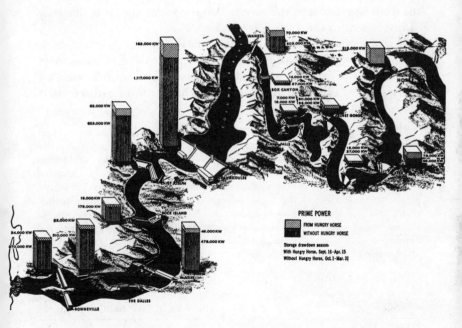

FIGURE 12. *Downstream External Economies for Power Production of the Hungry Horse Project (adapted from chart published by Bonneville Power Administration)*

as it contributes to the prime power generation of hydroelectric power plants downstream. For example, storage provided at the Hungry Horse site on the Flathead River of the Columbia River tributary system can be used to generate 212,000 kilowatts of prime power at the Hungry Horse powerhouse. Its contribution of prime power under co-ordinated system operation, at downstream plants currently built or under construction, is nearly three times as great. (See Figure 12.) Table 1 illustrates this in detail.

The difference between at-site prime power for which an enterprise unit could collect compensation under the assumptions of the competitive model, and the total resulting from the direct interdependence between investment undertaken at the Hungry Horse site and downstream power plants, suggests the extent of the difference between the private and the social marginal efficiency of investment in this hydroelectric site.

It is recognized that the hydraulic measurements in establishing stream-flow regulation provided by the storage depend on assumptions as to the quantity and time profile of additions to storage on the system.[23] Yet these are matters which are not essential for our

---

[23] For example, the data in the illustration above are based on the current seven-month critical period from the standpoint of storage releases for prime power generation. During the remaining five months, production at Hungry Horse is lower and other plants in the system carry the load. As additional storage is constructed in the Columbia Basin, the critical storage drawdown period will increase and the prime power from Hungry Horse will be smaller. If we take an alternative measure, dependable capacity at site (available in sixteen out of twenty years) and the average annual salable energy at site and downstream, the following data are indicative of the annual kilowatt-hours attributable to Hungry Horse by the two methods.

Site	Prime power (million kw-h)	Dependable capacity and salable energy (million kw-h)
Hungry Horse	1,857	700
Downstream federal plants, U.S.	3,399	783
Downstream private plants, U.S.	1,489	358
Downstream private plants, Canada	613	178
Total	7,358	2,019

Both sets of data, computed by alternative methods, clearly reveal that power made available by Hungry Horse storage downstream greatly exceeds the amount available at site alone.

present purpose of simple illustration. It is possible, however, to show the direct interdependence among units of a multiple purpose system designed for flood control, navigation, and power, in which most of the hydroelectric sites on the river have been developed. Table 2 lays this out for a system operated to maximize output under two constraints—minimum channel depths for navigation and a specified level of flood control at the focal point for the flood control operations. This represents an integrated operation of two fiscally independent systems[24]—the Aluminum Company of America and the Tennessee Valley Authority—under the direction of a single management unit. The TVA is responsible for co-ordinating storage releases so as to maximize system output over the critical period, subject to the legal constraints with respect to navigation and flood control.[25]

Both the columns and the rows of Table 2 have for their heading the names of the hydroelectric plants in the Tennessee River and tributary system. At the top of each column, under the corresponding power plant, is shown the prime power equivalent, discounting the contribution of upstream plants in the system. At the bottom of each column is the actual prime power associated with the plant, taking into account the contribution of upstream storage to primary power at the downstream plant. The differences between the two indicate the effects of the direct interdependence.

The rows reveal the contribution which each plant provides to downstream plants shown in successive columns moving to the right, and finally the at-site primary power revealed by the last entry in the row. Beginning with row one, for example, the one entry indicates that there are no downstream plants below Kentucky Dam. The single entry indicates the at-site primary power equivalent without the effects from upstream plants. Row two,

[24] The Aluminum Company of America's system of five hydroelectric plants on the East Tennessee and North Carolina tributaries of the Tennessee River, and the Tennessee Valley Authority's system of twenty-eight dams on the main stem and tributaries of the Tennessee River.

[25] In addition to the contribution of Alcoa's storage to downstream generation of the TVA hydroelectric plants, there are net increments to generation available from operating the fiscally independent systems as a hydraulically and electrically integrated system. From such co-ordinated management, there results some 22,000 kilowatts of additional dependable generation, which by agreement is shared equally between the parties.

headed Pickwick Landing, shows the contribution of the impound-
ment of Pickwick Landing to Kentucky powerhouse prime power
amounting to 0.3 megawatts (row two, column 1); while over into
the second column, the last entry for row two shows the at-site
primary power of Pickwick Landing, 87.6 megawatts, on the assumption Pickwick was not benefited by upstream storage. At the
bottom of column two, of course, the 102.8 megawatts shown for
Pickwick Landing indicate the actual at-site prime power, taking
into account the upstream storage contribution.

While this table is an illustration of the physical interdependence
among units of a system, a number of things are to be kept in
mind. In the first place, the operation of the hydroelectric system
is subject to constraints imposed by flood control and navigation
priorities. If the system were operated for power alone, the power
output would be somewhat larger because of the greater allowable
reservoir contents at the beginning of a critical dry period. Also,
without flood control limitations, there would be a longer critical
period. This must be kept in mind in any comparison of the data
in the table with a hypothetical operation of a single project for
power alone, which might in any particular case favor a single
project.

For example, when operated in the system, the net contribution
to system output at Norris is only 29,000 kilowatts. If Norris had
been built as a power project and operated for power only as an
isolated project, primary power would have been about 47,100
kilowatts. Of course, as indicated in Table 2, Norris also contributes to power production at downstream plants in the amount of
25,200 kilowatts, making the total Norris contribution 54,200 kilowatts.[26] This relationship is generally true for the storage reservoirs,
such as Fontana and Cherokee. In the case of Watauga and South
Holston, the power generated in downstream plants is much greater
than that generated at the plant itself.

Although the table will show how much the primary power at
run-of-river plants is increased by releases from storage projects

---

[26] Even the 54,200 kilowatts attributable to Norris would be larger if maximum
power output were the exclusive objective. Since the Norris facilities (dam and
reservoir) are operated to provide a "package" of services, of which power is
only one, the value of the product mix may exceed what the value of the power
would be if the system were operated for maximizing power output alone.

upstream, the figures for primary releases are not to be used as additions to both the upstream storage dams and the downstream run-of-river plants. For instance, if Wilson Dam were operated by itself before any of the rest of the system was in operation, it would have a primary output of only 39,000 kilowatts. But since it is part of the system, primary power generated there from natural stream flow and its own storage is 156,000 kilowatts. The much greater amount results from the higher minimum flow and the longer critical period of the system. Moreover, this is increased to 184,200 by co-ordinating storage releases from twenty upstream plants. The difference between 184,200 and 156,000 kilowatts, however, is not to be credited both to Wilson Dam and to the upstream plants.

There is, in addition, a third type of unit in the system, as represented by Apalachia, which is of interest. Table 2 shows that the plant provides 33,700 kilowatts of primary power from natural streamflow, which is increased to 42,800 kilowatts by co-ordinating storage releases from three upstream dams. However, if Apalachia had been built as an isolated project without the other dams in the system, it would have generated only 11,700 kilowatts of primary power.

Any hydroelectric plant constructed as an isolated structure will produce, in addition to primary power, a certain amount of secondary and dump power. This may be sold at only very low rates, if at all. Although the exact data are not available, it is nonetheless true that when operated in a system as large as the TVA's much of the secondary and dump power is converted into primary power through electrical integration, and enjoys a higher economic value than it would otherwise have. In the total TVA system, there is virtually no dump power.[27]

Direct interdependence on the scale discussed above creates investment indivisibility or, expressed differently, creates complementary investment opportunities. Efficient investment in river

[27] The preceding material relating to TVA's hydroelectric system is based on data supplied by the Project Planning Branch, Division of Water Control Planning, TVA. In using Table 2 for purposes of illustration, we have employed data which refer to primary power only. A comprehensive analysis would also require a complete study of the average annual energy and the capacity of the thirty-three-plant system, as well as the continuous prime power. Such an analysis, however, would require time and resources not available for this study. The previous observations, therefore, should be read with this limitation in

TABLE 2. *TVA-Alcoa Hydroelectric Projects: Relative Contribution of Each Project to System Hydro Primary Power (Thousands of kilowatts continuous)*

Power From \ Power At	Kentucky	Pickwick Landing	Wilson	Wheeler	Guntersville	Hales Bar	Chickamauga	Watts Bar	Fort Loudoun	Ocoee No. 1	Ocoee No. 2	Ocoee No. 3	Blue Ridge	Apalachia
Kentucky	105.8													
Pickwick Landing	.3	87.6												
Wilson	0	0	156.1											
Wheeler	.5	.4	.8	79.3										
Guntersville	0	0	0	0	53.3									
Hales Bar	0	0	0	0	0	43.5								
Chickamauga	.1	.1	.1	.1	0	.1	52.0							
Watts Bar	.1	.1	.2	.1	.1	.1	.1	54.6						
Fort Loudoun	.1	0	.1	0	0	0	0	.1	39.2					
Ocoee No. 1	.1	.1	.1	.1	.1	0	.1	..	..	4.9				
Ocoee No. 2	0	0	0	0	0	0	0	..	..	0	11.1			
Ocoee No. 3	0	0	0	0	0	0	0	..	..	0	0	14.9		
Blue Ridge	.5	.5	.9	.5	.4	.3	.4	..	..	1.0	2.1	3.1	3.0	
Apalachia	.1	.1	.1	.1	0	.1	.1	..	..	..	..	..	..	33.7
Hiwassee	.5	.5	1.0	.5	.4	.3	.4	..	..					3.9
Nottely	.3	.3	.4	.2	.2	.2	.2	..	..					1.9
Chatuge	.5	.4	.8	.4	.3	.3	.4	..	..					3.3
Norris	3.1	3.0	5.6	2.9	2.3	2.1	2.6	3.6	..					
Calderwood	0	0	0	0	0	0	0	0	..					
Cheoah	0	0	0	0	0	0	0	0	..					
Santeetlah	.4	.4	.7	.3	.3	.2	.3	.4	..					
Fontana	2.0	1.9	3.6	1.9	1.4	1.3	1.6	2.3	..					
Nantahala	.4	.3	.6	.3	.3	.2	.3	.4	..					
Thorpe	.2	.2	.3	.2	.1	.1	.2	.2	..					
Douglas	1.7	1.7	3.1	1.6	1.2	1.2	1.4	2.0	2.5					
Nolichucky	0	0	0	0	0	0	0	0	0					
Cherokee	2.3	2.2	4.2	2.1	1.7	1.6	1.9	2.7	3.4					
Fort Patrick Henry	0	0	0	0	0	0	0	0	0					
Boone	.4	.4	.7	.3	.3	.3	.3	.4	.5					
Wilbur	0	0	0	0	0	0	0	0	0					
Watauga	1.4	1.4	2.5	1.3	1.0	.9	1.2	1.6	2.1					
South Holston	1.3	1.2	2.3	1.2	.9	.9	1.1	1.5	1.9					
Great Falls	..	..	..	..	..	..	..	..	..					
Total Power At Plant	122.1	102.8	184.2	93.4	64.3	53.7	64.6	69.8	49.6	5.9	13.2	18.0	3.0	42.8

Source: Project Planning Branch, Division of Water Control Planning, Tennessee Valley Authority, September 1956.

Hiwassee	Nottely	Chatuge	Norris	Calderwood	Cheoah	Santeetlah	Fontana	Nantahala	Thorpe	Douglas	Nolichucky	Cherokee	Fort Patrick Henry	Boone	Wilbur	Watauga	South Holston	Great Falls	Total Power at Downstream Projects From Storage Releases
																			.3
																			0
																			1.7
																			0
																			0
																			.5
																			.8
																			.3
																			.6
																			0
																			0
																			9.7
																			.6
20.0																			7.5
1.1	3.4																		4.8
1.9		2.4																	8.3
			29.0																25.2
				41.0															0
				0	34.7														0
				1.6	1.4	16.7													6.0
				8.4	7.4		69.3												31.8
				1.5	1.3		2.5	21.5											8.1
				.8	.7		1.3		7.6										4.3
										24.0									16.4
										0	4.2								0
												20.6							22.1
												0	7.1						0
												.7	.5	12.5					4.8
												0	0	0	2.0				0
												2.7	1.8	3.2	1.8	14.5			22.9
												2.4	1.7	2.9			11.8		19.3
																		8.8	8.8
23.0	3.4	2.4	29.0	53.3	45.5	16.7	73.1	21.5	7.6	24.0	4.2	26.4	11.1	18.6	3.8	14.5	11.8	8.8	

basin development, therefore, must take account not only of the returns to individual undertakings, but also of the complex of interrelated facilities. Moreover, if the advantages of an integrated system are to be exploited efficiently, management must be coordinated so as to maximize system output rather than outputs at individual units in the interdependent system of complementary facilities.

It is here that the market mechanism may fail to allocate factors efficiently in the development of a system of works. If, for example, financially feasible development at site A requires development of sites E, G, and H, and investments in H and G are dependent on assurance of the development of sites E and A, none of these sites may be developed for lack of co-ordination in the investment decision-making process in a purely market economy. Instead, an alternative site B or C may be developed which independently may return full costs, but which may preclude the development of the optimum system. Under these circumstances, investment in a complementary set of facilities which will yield economic (and financial) returns greatly in excess of its opportunity costs may be foregone in favor of a relatively inefficient development of a river system's economic potential.

MULTIPLE PURPOSES: COMPLEMENTARY PRODUCTION, SUBSTITUTABILITY, AND COMMON COSTS

The foregoing discussion of departures from our assumptions of competitive equilibrium has been limited to four of the traditional major functions served by river basin development. The discussion has been confined to reviewing the indivisibility and interdependence among facilities assumed to serve a single purpose and to suggesting some basic reasons for the investment indivisibility encountered in the production of water derivatives. Another general area of interdependence, however, is relevant to understanding the

mind, realizing that a comprehensive study based on prime power, energy, and capacity would doubtless affect in some degree the relative magnitudes. Nevertheless, prime power is a significant part of the economics of such a system, and, to that extent, the illustration can be regarded as indicative of the ratio of increased value of plants in an integrated system as compared to their value as isolated plants.

interrelations among water derivatives and the resultant complex problems in river basin development.

Where surface sources must be relied on for the services which water derivatives perform, the value of a stream is enhanced significantly by regulating its flow over time. This is accomplished by impounding wasteful excess runoffs that may also threaten damage, and by releasing water during periods when natural conditions would provide only subnormal flows. Diverse objectives of water control, such as flood prevention, navigation, salinity control, pollution abatement, residential and recreational uses, as well as head to move turbines, may all require storage. If storage is provided to regulate stream flows for one purpose, it may also be useful, within limits,[28] to meet the requirements of some of the other purposes. Viewed from the standpoint of a single activity—for example, flood control—investment in land acquisition and dam construction for storage provides factor services for each of the other activities served by common storage in a multiple purpose system. In a sense, the value of these factor services represents an economy for the other functions, which is external to the flood control activity considered independently. If all of the related activities which common storage capacity serves are integrated into a single fiscal unit, however, such external economies become "internalized" and appear on the economic accounts of the enterprise. We then have the familiar case of the plant with multiple products, established to achieve economies of scale.

Consider the economic nature of the river basin program described in Chapter I. Such a program, viewed in its entirety, in some respects performs economic activities akin to a large enterprise with multiple products and multiple plants, not unlike some of the integrated firms in the actual market economy. In other respects, however, it differs significantly in ways which preclude market mechanics from organizing efficiently the production and distribution of water derivatives. For one thing, a river basin pro-

---

[28] Within limits, a complementary relation exists between hydroelectric production and flood control; beyond the complementary range, a relationship of substitutability exists. That is, more power can be provided only at the expense of flood protection, and vice versa. Complementarity and substitutability within different ranges characterize the relationship among many of the water derivatives produced by a multiple purpose river system.

gram converts a migrating resource into forms which can satisfy a number of complementary and competing wants. At any stage in a river's seaward movement, its conversion into water derivatives may entail gains (external economies) for complementary uses, or inflict losses (external diseconomies) for competitive uses, outside the intermediary of the market. Moreover, the gains or losses for complementary or competitive uses downstream are not independent of the product mix at upstream plants during low-flow seasons or adverse hydrologic periods, when common storage must be used outside the range of complementary production. Accordingly, rather extreme, direct interdependence prevails among the complementary facilities representing a multiple purpose river basin development. This is true not only of the various production functions within the integrated system, but also to a considerable extent of the relationship between the system's production functions and those of fiscally independent enterprises employing the services of water derivatives as factor inputs. Direct interdependence, of course, eliminates the intermediary of the market so that, unless all of the interdependent economic activities are integrated into a single fiscal unit, not all of the costs and gains relevant to a socially efficient investment decision will be taken into account.

Integrating all directly interdependent activities is an extreme solution, however. Such integration would include under one umbrella hydroelectric power generation and the anadromous fishing industry; the water development agency which regulates stream flows for navigation and processing firms along the stream that profit from pollution abatement; and so on. This country has been loath to permit such a concentration of economic power, whether in a private or public body, as reflected in the national attitudes toward private monopoly and antipathy to so great a concentration of economic power in a public organization. Moreover, even this degree of integration would not meet the problem in cases where a significant proportion of the economic gains are nonmarketable. Thus, within the range in which there is a competitive relation between marketable and nonmarketable derivatives among the system's production possibilities, market mechanics cannot assure the economically most efficient product mix from multiple purpose projects. This poses not only a problem that market mechanics cannot solve efficiently, but also some difficult problems for specifying economic efficiency criteria.

Social Marginal Productivity Criterion
and Benefit-Cost Analysis

What are the implications of collective wants, indivisibility in production, and direct interdependence in resource use for the provision of water derivatives?

In the market economy, economic efficiency would require that every enterprise employ factors to the point at which marginal costs (cost of marginal inputs) would equal the product price (market valuation of the marginal unit of output). Economic efficiency would be achieved in this manner, however, only if: (a) every product for which factor costs had been incurred were marketable; (b) the market price of the enterprise's products were independent of its rate of output; (c) the market price of the factors employed were independent of the rate of output. These conditions could obtain in a free market if there were no product indivisibility (collective goods), input indivisibility (internal economies of scale), or physical interdependence among the production functions of fiscally independent enterprises (technological external economies).

If these departures from the assumptions of the competitive model existed, there would be differences between the sum of financial returns from the sale of marketable output and the total economic gains attributable to a socially efficient allocation of resources. There would be a divergence between the private and social valuation of the marginal products of the factors employed. And—since private returns are the indicators which guide resource allocations in a pure market economy—the divergence between actual results and efficient results would permit a reshuffling of resources such that the gainers could compensate the losers and still have something left over.

Thus there is an opportunity to improve economic efficiency by collective action through extra-market devices. Public bodies, through their authority to tax and levy assessments, have access to financial resources which is independent of the marketability of the commodities or services such resources can provide. When the public budgeting process supplements the allocative function of factor markets, however, criteria are needed to aid in achieving the efficiency objectives for which such public revenues have been used. A great deal of attention has been directed in recent years to specifying the needed criteria.[29] Such criteria normally require equating the value of the social marginal product of a factor to its social cost, in contrast to balancing private costs and gains at the margin, as in a purely market economy. The valuation of the social product, or benefits, takes account of the divergences between the private and social product which arise when conditions in the actual economy depart from those of the competitive model. On the cost side, the principal problem is that of estimating the social cost of public funds, except under circumstances of unemployment.[30]

The rationale underlying the evaluation of benefits and costs for purposes of this study is as follows: Since we are concerned only with multiple purpose projects of considerable size, we recognize that the collective action which is relevant, and hence the public funds which are primarily at issue, are federal. If federal resources are involved, we assume the objective of their use is to improve national economic efficiency.[31] Moreover, we restrict our attention to improvements in national economic efficiency that can be secured through use of federal funds for influencing factor

[29] A pioneering attempt is the 1950 report to the Federal Interagency River Basin Committee, *Proposed Practices for Economic Analysis of River Basin Projects,* prepared by the Subcommittee on Benefits and Costs. More recent contributions in this area have been made by Roland McKean, *Cost Benefit Analysis and Efficiency in Government* (Santa Monica: Rand Corporation Research Memorandum, 1955), and by Otto Eckstein, *Water Resources Development: The Economics of Project Evaluation* (Cambridge: Harvard University Press, 1958). For application to underdeveloped areas, where problems of the nature discussed above appear in intensified form, see Hollis B. Chenery, "The Application of Investment Criteria," *Quarterly Journal of Economics,* February 1953; and Otto Eckstein, "Investment Criteria for Economic Development and the Theory of Intertemporal Welfare Economics," *Quarterly Journal of Economics,* February 1957.

[30] In this study, since we assume pursuit of an effective economic stabilization policy, consistent with the intent of the Full Employment Act of 1946, we need not concern ourselves specifically with this problem. It is true, however, that even under conditions of relatively full employment throughout the economy, pockets of underemployment in some areas or regions may occur. In this case, the market rates of hire for construction labor may not accurately reflect the opportunity cost of labor, and an appropriately downward adjustment for this component of construction cost would be required to reflect accurately social cost.

[31] This is not to deny that there can be other objectives—social, strategic, etc. —for which federal funds may be employed in the water resources field. It

allocations to the water resources field. In short, our efficiency criteria equating social marginal productivity and cost—or incremental benefits and costs—relate only to investment opportunities in the water resources field.[32]

EVALUATION OF BENEFITS

The estimate of benefits from multiple purpose river development must take account of collective goods, physical interdependence, indivisibility in production, and adjustment for miscellaneous market imperfections.

An estimation of the value of collective goods—principally flood protection, within the context of multiple purpose river development—needs to reflect the sum which beneficiaries would be willing to pay for such protection if they were given a choice. Normally, if beneficiaries behaved rationally in this respect, they would be willing to pay no more than the cost that they would be prepared to incur for repairing flood damages and avoiding the inconveniences associated with flooding.[33] This would indicate the economic value of flood prevention, subject to the lack of an alternative approach—for example, flood management through zoning of flood

means only that in terms of the efficiency objectives with which we are concerned, the national economy is the appropriate frame of reference for the benefit-cost analyses.

[32] We recognize that a comprehensive efficiency criterion for investment would require that public funds be invested in every investment opportunity in which the economic returns would exceed the economic costs. For example, there may be investment opportunities in the private sector which, because of capital rationing or other market imperfections of an institutional (in contrast with a technical) nature, would provide returns to the investment of federal funds equal to or greater than returns available from remaining opportunities in the traditional public sector. However, we are aware that, given the prevailing economic-political philosophy in the United States, there are restraints on the extent to which the government can participate by direct investment. We therefore assume that other governmental policies with respect to increasing credit availability to certain groups, perfecting markets through policing monopoly activities, etc., are pursued to minimize the inefficiencies resulting from such conditions, rather than assuming that these sectors can be regarded as alternatives to government investment in the water resources field.

[33] For a complete discussion of the methods employed in flood control benefit estimation, see Eckstein, *Water Resources Development, op. cit.*, Chapter v.

plains, warning systems, and flood insurance—which would provide equally effective protection at lower aggregate cost.

Evaluation of benefits provided by a project involving direct interdependence with other fiscally independent production units requires crediting the value of external economies and debiting the cost of external diseconomies[34] from the estimate of project benefits otherwise taken into account. The value attributed to pollution abatement, salinity repulsion, increases in power generation, etc., resulting from stream regulation from a storage reservoir, can be taken as the sum which beneficiaries would be willing to pay to obtain the service if permitted a market choice. Again, of course, this could not exceed the lowest cost by which alternative, equivalent services could be obtained. Similarly, the debits from benefits otherwise estimated, that are required by the presence of external diseconomies, must reflect adequately the costs which are incidentally inflicted on third parties.

If the development of a multiple purpose project increases the supply of a marketable project service sufficiently to influence the price at which the total can be marketed, the drop in price calls for special treatment in estimating the value of the project output. The aggregate value of the increment in supply is represented by the amount which could be collected if each unit of the block of new output could be offered separately for sale at the price it could command. In short, successive units of output, during a specified marketing period, would command prices below the level of preceding units in the sequence. Accordingly, neither the price which would prevail in the absence of the project, nor the price which would be necessary to clear the last unit from the market, would directly indicate the value of each unit of output. If the demand function for the service were linear, however, the value of the total increase in supply could be approximated by using an average price midway between the price which would prevail with the project supply and without it.[35]

Similarly, if investment in a project occurred in a relatively underdeveloped region, where complementary facilities operated below capacity or within the range of decreasing average costs,

---

[34] This assumes that third parties cannot be compensated directly for costs that are incidentally inflicted.

[35] See McKean, *op. cit.*, Chapter 10, for a complete discussion of this question.

internal economies which would not be realized in the absence of the project represent an economic gain attributable to the project.

Marketable project services, which represent only marginal additions to the supply in the relevant market areas, can be valued by means of prevailing prices if such prices represent free market results. If—through public policies such as supported or subsidized prices, tariffs, import restrictions, etc.—the prevailing prices of substitutes for the project output do not mirror competitive equilibrium prices, appropriate adjustments to approximate equilibrium prices are required in properly estimating project benefits.

ESTIMATION OF COSTS

While evaluation of benefits often poses difficult problems in application, estimation of the costs of project construction is relatively more straightforward, and often little different from comparable estimation in the private sector. Markets exist for factor services needed in building projects; thus, market rates of hire for services and established prices for construction materials and items of equipment are generally available—or obtainable through estimation—by reference to relevant markets. In some cases, a project might increase the demand for localized factor services—for example, the increase in demand for workers might be sufficient to affect the rates of hire in the local labor market. Under such circumstances, costing the block of construction labor input would be symmetrical with the case involving valuation of the block of output discussed above. This is required, since the opportunity cost of the total input would be less than the amount obtained by costing all units of input at the level needed to attract the final unit required for the scheduled rate of project construction.[36] Moreover, if pockets of local unemployment or underemployment existed, the social cost of engaging otherwise idle resources would be less than the industry-wide wage rate established without reference to particular local labor supply conditions.[37]

Estimating the social cost of capital services for the project, however, represents a somewhat different kind of problem. Because only a part of the services of multiple purpose river projects are

[36] *Ibid.*, Chapter 10.

[37] For an alternative suggestion with regard to treating this problem in a practical situation, see Eckstein, *Water Resources Development, op. cit.*, Chapter II.

marketable, project capital is not obtained by competitive bidding in the market. In this study, we accept the fact that public revenues for project construction (and operation in part) typically are raised by taxation. Estimating the opportunity cost of tax-raised federal funds is a complicated task, however, which has not been systematically investigated in previous studies. Accordingly, we defer for the moment the treatment of opportunity cost of developmental funds needed to round out our benefit-cost criterion. This problem will be taken up for systematic, detailed treatment in the following chapter.

To complete the rationale underlying benefit-cost analysis used in this study, we argue as follows: Economic efficiency, as we define it, will require that a scarce resource be committed to a developmental opportunity (and to specific purposes within a multiple purpose project) up to the point at which the added benefits just compensate for the added costs. In deciding the scale of the project, if there are discontinuities in the project's expansion path, the more efficient scale will be the one that exhibits the larger total net gains—that is the excess of benefits over costs will be at a maximum, which is the point at which incremental benefits just equal incremental costs. If the benefits accrue to the same individuals that incur the costs, we can claim that the net gains represent an increase in social welfare. This is a possibility attending collective action when the public revenues in question are raised by means of special-purpose assessments, but will not ordinarily apply to the situations taken up in this study. However, if those who gain could and do compensate those who lose by the economic change stemming from a multiple purpose development, and if they will have a net gain remaining, our efficiency criteria will provide guides to achieving an increase in social welfare.[38]

If those who gain would be able out of their gains to compensate the losers, but do not do so because the administrative machinery for implementing multilateral compensation is not feasible, we do not argue that social welfare has been increased as a result of the development. We have no scientific bases for comparing one man's gain with another man's loss. A dollar's gain to one can be equated to a dollar's loss to another only if the marginal utility of money

---

[38] This abstracts from the cases in which the interrelation of consumer satisfactions could be significant.

is the same for both. Such a proposition cannot be demonstrated analytically. Hence, we cannot say that one man's gain though it be very large, increases the aggregate of welfare more than the decrease in welfare associated with the uncompensated loss of another's. Our efficiency criteria, in the practical case, will not lead unambiguously toward an increase in social welfare.

If systematically applied in the water resources field, however, our efficiency criteria will lead to an increase in social product valued at market (or imputed) prices.[39] That is, our benefit-cost criteria will lead to an increase in the social valuation of the total output, even though we cannot say that the resulting distribution of income will increase, diminish, or leave unchanged social welfare. But we know from empirical investigations that a rise in national output in modern societies has been attended by greater equality in its distribution.[40] Neither the rise in material output nor the greater equality of distribution of the social product offends the predominant ethical values of an equalitarian political democracy. Accordingly, there is reason—if not a scientifically demonstrable case—for believing welfare will be increased generally by systematic application of the economic efficiency criteria.[41] We claim no more for our efficiency criteria.

To the extent that multiple purpose river projects will normally require some financing out of tax revenues, we have to acknowledge the theoretical possibilities of tax effects on the marginal adjustments in the resource allocative process. This problem is not significant from the standpoint of considerations faced in this study. But financing by means of taxation has significant implications of another sort for our evaluation of costs in the efficient investment criterion. Accordingly, we shall take some time to arrive at an opportunity cost for water resources investment funds in the next chapter, which represents a different approach to the problem than any previously employed in benefit-cost analysis.

[39] This accepts the institutionally imposed restraint on public investment in the purely private sector.

[40] This point we owe to S. V. Ciriacy-Wantrup, "Concepts Used as Economic Criteria for a System of Water Rights," *Land Economics,* November 1956, p. 307.

[41] This does not deny exceptions or the application of "higher criteria" in particular cases. For a generalized defense of this position see Franklin M. Fisher, "Income Distribution, Value Judgments, and Welfare," *Quarterly Journal of Economics,* August 1956.

IV The Social Cost

of Federal Financing

We have seen how the interest rate in the competitive model serves as a price in the capital market, bringing the savings preferences of consumers into consistency with the investment plans of business enterprises. Let us now extend the examination to investment undertaken by government.

Most of the activities of government are devoted to satisfying collective wants, wants which cannot be met through goods and services sold in the market place. Whenever the ballot box and the political process replace market choice, investment decisions will not be made by comparing the rate of return of investments with the market rate of interest.[1] Many of the collective goods produced by public investments are valued qualitatively, precluding computations of the rates of return which underlie private investment decisions. The costs are more specific, however; resources employed in a public undertaking have alternative uses in the production of marketable commodities and will, therefore, have a price which measures their opportunity cost.

This cost cannot be measured directly from the borrowing cost, since the funds are raised by taxation, but within the competitive

---

[1] Some goods, such as electric power, supplied by government are marketable; others, such as flood control, though nonmarketable, can be valued at prices established in related markets. Yet the fact that the investment decision is made in a political context results in the introduction of other considerations and makes it unlikely that the decision will be made in accordance with the economic principle alone.

model the social cost can easily be imputed. An analysis based upon the competitive model would go like this: The cost of capital is measured by the interest rate. Insofar as the necessary taxes reduce marginal investments of firms, they prevent the creation of a stream of returns whose relationship to the foregone investment would have been just equal to the interest rate. Similarly, taxes which fall on consumption reduce the present levels of consumption for which people are willing to pass up the opportunity of collecting the market rate of interest. In other words, the consumer places the same value on the expenditure of the marginal consumption dollar as on a perpetual income stream equal to the interest rate. Thus, if government desires to place an economic value on the cost of raising capital through taxation, it can simply apply the market rate of interest.[2]

Unfortunately, the American economy does not fit the competitive model closely enough to permit use of so simple a procedure. The substantial risk premiums in the terms on which business can borrow, and the rationing of credit to some businesses and to most consumers, preclude the existence of a unique rate of interest and prevent consideration of any single actual rate as a measure of the social cost of capital. Yet, in considering alternative methods of financing water resource development and in evaluating the economic worth of projects, reasonable estimates of the social cost of federal funds are essential. Since the market cannot be consulted for the price of capital, as competitive theory would suggest, it is necessary to derive an estimate by more complicated empirical procedures which take account of some of the complexities of the process by which savings are actually channeled into investment.

That is the task undertaken in this chapter. First, as background for our inquiry, we shall examine the salient facts about saving and borrowing in the United States in a recent year. Then, through the use of models, we shall attempt to derive a figure that can serve as a measure of the social cost of public funds used in development of water resources.

---

[2] This assumes that the taxes are raised without causing any distortion in decision-making. If there are tax-induced distortions in the economy's allocation of resources, the true social cost of raising capital by taxation will be greater than the market rate of interest.

Saving and Investment in the United States

Before turning to our methods of estimation, let us take a quick look at some rather rough, but revealing, figures about the capital formation of the United States in the year 1955, which will serve as a background for the analysis. Table 3 indicates the total gross investment of the major sectors of the economy, defined somewhat more broadly than in the standard national income accounts—though even the set of categories used here misses large amounts of investment by government. The startlingly large figure for households, $52 billion, is offset to a significant degree by the depreciation of "durables" which last only a relatively few years, and

TABLE 3. *Gross Capital Formation in the United States, 1955*

Sector		($ billion)
Households:		
Residential construction	17	
Automobiles	17	
Other durables	18	52
Corporate business:		
Plant and equipment expenditures	25	
Inventory investment	4	
Other	1	30
Unincorporated business:		
Plant and equipment expenditures	4	4
Farms:		
Construction and equipment	4	4
Government:		
Federal construction	3	
State and local construction	9	12
Total		102

similarly for some of the other items. Yet it is clear that much investment occurs outside the business sectors; in fact each sector plays a significant part in the process of capital formation.

In the financing of these investments, there are significant departures from Chapter II's idealized picture, in which we assumed the savings of individuals to be the source of capital, with investors paying the market rate of interest on the requisite loans.[3] Households financed their purchases of automobiles in large part through installment credit, with the total outstanding increasing $4 billion over the year, an amount which is about half the net investment in cars after depreciation. About $15 billion of $17 billion of residential construction was offset by an increase in mortgages,[4] but the $18 billion of other durables was financed out of income for the sector as a whole. The Department of Commerce reports total personal saving to be $17 billion, but this figure does not reflect the borrowing done by households in the form of mortgages. If we subtract money borrowed in this way, we find that net personal saving is at most $2 billion or $3 billion. That is, the household sector—which in our theoretical model was to provide the savings for the business sector—actually saved little more than it invested in its own durables.

Of the $30 billion of real investment carried on by corporations, $15 billion came from depreciation and amortization allowances and another $9 billion from retained earnings. Only the remaining $6 billion was financed by new securities—$2 billion in common stocks and $4 billion in bonds and notes. And of this total, public utilities issued all but $400 million of the stock and $2 billion of the bonds and notes. There was also an increase of bank loans of $4.5 billion, and an increase of other liabilities of $1.5 billion, but this was more than offset by the increase in customer receivables. Thus the business sector as a whole, other than public utilities, borrowed no more than 8 or 10 per cent of the funds for its real investment.

Unincorporated business, which is typically small, and for which our figures are much more sketchy, invested about $4 billion in plant and equipment. Much of the investment of this sector, which consists primarily of retail and other service establishments, consisted of the construction and improvement of stores, which were financed largely by mortgages and bank loans. But the sector as a whole withdrew relatively little from the capital market; repay-

---

[3] See W. A. Salant, "Saving, Investment, and Stability," *American Economic Review*, May 1956, pp. 42-54.

[4] This figure includes mortgages issued on old houses.

ments of old loans and mortgages roughly offset new ones.

The picture in agriculture is quite similar; $4 billion of construction and agricultural implements was financed principally through bank loans and mortgages, but the repayments of other farmers were at least equal to the borrowing.

Finally, $12 billion of construction was carried on by government. The $9 billion share of state and local government led to the issuance of $5 billion of new securities, but surpluses run by other state and local bodies reduced the net deficit of the sector to $1.5 billion. The federal government invested at least $3 billion in construction, a figure which omits much military work, but this was entirely financed out of taxes, and there was a net cash surplus of $2.7 billion for the year. Foreign investment for the year was negative, with repayments exceeding new investments by $300 million.

It can be seen from these figures that the net borrowing of the various sectors is less than 10 per cent of the total capital formation for the economy as a whole. This is significant. On both the lending and borrowing side of the capital market we need to take a second look at the factors that determine the level of investment and of saving for each group of decision-makers.

The significance of the small amount of net borrowing or lending of the sectors depends, in part, on the degree to which the lenders provide funds for the borrowers within the same sector. To some extent, there is a common capital market for all sectors, in which some personal, business, and government savings are commingled through the activities of financial intermediary institutions. But, at least in the case of the household sector, we find the capital flows primarily within the sector. Of the $15 billion of mortgages, savings and loan associations acquired $5.4 billion; life insurance companies, $3 billion; mutual savings banks, $2.4 billion; individuals, $2.4 billion; and commercial banks, $1.7 billion. All but the last of these sources administer the savings of individuals and, even in the latter category, much of the money available for mortgages springs out of individuals' time deposits. As for the $5 billion of installment and other credit, the household credit corporations which handle the largest part of this paper raise their own funds by sale of their notes to insurance companies and other financial intermediaries who draw the bulk of their funds from individual savings.

For the other sectors, the case is not so clear. Corporate securities draw on a wide variety of sources. Unincorporated business is financed in part by bank loans—which, to a considerable extent represent money created by the banking system—and in part by loans from individuals who are willing either to invest in the business or to lend the owner money because of ties of friendship or family. The securities of state and local governments, because of their tax-exempt feature, are particularly attractive to individuals with very large incomes, and thus can be assumed to draw on individual savings. Capital for agriculture is supplied in the form of mortgages by banks and insurance companies and in the form of loans by commercial banks.

Interest Rates in the American Economy

There is no one interest rate—capital is offered on a very wide range of terms. Bonds, notes, and other debt instruments of governments and corporations find a ready market at rates ranging from 2 to 5 per cent, depending on the terms of the loan and the credit standing of the issuer. Mortgages of good quality are financed at rates between $4\frac{1}{2}$ and 6 per cent, though this rate is kept low by government guarantees of a large part of the total. Other consumer credit is expensive, ranging from 5 to over 25 per cent, with the typical automobile installment loan held by a large credit company costing 9 to 12 per cent. Yet the sales finance companies are able to raise their funds at rates below 4 per cent. The difference between their lending and borrowing rates is explained by the high cost of administration and collection, the pooling of many small, risky loans to reduce risk, and substantial profits. Bank loans to corporations and unincorporated business may cost from 3 to 6 per cent, depending on size, the region of the country, and the credit standing of the borrower, but their availability is strictly rationed to each firm. Loans to agriculture, while only slightly more expensive, are even more severely rationed to each farmer. Most personal saving, in the form of savings accounts, insurance, and pensions, receives a return of 3 per cent or so, with investments in common stocks the only substantial exception. And stock ownership is still restricted to a relatively small proportion of savers, who receive an income yield of only 4 per cent, but who have been receiving large capital gains.

Measuring the Social Cost of Public Capital: The Method of this Study

The task of discovering the true social cost of the capital devoted to water resource development under actual conditions is much more difficult than if our theoretical model applied in a straight-forward way. The model determines one interest rate for each period, a rate which indicates both the opportunity cost of capital in other fields and the rate at which consumers are willing to give up present income for a future income stream. In reality, there are many interest rates for both borrowers and lenders, and we are not free to fasten upon any one of them for our purpose. Yet the sound formulation of public policy requires some clear idea about this social cost. Use of a rate which is much too low may result in the waste of the nation's capital in a project yielding less satisfaction to consumers than if left in its alternative use. Use of an excessively high rate will leave water resources underdeveloped as compared to other resources in the nation's economy. For the typical problem of financing public investment by taxation, we, therefore, need to derive an appropriate estimate for the social cost of capital.

Our method will take account of the actual structure of capital flows in the United States. First, we shall try to determine where the tax money that provides the capital used for federal resource development actually comes from—that is, the incidence of the marginal tax dollars. This requires quantitative study of the revenues produced by different taxes, the persons and organizations who pay these taxes, and the extent to which taxpayers are able to shift their tax liabilities to others. It also requires that we assume in what proportion the various taxes would be increased were the program to be expanded, or which ones would be cut in the event of contraction. Once we know the sources of the money, we can proceed to the second stage and estimate what value attaches to these funds in their alternative uses.

When government imposes taxes in order to finance public investments, it levies a compulsory loan or forced saving on the community, which releases the resources for the undertaking. The taxes lead to a reduction of consumption by households, to a decline in investment, or both. The social cost of the capital raised from foregone investment is clear: the investments would have yielded a certain rate of return to the community which would have increased the future flow of real national income. The social cost, therefore, is equal to the foregone rate of return on private investments.

To estimate the cost of funds which would have been spent for consumption, we must turn to the saving and borrowing behavior of households. Each individual has certain preferences about the allocation of his expenditures over time, more particularly, the allocation between present and future consumption. If he postpones consumption, he earns interest on the resultant saving; if he pays outstanding debts he reduces his interest payments accordingly. A rational consumer will allocate his expenditures over time in such manner that the rate at which he is willing to give up present consumption for the income stream made possible by the resultant increase of his saving will be equal to the interest rate which he faces in making this choice. Thus, a saver will push his consumption to the point where the satisfaction of a future income stream equal to the interest rate is exactly equal to the satisfaction he derives from the marginal dollar of consumption. Similarly, a borrower will derive satisfaction from his marginal dollar of consumption equal to the stream of interest payments he must make on this marginal expenditure dollar which he has borrowed.[5]

Figure 13 illustrates this optimum condition of consumer behavior. It shows the consumer's indifference map between present consumption expenditures and increases of his future annual consumption streams.

If the consumer's income in the present period is represented by point *a* (Figure 13-a), then he can reach any of the points on the two line segments, *ad* and *ae*, which start at that point. Moving to

---

[5] This formulation does not detail the intertemporal optimum conditions between all present and future periods and, hence, cannot describe the entire future time profile of an individual's consumption. It is sufficiently detailed for our limited purposes, however, and we seek to keep our assumptions as simple as possible. The same reasoning can be applied to the rate of substitution of consumption expenditures between any two periods, provided the entire structure of future interest rates is also known for the individual.

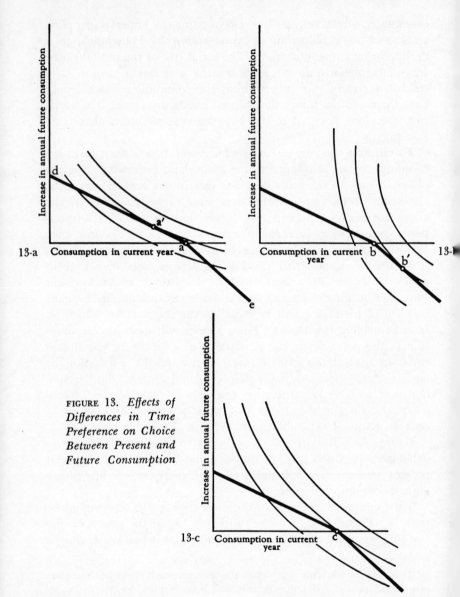

FIGURE 13. *Effects of Differences in Time Preference on Choice Between Present and Future Consumption*

the right along the steeper line means that he is borrowing to increase his present consumption at the expense of future diminished consumption; the slope of this line reflects the relatively high borrowing rate. Moving to the left on the less steep line represents saving out of present income at the relatively low interest rates that can be earned on savings accounts and other assets. It can be seen from the diagram that point a', the point of tangency between the saving line and an indifference curve, is the preferred point that this individual can reach: it is on the highest attainable indifference curve. Point b (Figure 13-b) illustrates the case where the individual will borrow and thereby reach the preferred point b', while point c (Figure 13-c) represents a situation where the individual does not find it worthwhile to lend at low rates or to borrow at high rates, and so simply spends his current income.

There are several fundamental factors which determine the general shape of a particular consumer's indifference map in any one period. First, there is the phase of the consumer's life cycle of earnings and of expenditure needs. A young married person— with an expectation of a rising income, with dependent children, and with large needs to fully equip his household with standard durables—has a high preference for current consumption expenditures. An older person, expecting a falling income and retirement, saves to increase his consumption later on, and so on. Second, an individual's attitude toward satisfaction enjoyed at different points of time will be reflected in this preference map. People with a very short horizon will have strong preferences for present consumption, while misers will favor the reverse. Third, a person's need and desire for providing for financial contingencies will help to determine these preferences. Many other factors could be cited, but this brief list at least indicates their general nature.

Much of consumer borrowing is for the sake of purchasing durables before sufficient cash can be set aside to pay for them; all mortgages and most installment paper fall in this category. Such borrowing, in a sense, is for investment rather than consumption, for in each instance the asset yields a return to the owner. The return may be monetary; a house, for example, reduces rent payments. It may be a saving of labor, as in the case of washing machines. The rest of the return may be in the form of satisfaction enjoyed directly, sometimes as extra convenience, often as the enjoyment of consumption through use of the durable. But whatever the form of the return, a rational consumer will borrow at a given interest rate only if his enjoyment of the return is at a rate at least as great as his interest payments. Thus, we can assume that a person who is willing to pay 12 per cent interest on the purchase of a car on credit, or a homeowner paying 5 per cent on the mortgage on his house, presumably is enjoying satisfaction from these assets at rates at least equal to these figures.

In order to determine the social cost of funds raised through taxation of an individual with given preferences about his saving-borrowing behavior (or with given opportunities for investing in durables), we must ascertain the interest rates which he faces. A dollar of taxation is a reduction of his current income. If we can assume that the marginal dollar an individual spends for present consumption, or the dollar he saves, would be worth a future annual income stream equal to his interest rate, then the same interest rate would apply to the dollar required to pay an increase in taxes. Conversely, a tax reduction of a dollar can be converted into a future income stream equal to his interest rate. Interpreting taxation for public investment as a compulsory loan for the sake of future benefits, the social cost of this investment is equal to the interest rate which the government would have to offer to the taxed individuals to induce them to grant the loan voluntarily. Our analysis does not assume that all of the taxed money would have been saved voluntarily; presumably part of it would have been consumed. We assume only that the decision about the fraction to be saved is made rationally and in the light of the opportunities for changes in future income which the interest rate measures. These assumptions are sufficient to derive the value of marginal income in terms of a future stream which can be expressed as an interest rate. We can then apply this reasoning to marginal changes of income which are caused by taxation.

A further requirement for the estimate of the social cost of marginal tax dollars is to discover how these dollars are apportioned among the major categories of decision-making units that face different interest rates. This means allocation of the taxes between businesses and households, between borrowers and lenders, between borrowers at high rates and borrowers at moderate rates, and so on. For households, we use three categories—lenders, borrowers at mortgage rates, and borrowers at short-term credit rates—combined with a breakdown by income class. In the case of business, we estimate the effect on investment and its potential return, in accordance with the size of assets of the taxpaying firms.

Our analysis necessarily is confined to small changes in expenditures and taxation relative to the over-all levels of the federal budget. Large tax changes, such as a 30 per cent reduction in income taxes, would lead to such substantial shifts in consumers' decisions and in the rate-of-return schedules of business that assumptions of the present relationships between incomes, prices, interest rates, and rates of return would no longer be valid. There might be effects on consumers' incomes which would convert borrowers into savers, effects on the total amount of saving and of investment which might alter and shift the interest rate structure, and changes in the relative prices of consumer goods and capital goods which would result in a shift from investment to consumption in the private sector. Since all of water resource development absorbs little more than 1 per cent of the federal budget, any tax changes made possible by changes in this program would be so small as to be truly marginal; no limitation to the applicability of our analysis to this field is imposed by these considerations.

As with other criteria of economic efficiency, our measure abstracts from changes in the distribution of income. We view the public investment as a loan by society to itself in order to build certain physical investments. That is, we assume that it does not matter to whom benefits and costs accrue. In fact, much of the cost is usually borne by individuals who do not benefit from the investment, so that the distribution of income is changed. If we attached a different value to a dollar of cost or benefit for different groups, our efficiency measure would need to be modified. In the present context, the value of the addition of a dollar to the future income stream is assumed to be the same for all taxpayers and beneficiaries. And if we go beyond the measurement of cost and compare it with benefit, we make the additional assumption that who receives the benefits and costs is a matter of indifference. These are ethical judgments which each person is free to accept or reject. Insofar as our interest is focused on the increase in total national income and on the efficiency of particular programs in promoting this objective, this assumption serves as a means of isolating this facet of the problem from redistributive issues.[6]

---

[6] For further discussions of this question, see the last sections of Chapters II and III. In the water resource field, this value judgment has been made explicit by the Congress in the Flood Control Act of 1936, where it is specified that benefits must exceed costs for a project "to whomsoever they may accrue," in order for a project to have economic feasibility and to be eligible for authorization.

Our quantitative analysis could be presented, with no substantive difference, either as an expansion of investment and a tax increase or as a contraction of investment and a tax cut. It is the change in taxes which is significant; it does not matter whether the public investments would increase existing taxes or prevent a possible reduction. Since the actual tax policy issues have appeared in terms of tax reductions in recent years, we consider the problem from this point of view.

In order to measure the cost of capital for a wide range of taxes, we present two models using different sets of assumptions about the potential tax cuts which are forestalled by the public investments. In Model A, we assume that the personal income tax is reduced in a manner most advantageous to low-income families and that sales taxes are lowered. These tax cuts would primarily boost consumption. Model B consists of a reduction of the personal income tax with emphasis on upper-income brackets, combined with a reduction of the corporation income tax. This model would increase investment.

Throughout the analysis it is assumed that the government runs a successful stabilization policy. This is not to say that full employment and stable price levels prevail constantly, but only that neither major unemployment nor severe inflation is allowed to develop. This assumption accords both with the avowed objectives of the government and with the general setting assumed for federal resource development programs, and it corresponds with the record of recent years. Most of the data for our quantitative analysis are based on the year 1955, a year in which employment was high and prices stable, and the money supply was moderately tight.

In this context, a reduction in a specific government expenditure must be considered an autonomous change that must be offset by some weapon in the arsenal of the stabilizers. It is this reasoning which forces us to derive our estimates of social cost on the basis of specific counteracting fiscal or monetary policies.[7]

[7] Thus our procedure measures what Musgrave calls the "differential incidence" of expenditures (See R. A. Musgrave, "General Equilibrium Aspects of Incidence Theory," *American Economic Review*, May 1953, pp. 504-17). A reduction of expenditures by $1.00 may require an offsetting tax cut of less than $1.00, because the multiplier effects of the former may exceed the effects of tax reduction (see H. C. Wallich, "Income-Generating Effects of a Balanced Budget," *Quarterly Journal of Economics*, 1944, pp. 78-91). In our quantitative

This may seem to be a cumbersome procedure for deriving one number—the opportunity cost applicable to resource development funds. But there is no short cut. With capital coming from many sources, which face widely differing borrowing and lending rates of interest and whose saving and investment decisions are conditioned by altogether different factors, the actual impact of federally financed projects on the economic activities of the other sectors of the economy varies widely. It has been argued, for example, that the true opportunity cost of capital is the rate of return earned on the marginal investments of the most successful private firms, such as DuPont or General Motors, rates which before taxes are in excess of 20 per cent. But this is not the true opportunity cost; reduction of the federal program by $100 million would not result in expansion of investment by such firms of an equal amount. It has also been argued that the interest rate on long-term government bonds measures the social cost of public capital.[8] This rate is also inappropriate, because it presupposes that the entire cost of projects is financed out of voluntary bond purchases and that the risks attached to projects are borne by the buyers—two conditions that do not hold. A number of other easily derived rates can be supported by plausible arguments, but in the end the arguments break down. A sector-by-sector approach, assuming a specific incidence of marginal taxation, is far more trustworthy because it corresponds to the actual conditions under which public capital is raised.

Before embarking on our detailed quantitative study, a few precautionary comments should be made about our basic assumptions. We take it as axiomatic that a measure of the social cost of capital which is consistent with an economic efficiency approach must accept the sovereignty of consumers' choice, even in matters of

---

study, we assume that the fiscal authorities reduce taxes by the appropriate amount, i.e., an amount sufficient to result in the utilization of a bundle of resources equal to the quantity released by the reduction of expenditures. Thus, we assume constancy of effective demand. We also assume that our result is not affected by any redistributions of income attributable to the multiplier effects of the two offsetting changes in the budget.

[8] The practice of most agencies and the recommendations of Budget Bureau Circular A-47 and of the Sub-Committee on Benefits and Costs of the Federal Interagency River Basin Committee imply this position. See Otto Eckstein, *Water Resource Development: The Economics of Project Evaluation* (Cambridge: Harvard University Press, in press), Chapter IV, for a survey of actual practice.

allocation of expenditures over time, and particularly with regard to their decisions on how much to consume and how much to invest. It has been widely contended that consumers' sovereignty should be rejected for intertemporal choices because of the myopia of individuals,[9] which leads to inadequate amounts of saving and investment for society as a whole from a long-run point of view. It has also been contended that it is not the function of government slavishly to follow individual desires, but to act for unborn generations, to take the lead in providing for the future.

We do not reject these considerations and shall return to them later in this chapter. In some instances, they will be reflected in the higher social criteria which may supersede the efficiency criteria as we have defined them. But, throughout this study, we take the view that economic efficiency is one of the significant criteria and that it requires measurement of gains and costs in terms of the subjective valuations of the individuals who constitute our society. In the case of the cost of capital, we also look to individual preferences, and it is on this basis that we proceed.

Model A: A Tax Cut Stimulating Consumption

Our first tax model estimating the social cost of capital consists of reductions which are particularly favorable to low-income families. In Model A, 80 per cent of the tax cut is in the form of an increase in the personal exemption of the federal income tax. The other 20 per cent is assumed to go into a reduction of those federal excises which would, in fact, be most likely to take place. When our computations for each of these tax cuts are completed and the results combined, we arrive at the following applicable interest rates:

[9] M. Dobb, *On Economic Theory and Socialism* (New York: International Publishers, 1955), pp. 38-41, 73-77, 244-45, and 258-60; A. C. Pigou, *The Economics of Welfare* (4th ed.; London: Macmillan Company, 1932), pp. 22-30; W. J. Baumol, *Welfare Economics and the Theory of the State* (Cambridge: Harvard University Press, 1952), pp. 91-92; and R. H. Strotz, "Myopia and Inconsistency in Dynamic Utility Maximization," *Review of Economic Studies,* 1955-6, pp. 165-180.

	Per cent
Increased personal exemption	5.87
Reduced excises	5.49
Weighted average for Model A	5.79

INCREASING THE EXEMPTION OF THE PERSONAL INCOME TAX

A tax cut in the form of a higher exemption frequently has been proposed in Congress. Assuming that the income tax liabilities are not shifted, it is easy to compute the incidence of the tax cut by income classes. Let us suppose the exemption is raised by $1.00. The tax saving on the typical return in each income class depends upon the marginal tax rate paid; the saving for the income class also depends upon the number of exemptions claimed. It can be seen from Table 4 that most of the tax saving accrues to those with low and middle incomes—those with incomes of $5,000 or less.

TABLE 4. *Incidence by Income Classes of an Increase in the Personal Exemption*

Income class ($ thousand)	Number of exemptions [a] (000)	Tax saving per dollar [b] (cents)	Total tax saving ($ thousand)	Per cent distribution of tax saving
0 to 3	24,472	21	5,139	19.5
3 to 5	44,557	24	10,694	40.6
5 to 7.5	23,066	27	6,228	23.6
7.5 to 10	4,906	33	1,619	6.1
10 to 15	2,705	41	1,109	4.2
15 to 20	984	50	492	1.9
20 to 30	839	59	495	1.9
30 to 50	507	67	340	1.3
50 to 100	223	79	176	.7
Over 100	63	90	57	.2

[a] U. S. Treasury Department, Internal Revenue Service, *Statistics of Income for 1951*, 1955, based on returns with taxable income.

[b] Marginal tax rates at average income tax liability reported in each class.

Discovery of the rates at which each income class saves or borrows requires examination of its asset and credit position. The

Survey of Consumer Finances provides relevant data on this question; they are summarized in Table 5. It shows, for each income class, what percentage of spending units have a significant amount of short-term consumer debt and mortgages.

TABLE 5. *Asset-Debt Position of Consumer*

	Income class		
	$0 to $3,000 (per cent)	$3,000 to $5,000 (per cent)	Over $5,000 (per cent)
Owed more than $100 of consumer debt	33	52	52
Owed mortgages only	5	8	11
Owed neither kind of debt	62	40	37

Source: 1956 Survey of Consumer Finances, "Consumer Indebtedness," *Federal Reserve Bulletin,* July 1956, p. 702.

To derive the interest rates on which consumers make their marginal borrowing-saving decisions, we must estimate the rate of return earned on their assets and the rates paid on their debts. Let us assume that the interest paid on the assets held by debt-free households is 3 per cent, a rate typical of the savings accounts and U. S. government bonds into which most households in the lower-income brackets put their savings. To take account of the higher returns earned on common stock by 15 per cent of the class with incomes above $5,000,[10] we increase this rate to 3.75 per cent for the class with no debts.

A rate of 5 per cent is applied to mortgage loans. This rate is somewhat above that charged on loans guaranteed by the Federal Housing Administration or the Veterans Administration, but corresponds to rates on conventional first mortgages and allows for the considerably higher rates which prevail on second mortgages.[11]

As for interest on short-term consumer credit, rates vary widely, from less than 6 per cent on some personal bank loans (and 0 per

[10] 1955 Survey of Consumer Finances, "The Financial Position of Consumers," *Federal Reserve Bulletin,* June 1955, p. 621.

[11] This rate corresponds to the findings of Morton for 1947. See J. E. Morton, *Urban Mortgage Lending Experience,* National Bureau of Economic Research (Princeton: Princeton University Press, 1956), pp. 80-81.

cent on loans within families) to over 30 per cent on some small loans of finance companies. This range can be narrowed by studying the composition of personal debt. Of the $36 billion outstanding at the end of 1955, $14 billion was automobile paper.[12] The rates of most automobile paper were between 8 and 12 per cent, with that held by banks near the lower figure and by finance companies near the higher one. Another $6 billion was for other consumer goods paper, which has comparable rates. Personal loans constituted $8 billion. Of these the small loans which bore very high rates were offset to some degree by low rates on bank loans available to the best of the credit risks. Of the remaining, about half were charge accounts and the rest were service credit and repair and modernization loans. The rates on these categories tended to be relatively low, ranging from 6 per cent on regular charge accounts to 9 per cent on modernization loans. The average rate for personal debt suggested by these figures is about 10 per cent. A breakdown by type of holder is consistent with this estimate, since banks hold 33 per cent, credit unions 5 per cent, stores 25 per cent, sales finance companies 28 per cent, and others 9 per cent. It would be incorrect, however, to assume that all income classes pay the same rates. Generally, poorer people obtain small loans at very high rates and borrow from sales finance companies for their durable goods purchases; those with higher incomes are able to obtain bank loans and have charge accounts. To allow for this factor, we assume a rate of 12 per cent for consumer credit for those with the lowest income and a rate of 9 per cent for the rest.

Interest payments are deductible from federal income taxation. This implies that the actual rate which governs the choice of consumers is not the rate paid, but the rate adjusted for the saving in taxes. But the applicability of this reasoning is limited by the wide use of the standard deduction in income tax returns. Itemized deductions were made on only 8 per cent of the returns for $3,000 or less; 24 per cent for $3,000 to $5,000; and 40 per cent for $5,000 and over. Because the tax saving from this source is usually more significant in the case of mortgages, we use the borrowing rate after taxes only in the case of households with mortgages.

[12] U. S. Department of Commerce, *Survey of Current Business,* March 1956, p. S-16.

Interest receipts, on the other hand, are taxable income, which again argues for the use of interest rates after taxes. But the amounts of interest received are relatively small for most households and frequently are not reported to the tax collectors. Only 7 per cent of returns with incomes below $5,000, and 20 per cent with higher incomes, reported interest receipts.[13] Therefore, we use the before-tax interest rates except for half of the interest recipients with top incomes.

Our set of categories for assigning interest rates to households does not properly describe one group in the debt-free households. The fact that the largest percentage of debt-free households is found among the lowest incomes does not mean that low-income families have less need for credit. Rather, many of these families are not sufficiently good credit risks to get any loans except small loans at very unattractive terms. It would be incorrect to assume that these families make their borrowing-saving decisions on a rate of 3 per cent. For a sizeable group of low-income families, the lack of the use of credit can be explained on other grounds. Unskilled workers are heavily represented; because their income reaches a peak relatively early in life, they have relatively little inducement to borrow. Still other low-income families consist of older people who are living on their capital; they also have no incentive to borrow. To take account of the group who wants credit but is too poor to obtain it, we assume that 20 per cent of the nonborrowers have a high time-preference and, if they were free to do so, would make use of short-term consumer credit at the usual rate of 12 per cent.

Table 6 gives the rates derived in the manner we have indicated, with adjustments for taxes incorporated in the figures. Table 7 gives the distribution of households by income class, asset-debt position, and by their marginal borrowing or lending rates. Those who owe both consumer debt and mortgages are considered to be paying the higher borrowing rate (that for consumer debt), which is the rate that must be considered marginal. Low-income families unable to borrow at reasonable rates are listed separately.

[13]U. S. Treasury Department, Internal Revenue Service, *Statistics of Income for 1952, Preliminary Report*. These figures include returns reporting miscellaneous income on the federal income tax form 1040a. We apply after-tax interest rates to one-half the interest recipients in the top class because that is the degree of compliance suggested by our asset-debt data.

TABLE 6. *Interest Rates Faced by Households in Their Saving-Spending Decisions*

	Interest rates for income class		
	$0 to $3,000 (per cent)	$3,000 to $5,000 (per cent)	Over $5,000 (per cent)
Owed more than $100 of consumer debt	12.0	8.3	7.3
Owed mortgages only	4.0	3.9	3.5
Owed neither kind of debt and held savings	3.0	3.0	3.2
Unable to borrow at reasonable rates	12.0	..	..

Source: See text.

The table also gives the average rate for each income class and the distribution of tax savings caused by an increase of the personal exemption. The final figure, computed by weighting the average rates applicable to the three income classes by their shares of tax savings, is equal to 5.87 per cent.[14] This is the rate which our quantitative analysis suggests as the proper measure of value to consumers of the tax savings made possible by an increase in the exemption of the personal income tax.[15]

[14] The use of income classes as defined by the Internal Revenue Service in combination with the definitions of the Survey of Consumer Finances introduces a slight upward bias into the estimate. The Survey's "spending unit" includes all related persons living together who pool their incomes, while the Internal Revenue Service gives its figures in terms of tax returns. Since some spending units will file several tax returns, relatively fewer spending units will fall into our lowest-income class. This bias is accentuated by the fact that our tax data pertain to 1951, when incomes were lower than in 1955. Data for the distribution of income from the two sources suggest that as many as one-half of the returns filed in the lowest-income class in 1951 should be assigned to "spending units" in the next income class in 1955. Similarly, the data suggest that one-third of all returns filed in the middle-income class in 1951 belonged to "spending units" in the highest class in 1955. On these assumptions, our estimate for the interest rate would fall to 5.70 per cent. This probably overstates the bias since the Survey's sample appears to underrepresent low-income "spending units."

[15] Our analysis has not endeavored to impute a rate of return to the investments made possible by the increased savings of consumers. Presumably, a return greater than the borrowing cost is earned on these investments, which serves as an inducement for the investor. An estimate of this extra return requires identification of the marginal borrowers to whom these investible funds

TABLE 7. *The Average Interest Rate Applicable to the Distribution of Tax Savings From Increasing Personal Exemption Based on Distribution of Spending Units by Income Class, Asset-Debt Position, and Marginal Borrowing or Lending Rates of Interest*

	Income class					
	$0 to $3,000		$3,000 to $5,000		Over $5,000	
Item	(1) Per cent of units [a]	(2) Interest rate [b] (per cent)	(3) Per cent of units [a]	(4) Interest rate [b] (per cent)	(5) Per cent of units [a]	(6) Interest rate [b] (per cent)
Owed more than $100 of consumer debt ..	33	12.0	52	8.3	52	7.3
Owed mortgages only	5	4.0	8	3.9	11	3.5
Owed neither kind of debt	50	3.0	40	3.0	37	3.2
Unable to borrow at reasonable rates [b]	12	12.0	—	—	—	—
Average rate for each income class		7.0		5.8		5.4
Percentage distribution of tax saving [c]		19.5		40.6		39.9
Average applicable interest rate						5.87

[a] 1956 Survey of Consumer Finances, *op. cit.*
[b] See text.
[c] *Statistics of Income for 1951, op. cit.*

REDUCING SELECTED EXCISE TAXES

In addition to the increase in personal exemption, amounting to 80 per cent of the tax cut, our Model A calls for a cut in excise taxes sufficient to make up 20 per cent of the decline in government revenue. We assume a reduction for only those commodities which seem likely to be affected by an actual move to cut excises. Thus, all road-user taxes are excluded because they have been set aside to finance the expanding federal highway program. Taxes on alcoholic beverages and tobacco are ruled out because they are imposed, in part, for noneconomic reasons and have a long-accepted place in the federal revenue structure. We treat the remaining excises as if they were cut proportionately, and assume that the price elasticity of consumer demand is such that the relative increase in sales will be the same for all commodities in question. These two assumptions imply that the proportionate cut in tax rates leads to a proportionate fall in the revenues from the various excises.

The incidence of excise taxes is usually assumed to fall on the consumer.[16] The incidence by income classes, then, depends on the distribution of the tax cut among commodities and on their income elasticity. Table 8 sheds some light on this question. It lists the major federal excises, shows the revenues derived from them and their percentage distribution, and gives estimates of the income elasticities of the commodities which have been made by the U. S. Department of Commerce. Using the distribution of taxes as weights, an average income elasticity is computed for the entire excise tax cut. Both the prewar and postwar figures produce an

---

would be made available, a task we shall not assay. Were we to assume that the return above borrowing cost is 3 per cent—a liberal figure in view of the low- and middle-income sources of these savings and the channels into which their savings usually flow—and were we to apply marginal propensities to save by income classes (see footnotes to Table 14) to estimate the share of the tax cut that would be saved, we would increase our estimate by .12 percentage points, resulting in a figure of 5.99 per cent.

[16] Musgrave and Tucker followed this assumption in their studies of tax incidence. (See R. A. Musgrave, J. J. Carroll, L. D. Cook, and L. Frane, "Distribution of Tax Payments by Income Groups: A Case Study for 1948," *National Tax Journal*, March 1951; and R. S. Tucker, "Distribution of Tax Burdens in 1948," *ibid.*, September 1951.) This assumption is only a first approximation and overlooks the effects of product substitution.

TABLE 8. *Excise Taxes and Income Elasticities for Selected Goods and Services*

Commodity	Tax revenue [a] ($ million)	Per cent of tax revenue	Income elasticity [b] 1929-40	1947-54
Musical instruments and radios ..	248	12.3	2.5	1.1
Records	8	.4	2.5	1.1
Appliances	107	5.3	1.3	0.3
Cameras	15	.7	1.5	0.6
Jewelry	142	7.1	1.8	0.3
Furs	27	1.3	1.5	1.5
Toiletries	72	3.6	0.8	0.5
Luggage	51	2.5	1.1	1.3
Admissions	189	9.4	0.8	−0.4
Telephone	520	25.9	0.5	1.7
Transportation	632	31.4	1.1	1.1
Average elasticity			1.15	1.00

[a] U. S. Treasury Department, *Treasury Bulletin*, March 1956. Figures are for fiscal 1955.

[b] U. S. Department of Commerce, "Consumer Expenditure Patterns," *Survey of Current Business*, September 1955, pp. 23-32. These estimates are based on time series analysis and are of questionable statistical validity in view of the small number of observations and the strong trends in some of the series. But the similarity of the results for the average of the two periods offers considerable evidence that the actual value is not far removed from 1.0. It may appear puzzling that these luxuries do not have a higher elasticity; but the result can be explained by the wide range of goods and prices offered in each category.

estimate very close to 1.0, which implies an incidence of the taxes among income classes similar to the distribution of income.[17]

Table 9 shows the distribution of family income and the interest rates applicable to the tax saving in each class. Averaging the rates by using the income distribution as weights, gives us the

[17] Rolph has put forth the view that factors of production bear the cost of excise taxes through backward shifting. Our computation is consistent with this assumption if the changes in factor payment are proportional, for this will distribute the tax saving among income classes in accordance with the distribution of income. See E. R. Rolph, "A Proposed Revision of Excise Tax Theory," *Journal of Political Economy*, April 1952, pp. 102-17.

interest rate applicable to this form of tax cut.[18] This rate turns out to be 5.49 per cent.

Averaging the 5.87 per cent rate for the increased personal exemption and the 5.49 per cent for excise cuts, weighted by their relative importance, we get an over-all estimate of the applicable rate under the tax assumptions of Model A, which is equal to 5.79 per cent.

TABLE 9. *Reduction of Selected Excise Taxes: Distribution of Income and Applicable Interest Rates, 1955*

Family income class ($ thousand)	Family personal income [a] ($ billion)	Per cent distribution before tax	Per cent distribution after tax [b]	Applicable interest rate [c] (per cent)
0 to 3	25.0	9	10	7.0
3 to 5	59.1	21	22	5.8
5 to 7.5	81.6	28	28	5.8
7.5 to 10	47.1	16	16	5.4
10 to 15	29.3	10	10	5.0
Over 15	46.0	16	14	4.6
Average applicable interest rate				5.49

[a] S. F. Goldsmith, "Income Distribution in the United States, 1952-55," *Survey of Current Business, op. cit.*, June 1956, pp. 9-16. Our income classes have to be defined as income before tax because the *Survey* data on which our interest rates are based are given that way.

[b] Since the income elasticities were derived from regressions on disposable, or after-tax, income, it is the distribution of income after taxes which supplies the proper weights for our average interest rate. The distribution after taxes was computed by applying the average tax rate for each income class (given in the Goldsmith article cited above) to the before-tax income.

[c] The rates for the lower brackets are carried over from the preceding section. The breakdown in the upper brackets is derived in detail in the discussion of Model B.

[18] A reduction of excise taxes is less likely than a reduction of income taxes to result in accrual of additional returns to marginal investors to whom additional private savings are made available. This is because the tax cut leads to price reductions of consumer goods and hence induces some substitution of consumption for saving. While we cannot be sure that the substitution effect will exactly cancel the income effect on consumption, it is unlikely that the net result will be significant. The distribution of the tax cut among income classes, and particularly to high-consumption families, strengthens this conclusion.

Model B: A Tax Cut Stimulating Investment

In Model B, we make quite different assumptions about the tax cuts made possible by a reduction in expenditures, though we again try to cast our assumptions in a plausible form from a political point of view. We assume that 50 per cent of the reduction will be taken by reducing the rate structure of the personal income tax. Rather than assume a new rate schedule, we assume that it is the objective of the rate changes to reduce the tax bill of each taxpayer in the same proportion. Income tax payments represent a larger percentage of the income in higher brackets; therefore, such a tax cut would produce a more than proportionate increase in after-tax incomes in the higher-income classes and would, therefore, reduce the degree of progression of the personal tax structure. The remaining 50 per cent of the reduction is assumed to take the form of a cut in corporate income taxes, distributed among corporations in proportion to their tax liability. Combining the interest rates applicable to each of these tax cuts, we derive our over-all estimate for Model B as follows:

	Per cent
Proportionate reduction of personal income taxes	5.29
Proportionate cut in corporation taxes	5.59
Weighted Average for Model B	5.44

REDUCING PERSONAL INCOME TAX LIABILITIES PROPORTIONATELY

Much of the method applied in Model A can be used for the personal income tax cut favoring upper-income families. Let us first look at the distribution of tax savings among income classes, given in Table 10. Comparing the incidence of this tax cut with the incidence of an increase in the exemption, we find that much more of it accrues to high-income classes, 59 per cent of it to incomes over $7,500. Where Model A emphasized the asset-debt position of families with low and middle incomes, for whom the Survey of

Consumer Finances provides good coverage, Model B must give much more detailed estimates for the upper-income classes. Insofar as the tax cut does accrue to families with incomes below $5,000,

TABLE 10. *Incidence by Income Classes of a Proportionate Reduction of Income Tax Payments, 1954*

Family personal income ($ thousand)	Per cent distribution of income tax liability [a]
0 to 3	3.6
3 to 5	13.2
5 to 7.5	24.0
7.5 to 10	14.4
10 to 15	10.3
15 to 20	5.0
20 to 30	6.5
30 to 50	7.8
50 to 100	7.7
Over 100	7.5

[a] Goldsmith, *op. cit.*, p. 15. The breakdown of the 34.5 per cent paid on incomes above $15,000 is in proportion to the tax liabilities of these classes in 1952, as given in the *Statistics of Income for 1952, Preliminary Report*, U. S. Treasury Department, Internal Revenue Service.

we can simply use the interest rates derived earlier. But a somewhat different approach is required for the upper-income groups. In the lower brackets, the diversity of interest rates is explained primarily by the presence or absence of debt and by the kind of debt owed. In the upper brackets, the form of the assets from which income is derived and the rates at which such income is taxed are the most important variables.

First, we determine what proportion of families in each class has debts in such amounts that borrowing rates would dominate choices between spending and saving, and then estimate the relevant borrowing rates. For the remaining families, which include a rapidly increasing share as we go up the income scale, we try to determine the kind of earning assets from which they derive their nonwage income and at what rates of return this income is received. Again, combining the distribution of incidence of the tax cut with the interest rates applicable to different income classes, we derive an average rate which measures the value of the money released by the postulated tax cut.

Table 11 presents the asset-debt position of households with incomes greater than $5,000. It shows a wide prevalence of debt, which results from lumping all incomes above $10,000 into one bracket. Since debt for consumption purposes falls rapidly in the higher brackets, in our subsequent analysis the figures for the bracket over $10,000 are applied only in the range $10,000 to $15,000. Also, in the higher brackets, the relevance of the borrowing rate ceases, because the rate of return on assets increases while the borrowing cost falls, until at some point on the income scale, the borrowing rate is no longer marginal—the return on assets playing the role instead. When that point is reached, consumer credit is likely to be in the form of charge accounts owed as a matter of convenience, and mortgages owed—in part—in order to raise funds for investment purposes.

Table 11 also shows the interest rates applicable to debtors in these income classes. As in Model A, rates of 9 per cent on short-term debt and 5 per cent on mortgages are used in deriving these rates, but in the case of the upper-income classes, it is assumed that interest payments are deducted from the tax liability and the rates are adjusted accordingly.

To derive the rates of return which upper-income families earn on their assets, we estimate asset holdings by income class and the rates applicable to each asset category. Table 12 shows in what form upper-income classes receive property income as reported in income tax returns.

TABLE 11. *Debt Position of Families with Incomes Over $5,000*

Income class ($ thousand)	Per cent owed more than $100 of short-term debt [a]	Per cent owed mortgages only [a]	Per cent owed neither kind of debt	Interest rate applicable to debtors (per cent)
5 to 7.5	56	11	33	6.2
7.5 to 10	52	22	26	5.6
Over 10	41	22	37	4.9

[a] 1956 Survey of Consumer Finances, *op. cit.,* pp. 701-03.

In the case of business and professional income, part is actually managerial wages or income earned for supplying professional services. While we have no direct data on this breakdown, the Department of Commerce has estimated that, in 1949, 11.3 per cent of all incomes of \$5,000 and over was professional income; 37.8 per cent, from farms; and the remaining 50.9 per cent from unincorporated business.[19] We consider all of the professional income to be a form of wages.[20] As for the income from farms and unincorporated business, we allow 50 per cent of the income as managerial

TABLE 12. *Percentage Breakdown of Nonwage Income in Upper-Income Classes* [a]

Income class (\$ thousand)	Business and professional	Dividends plus retained earning	Rent	Interest	Income from trusts
5 to 7.5	69.9	14.2	8.9	5.0	2.1
7.5 to 10	67.0	17.0	6.9	6.2	2.7
10 to 15	67.0	18.4	6.7	4.5	3.4
15 to 20	66.3	19.6	6.1	4.2	4.0
20 to 30	62.7	21.8	5.9	4.2	5.3
30 to 50	58.6	26.1	5.5	4.0	5.8
50 to 100	46.3	36.4	5.5	3.9	8.2
Over 100	22.2	56.8	4.3	2.9	13.9

[a] *Statistics of Income for 1952, Preliminary Report, op. cit.* Direct data on the holdings of assets of investors, not derived from tax information, are generally consistent with the figures given here. See J. K. Butters, L. E. Thompson, and L. L. Bollinger, *Effects of Taxation on Investment by Individuals* (Boston: Graduate School of Business Administration, Harvard University, 1953), p. 468.

TABLE 13. *Percentage Breakdown of Income from Assets in Upper-Income Classes*

Income class (\$ thousand)	Business	Dividends plus retained earnings	Rent	Interest	Income from trusts
5 to 7.5	56.4	20.6	12.9	7.2	3.0
7.5 to 10	47.5	27.2	11.1	9.9	4.3
10 to 15	47.4	29.4	10.7	7.2	5.4
15 to 20	46.5	31.0	9.6	6.6	6.3
20 to 30	42.7	33.5	9.1	6.5	8.2
30 to 50	38.2	39.0	8.2	6.0	8.6
50 to 100	27.5	49.0	7.4	5.2	10.9
Over 100	10.9	64.2	5.1	3.3	15.8

[19] U. S. Department of Commerce, *National Income, 1954 Edition, A Supplement to the Survey of Current Business,* p. 76.

[20] While many professions require considerable investment in equipment, a reduction in income would not be likely to affect this kind of investment.

wages and the remainder as income earned on assets. Table 13
gives the distribution of income from assets which is implied by
these assumptions.

Turning to the rates of return, Figure 14 throws considerable
light on prevailing rates in unincorporated business. Each dot on
the frequency distribution indicates the median rate of return of a
sample of firms in an industry. Most of the firms have assets in
excess of $50,000—the proper size to yield incomes which fall into
the brackets with which we are concerned. Both the means and
the medians of the industry medians fall very close to 6 per cent [21]

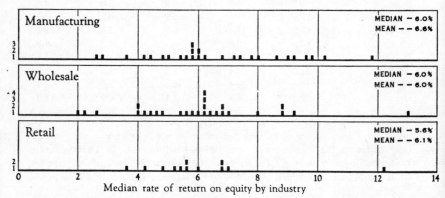

FIGURE 14. *Rates of Return in Small and Medium-Sized Firms*
Source: *Dun's Review,* October, November, and December 1955. Data compiled
by Roy A. Foulke.

for all three categories of data; we use this figure as our estimate.
In the case of farming, the average rate of return on investment,
after allowing for the value of operator and family labor, has been
estimated at 4.9 per cent for the year 1949, although the return in
38 per cent of the regions of the United States is in excess of 6 per
cent.[22] The subsequent deterioration of farm prices has lowered
the average return. But we are concerned with farms yielding an
income in excess of $7,500, earned only on the farms which are the

[21] Use of the median assures that the presence of a few large firms or of a
few extreme values will not bias the estimates.
[22] E. G. Strand, E. O. Heady, and J. A. Seagraves, *Productivity of Resources
Used on Commercial Farms,* U. S. Department of Agriculture, Technical Bulletin
No. 1128, November 1955, p. 50.

largest and most successful, and located in the better regions, and so we assume a rate of return of 6 per cent to apply.

Treatment of the returns on stock poses severe problems. The *ex post* rate of return has been extremely high in recent years because of the doubling of common stock prices. If we considered all capital gains to be income, the annual rate of return of recent years would exceed 15 per cent. But in making decisions, individuals did not fully anticipate these capital gains, nor would it be realistic to suppose that this rate will continue indefinitely. Yet, it also would be unrealistic to exclude all capital gains, since the high rate of income retention of corporations makes likely the continued growth of the value of stocks. To take account of this factor, we assume that the yield on stocks is equal to dividends plus retained earnings. In 1955, the average dividend yield on all common stock was 3.93 per cent; since only 50 per cent of earnings was paid out, we assume a total rate of return of 8 per cent.

Income from rent, interest, and trusts represents relatively small shares of total property income. For the rate of return on real estate, we use two sources. The first is profits of corporations whose main business is the holding of real estate. This has been at the rate of 12 per cent before taxes,[23] a figure which primarily represents commercial property and apartment houses. Second, for residential property as a whole, some unpublished investigations of R. Muth suggest an average rate of 5.5 per cent.[24] Since commercial property and residential property of above average profitability are likely to be held by individuals in the upper-income brackets, we assume that rental income is earned at a rate of return of 8 per cent. For interest, a rate of 3 per cent is assumed. This is slightly higher than the rates of 2.8 to 2.9 per cent which prevailed on government bonds in 1955, but lower than the average yield of 3.25 per cent on corporate bonds.[25] Finally, we assign an interest rate to income from trusts. Since the trusts represent various combinations of other assets, we simply assume that their rate of

[23] U. S. Treasury Department, Internal Revenue Service, *Statistics of Income for 1951* (Washington, D. C.: Government Printing Office, 1955), and *Statistics of Income for 1952, op. cit.*

[24] For an abstract, see R. F. Muth, "The Demand for Non-Farm Housing," *Econometrica*, April 1957, p. 365.

[25] Board of Governors, Federal Reserve System, *Federal Reserve Bulletin*, May 1956, p. 477.

return is equal to the average rate of return earned by the income class.

These rates have been stated before taxes. In the case of funds actually used for investment, this rate measures the social opportunity cost since the assets which the money makes possible yield this return. But in determining a rate of interest which measures the value of the funds used for consumption, we must use the rates of return that could be earned after taxes, since these are the rates which households actually face in making decisions. Table

TABLE 14. *Rates of Return Earned by Households, Adjusted for Taxes by Upper-Income Classes and Form of Property*

Income class ($ thousand)	Rates of return for form of property income (per cent)				
	Business income	Dividends plus retained earnings	Rent	Interest	Average rate of return [a] (per cent)
Rate of return before tax [b]	6.0	8.0	8.0	3.0	—
Rate of return after taxes by households [c] for:					
5 to 7.5	4.5	6.5	6.0	2.2	5.0
7.5 to 10	4.2	6.2	5.7	2.1	4.7
10 to 15	3.8	5.8	5.1	1.9	4.4
15 to 20	3.2	5.1	4.2	1.6	3.8
20 to 30	2.5	4.6	3.2	1.2	3.2
30 to 50	2.1	4.4	2.8	1.0	3.1
50 to 100	1.4	4.0	1.9	1.2	2.9
Over 100	0.7	3.4	0.9	0.9	2.8
Applicable rate of return [d] for:					
5 to 7.5	4.5	6.5	6.0	2.2	5.0
7.5 to 10	4.4	6.4	6.0	2.2	4.9
10 to 15	4.4	6.4	5.9	2.2	5.0
15 to 20	3.9	5.9	5.2	2.0	4.6
20 to 30	3.9	6.0	5.1	1.9	4.6
30 to 50	3.7	5.8	4.9	1.8	4.6
50 to 100	3.2	5.6	4.3	2.3	4.6
Over 100	2.8	5.2	3.7	1.9	4.6

[a] The average is weighted by the distribution of property income within the income class.

^b See text.

^c The following marginal tax rates are applied to the respective income classes: .25, .29, .36, .47, .59, .65, .76, and .89. These rates represent the marginal rate in each income class as indicated by the average tax liability reported for the class. In applying the rates, half of the income from stock is considered long-term capital gain. Also 25 per cent of the interest income in the top two brackets is considered to be from tax-exempt bonds yielding an average of 2.6 per cent; this assumption is based on the findings of Butters, Thompson, and Bollinger, *op. cit.*, p. 468.

^d These rates are derived as follows: We assume the following marginal propensities to save: 0, 12, 26, and 26 per cent respectively on the first four brackets, and 40 per cent on all brackets over $20,000. (Source: Survey of the Bureau of Labor Statistics to revise the Consumer Price Index, 1950, as reported in *Business Week*, June 16, 1956, p. 104; the figure for the top bracket is based on the 1936 survey of the National Resources Committee, reported in M. Bronfenbrenner, *et al.*, "A Study in Redistribution and Consumption," *Review of Economics and Statistics*, May 1955, p. 153, adjusted downward in accordance with the shift of the known portions of the consumption function.) We apply the rates after tax to the portion of the tax cut that would be consumed and the rates before tax to the share that would be invested, and then compute a weighted average.

These rates can be given an alternative interpretation to that of the text. Where the government is considered a "partner" in the ownership of the assets, the return in excess of the after-tax rate can be considered to be the return earned by the government on the assets. The rate at which taxes are paid on the part of the tax cut which is invested measures the government's share of the returns.

14 first gives the rates of return after taxes, and then shows the adjusted rates of return allowing for the higher rates that must be applied to the portion of the tax cut which is actually invested. Taking these adjusted rates in combination with the distribution of various kinds of property income of Table 13, we derive the average rates of return applicable to the property holders in each income class (final column of Table 14). Combining the resulting rates with the rates given for debtors in Table 11, we derive the average interest rate for the entire income class (column 3, Table 15). Finally, bringing in the rates for low-income classes from Model A, and the distribution of the tax cut from Table 10, we compute the over-all interest rate for this form of tax cut. These computations, summarized in Table 15, show an over-all rate of 5.29 per cent.[26]

[26] If we assume that an additional return of 3 per cent above borrowing cost accrues to the investors to whom the additional savings are made available, our

TABLE 15. *Summary of Derivation of Interest Rate Applicable to Proportionate Reduction of Personal Income Tax Payments*

Income class ($ thousand)	(1) Interest rate applicable to debtors (per cent)	(2) Interest rate applicable to investors (per cent)	(3) Average rate for class (per cent)	(4) Per cent distribution of tax cut
0 to 3	—	—	7.0	3.6
3 to 5	—	—	5.8	13.2
5 to 7.5	6.2	5.00	5.8	24.0
7.5 to 10	5.6	4.93	5.4	14.4
10 to 15	4.9	5.03	5.0	10.3
15 to 20	—	4.56	4.6	5.0
20 to 30	—	4.64	4.6	6.5
30 to 50	—	4.58	4.6	7.8
50 to 100	—	4.56	4.6	7.7
Over 100	—	4.63	4.6	7.5
Average applicable interest rate				5.29

Source: See text.

REDUCING THE CORPORATION INCOME TAX PROPORTIONATELY

In order to discover the interest rate applicable to a cut in the corporation income tax, we must first analyze its incidence. To what extent is it passed on to consumers through lower prices and to workers through higher wages? There is little evidence on these questions. Colm argues [27] that the benefit of the reductions after World War II accrued primarily to profits and, to some extent, to wages, but that under less inflationary conditions more of the tax cut would be passed on to consumers. Musgrave,[28] in his study of the incidence of taxation, assumes that 33 per cent of the tax is passed on to consumers and 12 per cent to wage and salary earners, leaving 55 per cent as the increase in corporate earnings. We adopt his assumption for our tax cut.

estimate is increased by .61 percentage points to 5.9 per cent. This probably overstates the effect, since the return to the investor is identical with the return to the saver on a large part of the property incomes.

[27] Gerhard Colm, "The Corporation and the Corporation Income Tax in the American Economy," *American Economic Review,* May 1954, p. 493.

[28] Musgrave, Carroll, Cook, and Frane, *op. cit.,* p. 16.

The interest rate applicable to the share of the tax cut benefiting wage and salary earners can be derived from the distribution of this form of income by income classes and our earlier estimates of interest rates. Similarly, the part of the tax cut passed on to consumers can be allocated to income classes in accordance with the distribution of consumption, and then be combined with our interest rates. The rates derived from these computations, summarized in Table 16, are 5.81 per cent for wage and salary earners and 5.68 per cent for consumers.

TABLE 16. *Derivation of Interest Rates Applicable to the Shares for Wages and Salaries and Consumption of a Reduction in the Corporation Income Tax*

Income class ($ thousand)	Per cent distribution of wages and salaries [a]	Per cent distribution of consumption [b]	Applicable interest rates [c] (per cent)
0 to 3	15	12	7.0
3 to 5	33	24	5.8
5 to 7.5	29	29	5.8
7.5 to 10	11	15	5.4
10 to 15	5	9	5.0
Over 15	7	11	4.6
Average applicable interest rate (per cent)	5.81	5.68	

[a] *Statistics of Income for 1952, op. cit.*, adjusted for 1955 conditions by applying the pattern of change of the distribution of personal income as reported in Goldsmith, *op. cit.*

[b] Assumes average propensities to consume in the respective income brackets as follows: 1.1, .96, .90, .82, .75, and .60. These propensities are taken from M. Bronfenbrenner, *et al., op. cit.;* values for the four lower income classes are based on Federal Reserve Board data for 1950; values of the two upper income classes are from National Resources Committee data for 1935-6, adjusted upward in accordance with the drift of the known portions of the consumption function.

[c] See Tables 7 and 15.

Part of the unshifted portion of the tax cut is passed on to dividend recipients. We use the relationships between dividends and earnings established by Lintner to discover the share going to dividends. He found that an increase in earnings will lead to a gradual increase in dividends until the traditional payout ratio of the firm has been restored.[29] In the first year, dividends will rise 13.5 per cent of the increase in earnings; in subsequent years, the same percentage of the gap between the dividend paid in the previous period and the dividend called for by the firm's traditional payout ratio will be closed. For the country as a whole, the average payout ratio was about .50 [30] in 1955, so a reduction of the tax by $1.00 will increase dividends 13.5¢ in the first year, 23.4¢ in the second year, and so on until the increase would equal 50¢. An average of these payments over a period of 100 years—a period corresponding to the economic life of water resource projects —would be 47¢. So, of the 54 per cent of the tax cut which accrues to increased profits, 47 per cent is passed on to dividend recipients. The distribution of dividends by income classes is given in Table 17. Applying the interest rates derived earlier, we find that a rate of 4.96 per cent is applicable to this portion of the tax cut.

These allocations leave 29.2 per cent of the tax cut as the increase of retained earnings. How much will the investment of the taxed firms increase as a result? To answer this question, we consider firms with assets greater than $10 million separately from smaller firms. This division into "large" and "small" corporations is necessary because the influence of the availability of additional funds on investment varies sharply with the size of the enterprise. We assume that 75 per cent of the tax is paid by large firms, 25 per cent by the rest.[31]

In regard to large corporations, Lintner cites a number of reasons

[29] J. Lintner, "Determinants of Corporate Savings," Chapter 14 in *Savings in the Modern Economy*, W. Heller, ed. (Minneapolis: University of Minnesota Press, 1953); and Lintner, "Distribution of Incomes of Corporations among Dividends, Retained Earnings and Taxes," *American Economic Review*, May 1956, pp. 97-113.

[30] *Statistics of Income for 1952, op. cit.* The payout ratio of small corporations is lower, and we assume a ratio of .35. This figure is an average of the payout ratios by asset size, weighted by the distribution of tax payments, and allowing for a gradual approach to the average ratio.

[31] In 1951, corporations with assets over $10 million paid 70.4 per cent of the tax (*Statistics of Income for 1951, op. cit.*). Figures for all corporations for 1951 are not yet available, but we can make a good estimate from the data on manufacturing. In this sector, which pays two-thirds of the entire tax, the percentage paid by large corporations rose from 76 to 82 per cent from 1951 to 1955. Our estimate assumes a somewhat smaller increase of taxes paid by large corporations outside manufacturing.

TABLE 17. *Derivation of Interest Rate Applicable to the Share of Corporation Income Tax Cut Benefiting Dividend Recipients*

Income class ($ thousand)	Per cent distribution of dividends [a]	Interest rate [b] (per cent)
0 to 3	4	7.0
3 to 5	6	5.8
5 to 7.5	8	5.8
7.5 to 10	7	5.4
10 to 15	11	5.0
15 to 20	7	4.6
20 to 30	11	4.6
30 to 50	13	4.6
50 to 100	14	4.6
Over 100	19	4.6
Average applicable interest rate ..		4.96

[a] *Statistics of Income for 1952, op. cit.*
[b] See Table 15.

for believing that the effect on real investment will be small.[32] Most corporations are forced to maintain a certain level of investment. Failure to expand capacity or to maintain a steady rate of reduction of costs, by jeopardizing the firm's competitive position in the industry, would pose a serious threat to its long-run future. Investment for diversification, which is usually motivated by a desire to reduce the variability of production levels and earnings, would also be relatively immune to changes in tax rates. If internally generated funds are inadequate for these purposes, the firm borrows. The effect on investment incentives caused by a tax rate which takes away part of a firm's profits on successful ventures, is, to a large extent, offset by the government's bearing part of the losses through reduced tax liability in the event of failure. Finally,

[32] J. Lintner, "Effects of Corporate Taxation on Real Investment," *American Economic Review,* May 1954, pp. 520-34. For an analysis of the effect of taxation on the conditions of supply of capital see J. K. Butters, "Federal Income Taxation and External vs. Internal Financing," *Journal of Finance,* September 1949, pp. 197-205. In times of very tight money, the effect on internal investment will be larger, of course. For a somewhat stronger emphasis on liquidity as an investment-determining variable, particularly in recessions, see J. Meyer and E. Kuh, "Acceleration and Related Theories of Investment: An Empirical Inquiry," *Review of Economics and Statistics,* August 1955, pp. 217-30.

in many instances, the limit to a firm's rate of expansion is not set by the diminishing attractiveness of profit opportunities in relation to borrowing costs, but rather by its supply of managerial personnel. The firm undertakes as much investment as its staff can handle successfully. Lintner believes this analysis to be particularly applicable in periods of high employment. In depressions, firms hesitate to borrow for fear of inability to repay, and the relationship between the levels of taxation and of investment becomes much stronger. Since our analysis supposes that a successful stabilization policy precludes depression, we assume that an increase of retained earnings of $1.00 would lead to only 10¢ of added investment in the firm. A rate of return of 21 per cent, the average rate of return of large corporations in 1955 before taxes,[33] is assumed for the share of the tax cut that would be invested by the firm.

The liquidity of the large firm would be increased by the remaining 90¢ of increased retained earnings. Firms with a significant amount of debt would be able to lower it; firms which raise funds by financing their accounts receivable could reduce this practice; those which are creditors would be able to increase their financial assets—consisting in the case of large corporations primarily of government securities.[34] Thus, the major share of the increase of retained earnings would add primarily to that large pool of low-interest, low-risk, relatively liquid capital into which excess corporation funds are channeled, and from which the loans of large corporations, governments, and financial institutions are drawn. An increase in the supply of loanable funds in this market would have several effects. To some extent, interest rates on low-risk securities would fall and the severity of rationing would diminish, leading to some increase of mortgages and perhaps even a small

[33] This figure is derived as follows: 78 per cent of the tax cut goes to manufacturing, 17 per cent to utilities, and 5 per cent to trade. The average rate of return of large corporations in manufacturing was 23.8 per cent (reported in *Quarterly Financial Report for Manufacturing Corporations, Fourth Quarter 1955*, Federal Trade Commission and Securities and Exchange Commission, Washington, April 1956). The rate for utilities was estimated directly from prevalent standards of rate regulation to be equal to 10 per cent. The rate for trade, which is equal to 20 per cent, assumes that it stood in the same ratio to the rate in manufacturing as in 1952. (Figures for 1952 from SEC data.) A weighted average yields our estimate. The concept of rate of return used by the SEC may overstate the actual rate by 1 to 2 per cent.

[34] C. E. Silberman, "The Big Corporate Lenders," *Fortune*, August 1956, p. 112.

increase of business borrowing. The effect of the drop in low-risk interest rates would be gradually diffused through the credit structure, as banks and other financial institutions adapted their portfolios to the changed pattern of interest yields. Because the primary impact of an increased supply of funds is on the low-interest, low-risk sector of the capital market, and only the spill-over occasioned by secondary repercussions makes funds available to risky investments producing higher yields, we assume an average rate of 5 per cent to apply to this part of our tax cut.

The investment behavior of small corporations is considerably more sensitive than that of large corporations to changes in tax rates.[35] Companies with high growth potential are affected most adversely by corporate taxes, which prevent internal accumulation of the capital they need. External sources of long-term capital are available to small companies only at high cost in terms of both money and loss of control.[36] The corporation income tax also diminishes the attraction of risky investments, since a small firm is less likely to be able to take advantage of the loss-offset provisions to reduce the tax liability on profitable operations. But the significance of these arguments should not be overstated. Not all small business would grow rapidly in the absence of taxes; the need for new capital of many companies is small and can be satisfied. A recent survey of the Department of Commerce [37] found that of all the firms in their sample, 56 per cent had no desire for outside financing, 24 per cent obtained all the funds they desired, 13 per cent obtained some, and only 7 per cent failed to obtain any. New firms were somewhat less successful in raising capital and, most significantly, it was the demand for long-term and, particularly, for equity funds which failed to be met. On the basis of this evidence, we assume that 50 per cent of the increase in retained earnings is invested within the small firm; to this we assign a rate of 18 per

---

[35] Lintner, "Effects of Corporate Taxation on Real Investment," *op. cit.*, p. 533.

[36] For an analysis of the case of the growing firm, see J. K. Butters and J. Lintner, *Effect of Federal Taxes on Growing Enterprises* (Boston: Graduate School of Business Administration, Harvard University, 1945).

[37] Loughlin F. McHugh and Jack N. Ciacco, "External Financing of Small and Medium-Size Business," *Survey of Current Business, op. cit.*, October 1955, pp. 15-22.

cent.[38] The remaining 50 per cent, we assume, is used to reduce bank loans or to purchase liquid assets, at a rate of 5 per cent. The computation for this form of tax cut is summarized in Table 18. The interest rate applicable to a reduction of the corporation income tax is 5.59 per cent.[39]

TABLE 18. *Summary of Derivation of Interest Rates Applicable to Proportionate Reduction of Corporation Income Tax Payments*

Incidence	Per cent of tax cut	Applicable interest rate (per cent)
Shares of tax cut:		
Shifted to consumers	33.3	5.68
Shifted to wage and salary earners	12.5	5.81
Left as increased corporate earnings	54.2	
Large corporations—Distribution of 75 per cent of total increased corporate earnings:		
47 per cent passed on in dividends	19.1	4.96
53 per cent retained as earnings of which		
10 per cent invested in firm	2.2	21.00
90 per cent reduces debt or loaned in market....	19.4	5.00
Small corporations—Distribution of 25 per cent of total increased corporate earnings:		
35 per cent passed on in dividends	4.7	4.96
65 per cent retained as earnings, of which		
50 per cent is invested in firm	4.4	18.00
50 per cent reduces debt or loaned in market....	4.4	5.00
Average applicable interest rate		5.59

Source: See text.

[38] This rate is obtained as follows: In manufacturing, to which 54 per cent of the tax cut accrues, the average rate of return of small corporations was 18 per cent in 1955 (*Quarterly Financial Report, op. cit.,*); for utilities, which pay 9 per cent of the tax, the rate is about 10 per cent; and in trade, which pays 18 per cent of the tax, the rate is 20 per cent (footnote 33). The remaining 19 per cent of the tax cut goes to finance, services, and construction; we assume that the average rate for small corporations applies here. A weighted average of these rates yields our estimate.

[39] Again making an allowance of 3 per cent for the return accruing to the investors of the additional personal savings, our estimate is raised by .24 percentage points to 5.83 per cent. Were we to assume an extra return of 3 per cent on the funds made available to the capital market by corporations as well,

Combining this estimate with the interest rate of 5.29 per cent for the proportionate reduction of personal income taxes, we derive an over-all estimate for Model B of 5.44 per cent.

Interpretation of Our Results

The estimates of opportunity costs derived from our two models were quite similar, although the assumed changes in taxation were very different. This suggests that a value of the order of magnitude of our derived results could serve as a measure of the social cost of capital for federal investment. But before accepting this conclusion, it is necessary to examine possible errors in the assumptions and in the data of our quantitative analysis.

ACCURACY AND LIMITATIONS

A possible source of error is our analysis of the incidence and effects of taxation. Insofar as possible, we have tried to follow the views generally held by experts in this field. Changes in most of our assumptions would have only a moderate effect on the results. Experiments with somewhat different assumptions of incidence produced estimates similar to those obtained. Two exceptions, however, would upset our results. First, if it is assumed that a reduction in the corporation income tax will lead to an upsurge of investment by large corporations, then more of the tax cut would earn the high rates of profit which are prevalent. We have tried to show, however, that this effect is unlikely under the assumed economic condition of high employment. Second, it can be argued that the high levels of federal taxation lead to a large waste of economic resources caused both by the managerial efforts devoted to the tax problem and the distortions in economic decisions of firms and households resulting from a desire to avoid taxes. These considerations are not likely to have much relevance to the problem under study here because the magnitudes of the possible tax reduction are so small compared to the taxes which are needed to finance

the total estimate would rise to 6.59 per cent. In times of moderate monetary policy, the condition postulated for our analysis, these effects would not be of the magnitude indicated here.

defense and other programs. Our result is meant to apply only to small tax cuts.[40]

The rates of return which we assumed are another possible source of error. Through parts of the analysis, average rates were used to approximate marginal rates of return. Households were assumed to add to their assets in such proportion that the average rate of return of their property incomes would remain constant. For any one firm or household that is not likely to be a good approximation; but for large aggregates the error will be smaller. The typical household will not hold assets in the proportions of the group average; some households will make investments in their own business, others in common stocks, others in real estate— depending upon the experience of the head of the household and the opportunities to which he has access. Additional funds are likely to be put into the household's major form of asset. With the tax cut spread over all households in the income class, the money is likely to be invested proportionately to total holdings.

Similarly, business was assumed to make its additional investments at a rate equal to its average rate of return. In the case of industry, the tax cut is diffused over successful and marginal firms in many fields. This does not rule out a systematic bias between marginal and average rates, but the direction of bias is not clear. On the one hand, extra funds must go into investment opportunities

---

[40] We have made no allowance for effects originating in rounds of re-spending subsequent to the economic units on whom the initial impact falls. The increase in disposable income due to a tax reduction will have multiplier effects on the incomes of others, of course, but we have assumed that a correctly managed fiscal and monetary policy offsets these multiplier effects. Nevertheless, the multiplier effects and their policy offsets will lead to some redistribution of income, and it is logically possible that there are systematic differences between the time preferences of the gainers and the losers of this redistribution. This would affect our estimate. But since both the initial repercussions and their offsets are diffused more or less randomly through the economy, it is most unlikely that there will be systematic differences between the two groups in this regard. Further, the similarity of our estimates for different taxes argues that if there are systematic differences in the two groups with regard to important economic characteristics, the effect on the social cost of capital will still be small. For a full discussion of these effects, see A. H. Conrad, "The Multiplier Effects of Redistributive Public Budgets," *Review of Economics and Statistics*, May 1955, pp. 160-73; also see M. Bronfenbrenner, Taro Yamane, and C. H. Lee, "A Study in Redistribution and Consumption." *ibid.*, pp. 149-59.

which are considered marginal in comparison to the opportunities that are undertaken without the tax cut. On the other, new investment opportunities may yield generally higher returns than the reported average for old and new capital. Also, business will not undertake any investment unless the expected rate of return meets minimum standards that are sufficiently high actually to yield an adequate return for the particular kind of investment. Finally it should be stressed that most of Model A and a large part of Model B do not use this approximation.

Our results are not meant to apply in periods of serious inflation or depression. In an inflationary period, monetary policy is likely to be pursued with such vigor that the supply of investible funds to firms will be severely restricted, while the attractiveness of high returns on investments will exercise strong pressure to invest any funds that become available. Under these conditions, the increase in retained earnings made possible by a reduction in the corporation income tax would, in large part, lead to investment within the firm. Since large corporations tend to earn high rates of return on internal investments, the interest rate applicable to such a tax cut would be considerably higher than our estimates. Even the reductions in personal taxes are quite likely to have significant investment effects. For in periods of money shortage, when there is sharp competition among borrowers for funds, more personal savings are likely to find their way into business uses in which high rates of return prevail.

In years of depression, when government expenditures are designed to raise the total level of effective demand in order to employ idle resources, the social cost of capital is extremely low. Tax policy, in such periods, would endeavor to tax idle hoards of funds rather than money which would be spent for consumption or investment; and much of public expenditures would be financed by government loans designed to avoid competition with private demands for investible funds. In real terms, many of the resources absorbed by public investment would have been idle and, hence, would have an opportunity cost close to zero. Expressed as an interest rate, it is not at all inconceivable that the social cost of public capital would be negative in such circumstances.

The year 1955, for which our estimate was derived, can be considered typical of long-term conditions, however. Employment was high, though not to a point where inflation had set in. Fiscal and monetary policies were moderate, endeavoring to keep the economy within a narrow range of balance, without drastic inflationary or deflationary measures. Consumer indebtedness reached an all-time high, but the strong upward trend in the use of credit suggests that the debt position of 1955 will be typical for future years.

How wide then is the range of error of our estimates? We believe that the actual level lies within a range of 1 per cent of our estimates for the general economic conditions postulated for our analysis. This statement is based both on judgment and upon experiments in which those assumptions most open to question were varied. Combining all reasonable assumptions that would raise the rate yields an estimate of 7 per cent; conversely, all plausible assumptions that would produce a low rate yield an estimate of 5 per cent. It is our conclusion that the probable value for the economic conditions postulated lies between 5 and 6 per cent.

AN ALTERNATIVE: A TIGHTER MONETARY POLICY

So far, our analysis has assumed that the expenditures for water resource projects would be offset by taxation sufficient to preserve balance in the economy. Let us also consider briefly the case where monetary rather than tax policy is used to restore equilibrium. An expansion of the federal program would then have to be offset by a tightening of monetary policy of sufficient degree to release the quantity of resources needed for the program. To estimate the social cost of capital under this assumption, it is necessary to discover which economic activities would be curtailed by the diminished supply of credit.

It is unlikely that a change in monetary policy would be a permanent method of compensating for a change in expenditures, because this would reduce the remaining potential of this stabilizing weapon. But the initial offset might well be in this form, subsequently to be converted into a change of tax rates.

We shall not undertake a full-scale quantitative effort to measure the incidence of monetary policy. The kinds of assumptions required would be considerably more arbitrary than those of our tax study, and the rates of return that would be earned by the marginal borrowers to whom credit would be denied could not be estimated with sufficient accuracy. However, we can get some idea of the order of magnitude by listing the sectors affected by monetary policy and the rates of return prevailing in them.

Bank loans are the traditional, perhaps most important, form of credit that can be reduced through monetary policy. Loans to business, which totaled $31 billion in 1955, were made at nominal average rates of 4.2 per cent.[41] While we cannot estimate what rates of return would have been earned on curtailed loans, we know that the rate expected by the borrower must be at least 4.2 per cent. And it is probably more, in view of the somewhat higher interest rates charged to marginal borrowers and the return above borrowing cost which must be expected as an incentive to take the risk of the investment. Loans to individuals totaled $17 billion and were made at a wide range of rates—from as low as 4.5 per cent to over 10 per cent, depending upon the purpose, the collateral, and the credit worthiness of the individual. The marginal loans that would be refused because of a tighter monetary policy would have borne rates well above the minimum of the range.

The market for mortgages would also be tightened by monetary policy, both through a toughening of the terms and diminished availability of funds. Total outstanding mortgages were in excess of $130 billion, but the impact of the policy is concentrated on only a portion of the market. The rates on this category of credit largely fall between 4½ and 6 per cent and would apply to the mortgages that are precluded by the change in the monetary policy necessitated by a public investment. Debt issues of state and local governments would be curtailed, bearing very low interest rates, but often used to finance investments yielding higher returns, e.g., schools, hospitals, etc. Other forms of credit—such as brokers' loans on securities, corporate borrowing from sources other than banks, etc.—would also bear part of the impact, but the effect would be less important quantitatively.

These figures suggest that the social cost of federal capital raised in this manner is roughly of the same order of magnitude as the cost of releasing the necessary resources through taxation. Depending upon the exact combination of weapons employed by the

---

[41] "Business Loans of Member Banks," *Federal Reserve Bulletin, op. cit.,* April 1956, pp. 328-40. This rate makes no allowance for the common practice of requiring minimum account balances, which raises the effective rate of the loan by as much as 1 per cent.

monetary authorities and the circumstances at the time, the rate might be somewhat higher or lower; but the difference in cost under the two types of policies is moderate. The extent to which the resources will be drawn out of investment rather than consumption will differ more broadly, however.

AN ALTERNATIVE: SEPARATING RISK-BEARING FROM PURE INTEREST

So far, we have treated risk as a source of market imperfection, and have considered differences in interest rates caused by varying risk premiums to lead to a misallocation of resources. In the model we employ, a correct allocation of resources would require that the rate of return on marginal investments of all kinds be the same. If it were not, the total return could be increased by switching investments from fields with low marginal returns to fields with higher returns. In the real world, where there are differences in risk, a higher return is expected to prevail on the riskier investments, with part of this higher return a risk premium. This is a reward for taking risks, and may be needed to attract capital into risky uses. Yet our model would consider such differences inefficient; we assume that the riskiness of the returns on an investment do not detract from their contribution to real national income. That is, the satisfaction derived from the national output is independent of the total amount of risk taken on the nation's investments.

In the context of public investments, there is considerable justification for this assumption. From the point of view of the economy as a whole, the risks on investment are far smaller than the sum of risks of individual investments. Where one undertaking in one locality may fall far short of its expected outcome, other undertakings will succeed beyond expectations, and to some extent the failure of some assures the success of others. There is much cancellation of risks since the insurance principle of pooling reduces greatly the relative dispersion of outcomes for the nation's investment program as a whole. And, from the point of view of the long-run growth of the country, the increase of national income produced by risky investments on which a high return is to be earned, whatever the reason, will be greater than the increase of income to be expected from low-risk, low-return investments.

There are other reasons for adhering to our model's assumption. First, the empirical evidence on the relationship between risk-taking and individual welfare is scanty and unconvincing. While people purchase insurance to reduce risk, they also gamble.[42] Second, and more important, there are two very strong institutional factors in our economy which erode the relationship between high risk and high return. One is the giant corporation which undertakes so many investments that there is much pooling of risks within its own program. The suppliers of the corporation's capital bear only a fraction of the sum of risks of the individual investment projects, and the same is true of the company itself. The other institutional factor is our tax system, which makes risky investments particularly attractive to wealthy individuals, since they usually lead to capital gains rather than ordinary income. With much the largest part of the investable funds made available by personal sources [43] coming from taxpayers in the upper brackets, the differential between tax rates on capital gains and on ordinary income promotes the willingness to take risks to such an extent that the difference between the rates of return of risky and secure investments must be much diminished.

Let us briefly consider the cost of capital if risk premiums are treated as prices paid for the factor service of risk-bearing. Lenders are assumed to be rational in this respect, and the risk premium of a loan must be sufficient to compensate for the risk which is taken. On this assumption, a federal loan which displaces a risky private loan and invests the proceeds in a risk-free project would entail a lower social cost than the alternative since there is a reduction in risk-bearing. If we make the bold assumption that all differences in interest rates for the same period are risk premiums, then it might be argued that the true social cost of a risk-free federal investment is the pure interest rate alone—a rate which is probably best approximated by the yield on federal securities with a term equal to the life of the investment.

[42] Cf. M. Friedman and L. J. Savage, "The Utility Analysis of Choices Involving Risk," *Journal of Political Economy*, August 1948, pp. 279-304; and F. Mosteller and P. Nogee, "An Experimental Measurement of Utility," *ibid.*, October 1951, pp. 371-405.

[43] For a full discussion of this point, see J. K. Butters, L. E. Thompson, and L. L. Bollinger, *Effects of Taxation, Investment by Individuals*, (Boston: Gradu-

Actual resource projects are not free of risks, however. Where outputs are marketable, there is no assurance that the expected revenues will be collected; even in the case of nonmarketable out- puts, such as recreation and flood control, there is no guarantee that the expected benefits will actually accrue. In the case of water resource projects, there are always the risks caused by meteorologic and hydrologic uncertainties. Yields on government securities do not reflect these risks, since the federal taxing power stands behind the bonds and any losses on projects will be paid out of taxes.

To discover a risk premium which reflects individual willingness to bear risks, we would need to estimate the cost of raising money for water resource projects that would be incurred by a public corporation unable to employ the taxing power to guarantee its securities. The cost of financing some of the purposes, such as navigation, electric power, and municipal water supply, would be similar to the cost incurred by private utilities, since the service and the risk is almost the same. These companies typically could raise capital at an average cost of 4.5 per cent in 1955,[44] which serves as a first approximation for these purposes. The financing of irrigation would, in part, depend upon the security of the repay- ment contracts and, in part, on the likelihood that the settlers would realize the projected benefits. Nonreimbursable purposes, such as flood control, for which there are no comparable private industries, are subject to the risk that benefits will not be fully realized. To impute risk premiums for these purposes, we would need to take account of the fact that in some instances, particularly in the case of flood control, the projects also serve to reduce risks— a factor which should lower the interest rate. We shall not venture an estimate. Suffice it to say that, taking the water resource pro- gram as a whole, the interest rate derived from these assumptions would be well above the pure rate of interest as measured by the long-term government bond rate, but would be far below the highest rates prevailing in the private economy.

ate School of Business Administration, Harvard University, 1953) especially Chapters 2, 4-7, 9, 10, and 17.

[44] This assumes 50 per cent of the funds to come from bonds paying 3.22 per cent, 15 per cent from preferred stock paying 4.25 per cent, and 35 per cent from common stock with an earnings price ratio of 6.5 per cent. All figures are net of taxes. For a more detailed discussion of these figures see Chapter VII, Table 38.

A FINAL COMMENT

Our statistical analysis has provided an estimate which is designed to reflect the social cost of capital raised by federal taxation. We defined our concept of social cost in terms of the opportunities foregone in the private sector of the economy, either because of curtailed investment or of curtailed consumption. According to our results, if an efficient allocation of resources is the criterion, only those public investments that can produce a rate of return equal to the opportunity cost—or a rate of 5 to 6 per cent—should be undertaken. In operational terms, this would require that an interest rate of that order be used in the evaluation of projects.

Acceptance of this conclusion, however, requires that the exact meaning of the notion of efficiency in this context be made clear. As we pointed out in Chapter II, efficiency is a relative concept dependent on a specific distribution of income. An arrangement which is efficient with one distribution of income may be inefficient with another. The set of demands resulting from one income distribution will not be identical with the demands generated by a different income distribution, and so the prices which lead to efficiency in one case will not be appropriate to the other.

In considering the efficiency of an interest rate, this interdependence takes on particular significance. The interest rate indicates the relative value of output realized at different points in time, including the relative values for different generations. When we accept an interest rate determined by the preferences of the present generation—as we do in our quantitative models—we implicitly accept the time preference of the present generation of decision-makers. Children and unborn generations have no vote in the market place. With the power of the ballot distributed differently from the power of the purse, the community—when acting collectively through the political process—may decide on a distribution of consumption among generations different from the distribution it indicates through its saving behavior. There is no logical reason to give priority to one judgment over the other; our economic analysis must presuppose that the distribution of income and consumption implicit in the efficient allocation of resources is acceptable to society. Should an ethical choice be made through the political process to distribute more of the total consumption to future generations, our opportunity-cost measure of the interest rate would cease to be a proper indicator of social value. A lower interest rate might lead to a larger number of projects, would favor projects which are particularly long-lived, and would lead to the fuller development of the potential of many project opportunities.

The decision not to abide by the market judgment need not be based entirely on ethical considerations. As we have seen earlier, the capital market is imperfect because of the riskiness of investment and for various institutional reasons. Also, because of imperfect perception of future circumstances and the uncertainties surrounding individual lives, it is less likely that consumers make their saving-borrowing decisions as rationally as their choices among commodities. Consequently, the actual intertemporal choices in our economy, including the determination of the over-all level of saving and investment, are made in a rather haphazard manner.[45]

These arguments provide a point of contact between economic analysis and conservationist philosophy. Most of the policies advocated in the name of conservation are designed to make stronger provision for the future than the market mechanism would call for. Resource development is a particularly potent area for the kind of investment designed to benefit future generations. There are opportunities for development of extremely enduring, in some cases perpetual, additions to the nation's capital stock, which will increase in value as population and the economy grow. It may well be that the desire to redistribute income toward future generations can provide some rationale for continued use of a low interest rate.

But this line of argument has limitations. Insofar as a low interest rate leads to the justification of some projects at the expense of others which can produce a better return, the rate will result in a social loss even within water resource fields. Also, if the fundamental objective is the redistribution of income toward the future, the critical variable is not so much the interest rate as the over-all level of investment.[46] The best policy to meet this objec-

[45] It is not clear whether the actual level of saving is higher or lower than the ideal (defined in terms of the judgment of the present generation). On the one hand, the large gap between borrowing and lending rates indicates that the level is too low; on the other, the saving carried on by corporations may far exceed the level desired by their stockholders.

[46] For a fuller discussion of this point, see Otto Eckstein, "Investment Criteria

tive is to increase the amount invested every year and to put the funds into those lines of activity in which the rate of return is greatest. In this way, the contribution to future output is maximized and, should the time profile of output made possible by the investment place too much of the output in early years, an appropriate share of it can be reinvested. A series of reinvestment cycles, each at a high rate of return, will make a greater contribution to the welfare of future generations than investment in one very durable project which yields a low rate of return. It may be possible that the federal government is limited in the fields in which it can employ the desired extra investment; that resource projects yielding low rates of return must be undertaken because of a lack of better opportunities. But this argument holds only if the additional ethical judgment is made that the extra investment must be carried on under federal aegis.

There are other reasons for using a low interest rate. It may be a means of subsidizing new regions in a manner designed to promote their growth to maturity. In some instances, the low interest rate helps to justify projects needed as stand-by capacity for defense purposes. Or it may be a means of increasing the economy's rate of growth for the sake of preserving a lead over the Russian economy. But in these situations, the low interest rate serves to obscure the true issues. The public will be better informed and will be able to come to a more soundly based judgment if the costs of meeting these purposes are made explicit.

Note to Chapter IV

We present a brief formal derivation of the model employed to measure the social cost of capital drawn from consumption.

Let C_l = consumption expenditure of individual l in the present period,

S_l = net saving of l in the present period,

Y_l = disposable income of l in the present period,

i_l = interest rate faced by l for his marginal saving-borrowing decisions,

for Economic Development and the Theory of Intertemporal Welfare Economics," *Quarterly Journal of Economics*, February 1957.

and A_l = perpetual future consumption stream that l can enjoy.

Two identities are implicit in these definitions:

(1) $Y_l = C_l + S_l$, and

(2) $i_l \Delta S_l = \Delta A_l$.

The identity (2) defines the rate at which saving produces a future consumption stream. We assume a utility function

(3) $U_l = U_l(C_l, A_l)$,

which reflects l's present valuation of current consumption and consumption in the future. He maximizes his utility function subject to his income and interest constraints. This is equivalent to maximizing the Lagrangean expression

(4) $\phi = U_l(C_l, A_l) - \lambda(Y_l - C_l - S_l) - \mu(i_l \Delta S_l - \Delta A_l)$,

which has the first-order maximum conditions

(5) $\dfrac{\partial U_l}{\partial C_l} + \lambda = 0, \quad \lambda - \mu i_l = 0, \quad$ and $\quad \dfrac{\partial U_l}{\partial A_l} + \mu = 0.$

Therefore,

(6) $\dfrac{\partial U_l}{\partial C_l} = -\mu i_l \quad$ and $\quad \dfrac{\partial U_l}{\partial A_l} = -\mu,$ and so

(7) $\dfrac{\dfrac{\partial U_l}{\partial C_l}}{\dfrac{\partial U_l}{\partial A_l}} = i_l, \quad$ or $\quad \dfrac{\partial U_l}{\partial C_l} = i_l \dfrac{\partial U_l}{\partial A_l}.$

A change in taxation is a change in disposable income, part of which will change consumption, part saving. Thus,

(8) $\Delta Y_l = \Delta C_l + \Delta S_l$,

and the change in l's utility is

(9) $\Delta U_l = \dfrac{\partial U_l}{\partial C_l} \Delta C_l + \dfrac{\partial U_l}{\partial A_l} \Delta A_l$,

neglecting higher order terms on the grounds that they will be of the second order of smalls. (9) is equivalent to

(10) $\Delta U_l = i_l \dfrac{\partial U_l}{\partial A_l} \Delta C_l + \dfrac{\partial U_l}{\partial A_l} i_l \Delta S_l$, or

(11) $\Delta U_l = i_l \dfrac{\partial U_l}{\partial A_l} \Delta Y_l$.

We define a Social Welfare Function for all the individuals l in the economy.

(12) $W = \Sigma_l\ U_l$.

Then

(13) $\Delta W_c = \Sigma_l \dfrac{\partial U_l}{\partial A_l} i_l \Delta Y_l$, where c refers to costs.

We assume that $\dfrac{\partial U_l}{\partial A_l}$ is the same for all individuals and equal to the arbitrary constant α. Then

(14) $\Delta W_c = \alpha \Sigma_l i_l \Delta Y_l$.

ΔW_c measures the costs in the analysis. The benefits are a flow of future annual income accruing to various individuals, or

(15) $B = \Sigma_l \Delta B_l$.

Assuming the value of marginal future income the same for beneficiaries as for taxpayers, we have

(16) $\Delta W_b = \alpha \Sigma_l \Delta B_l$.

In order for a project to represent a favorable economic change, the value of benefits must exceed the value of costs, or $\Delta W_b > \Delta W_c$. This requires

(17) $\alpha \Sigma_l \Delta B_l > \alpha \Sigma_l i_l \Delta Y_l$.

This inequality is unaffected by the value for α. For convenience, let $\alpha = 1$. Then the criterion becomes

(18) $\Sigma_l \Delta B_l > \Sigma_l i_l \Delta Y_l$ or

(19) $\dfrac{\Sigma_l \Delta B_l}{\Sigma_l i_l \Delta Y_l} > 1$.

Use of the interest rate that our analysis seeks to estimate for benefit-cost analysis is equivalent to criterion (19). We have estimated $\Sigma_l \, i_l \dfrac{\Delta Y_l}{\Sigma_l \, \Delta Y_l}$; the benefit-cost criterion then becomes

(20) $\quad \dfrac{\Sigma_l \, \Delta B_l}{\Sigma_l \, i_l \dfrac{\Delta Y_l}{\Sigma_l \, \Delta Y_l} \cdot \Sigma_l \, \Delta Y_l} \qquad > 1,$

which is identical to (19).

Part 2

APPLYING THE ANALYSIS:

selected case studies

Introduction

Previously we have been concerned with general considerations basic to evaluating the economic efficiency of alternative courses of action in actual cases involving water resource development. In Chapter II, we outlined a theory of efficient resource allocation in a perfectly competitive market economy, specifying the conditions among all the decision-making units in the economy that would have to be met in order to achieve efficient production and distribution of the resulting output. We recognized, however, that the attainment of efficiency goals theoretically obtainable within the framework of a purely market economy is inhibited by certain conditions in the actual economy. These departures from the competitive model were elaborated in Chapter III, with special regard to the provision of water-derived commodities and services. This suggested that a perfectly competitive market economy would be unable to satisfy group wants, or to make allowances for the divergence between private and social marginal productivity of resources where direct interdependence among production processes short-circuited the market. Furthermore, the unadjusted competitive model did not adequately cover the case where public budgeting, by collective choice, entered into the determination of the actual allocation of resources.

We were then compelled to tinker with the machinery of the model to provide more appropriate criteria for evaluating economic efficiency. The methods that can be employed for evaluating economic benefits have been elaborated in other studies,[1] and thus we avoided dwelling on this aspect of the efficiency criteria. But such studies have not undertaken a systematic empirical investigation of

---

[1] For example, Otto Eckstein, *Water Resources Development: The Economics of Project Evaluation* (Cambridge: Harvard University Press, 1958).

the opportunity cost of capital employed by the federal government in current water resource development activities. We recognize that federal funds are not likely to be raised by the government in a competitive capital market, but rather by taxation. Approaching the problem from this perspective, we derived an empirical estimate of the opportunity cost of tax-raised federal funds under realistic assumptions as to the structure of taxes which are likely to be involved. This provided us with a social cost of public capital which must enter into the benefit-cost efficiency criterion.

We are now prepared to analyze the comparative efficiency of alternative approaches to river basin development. In the next three chapters, we shall analyze critically a few selected experiences of recent decisions on water resources development within the framework of analysis outlined in Chapters II, III, and IV. The greatest difficulty in achieving efficient development is encountered on the level of multiple purpose, integrated systems where the problems of direct interdependence, indivisibility, and collective— or nonmarketable—project services are encountered in their more extreme forms. It is in these large multiple purpose opportunities that the federal government has found the greatest need to participate actively. This participation has taken two forms: The federal government, through one of its several water resource agencies, has directly developed streams for multiple purpose objectives. It has licensed others, consistent with provisions of the Federal Water Power Act of 1920,[2] to undertake such development. Although this Federal Power Act was an instrument of public intervention, and provided for preferential treatment for local public bodies in the development of river sites,[3] it did not require public development[4] or prohibit development under private auspices if granted a license by the Federal Power Commission.

Under provisions of the Federal Power Act, development of the nation's rivers can be undertaken by a number of approaches: from the entire gamut of public development—federal, state, municipal,

[2] Prior to the Federal Water Power Act which established the Federal Power Commission, nonfederal development was authorized by the Congress, subject to the provisions of the General Dam Act and the Dam Act of 1906, and to the approval of the Secretary of War and Chief of Engineers.

[3] Federal Water Power Act, Section 7 (a).

[4] Except under special conditions in which development was reserved to the federal government, *ibid.*, Section 7 (b).

and public utility districts—to private development by regulated monopolies under an FPC license. Nonetheless, even under private development, an efficiency goal of the Act requires:

> Section 10 [as amended August 26, 1935]. All licenses issued under this Part shall be on the following conditions:
> (a) That the project adopted, including the maps, plans and specifications, shall be such as in the judgment of the Commission will be best adapted to a comprehensive plan for improving or developing a waterway or waterways for the use or benefit of interstate or foreign commerce, for the improvement and utilization of water power development, and for other beneficial public uses, including recreational purposes; and if necessary in order to secure such plan, the Commission shall have authority to require the modification of any project and of the plans and specifications of the project works before approval.

With this background on the agency for public intervention (aside from state regulatory commissions) and some of its responsibilities and authority as a backdrop, we are in a position to address one of the main questions to which this study is pointed: What is the comparative efficiency of alternative ways of developing multiple purpose river basin sites?

v   The Hells Canyon Case:

COMPARATIVE EFFICIENCY OF ALTERNA-

TIVE APPROACHES TO DEVELOPMENT

The Hells Canyon case, among water resource development projects, is one in which the project services are predominantly marketable, and even those which are not can be evaluated by conventional benefit-cost techniques.

In this chapter, we examine the alternatives open for the development of the Hells Canyon Reach of the Snake River. We begin by
reviewing the main features of the plan of development recently
undertaken under license from the Federal Power Commission by
the Idaho Power Company. To provide the bases for comparative
analyses, we also describe the federal plan of development for Hells
Canyon within the context of the comprehensive plan of development for the system made up of the Columbia River and its tributaries. We then analyze the comparative efficiency of the two plans
of development.

From this analysis, we conclude that neither plan appears to be
the most efficient economically—that the full range of meaningful
alternatives has not received serious consideration, and that a plan
of development that would be more efficient than the one licensed
was not required of Idaho Power Company by the FPC. Trying
to discover by means of economic analysis why the economically
most efficient plan was not undertaken voluntarily by the regulated
private monopolist, we find that a large part of the problem can
be traced to indivisibility, direct interdependence, and nonmarketable output. We then attempt a crude approximation of the sum
of the divergences between private and social product, and consider

possibilities under which this economic gain could be used to induce a private firm to undertake the socially more economic scheme of development.

The Hells Canyon Reach of the Columbia River and Tributary System

In August 1955, the FPC licensed Idaho Power Company to undertake a three-dam development along the Hells Canyon Reach of the Snake River. (See Figure 15.) The three rock-fill dams proposed by the company would develop the 602 feet of fall in that reach. Brownlee Dam would have a maximum head of 277 feet, usable storage of a million acre-feet for flood control, and an initial installation of 360,400 kilowatts with provision for an additional 180,200 kilowatts. Oxbow Dam, downstream, would have a head of 117 feet, usable pondage of 6,200 acre-feet, and an initial installation of 151,000 kilowatts with provision for an additional 75,000 kilowatts. A "Low" Hells Canyon Dam would be the third structure in the Idaho Power Company plan, with a head of 208 feet, usable pondage of 11,200 acre-feet, and an initial installation of 272,000 kilowatts with provision for an additional 136,000 kilowatts. The capacity installed at the sites of the three dams would therefore total 783,400 kilowatts initially, and somewhat over a million kilowatts ultimately. Moreover, it has been estimated that the storage provided in the Hells Canyon Reach would warrant installing approximately 181,000 kilowatts of additional capacity at downstream run-of-river plants.[1] The present generating capacity of the Idaho Power Company's system is 374,000 kilowatts, or

---

[1] The data in the Hells Canyon case were drawn from the Federal Power Commission's voluminous record of the case—extending from December 1950 to the issuance of the license in August 1955—*In the Matters of Idaho Power Company; Project No. 1971, No. 2132, and No. 2133,* including particularly: *Transcript of Hearing, Exhibits, Brief of Commission Staff Counsel,* and *Decision.* For a more detailed explanation of the particular estimates selected, see Note to Chapter v. The estimate of additional capacity for downstream, run-of-river plants was taken from the FPC's *Staff Brief,* Appendix A, p. 5. We assume the downstream plants to be the following (either existing, under construction, or proposed) federal installations: McNary, John Day, The Dalles, Bonneville, Ice Harbor, Lower Monumental, Little Goose, and Lower Granite.

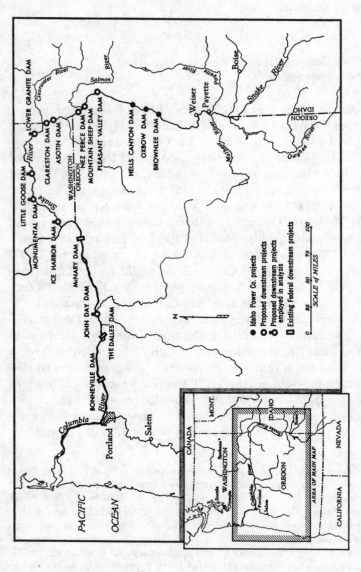

FIGURE 15. *Idaho Power Company Dams in Relation to Existing and Proposed Structures on Lower Snake and Columbia Rivers*

only about 30 per cent of the total capacity of the system upon completion of the initial plan of development.[2]

The Idaho Power Company three-dam development will occupy lands of the United States government and will pre-empt the site for the "High" Hells Canyon Dam, which represented a key structure in the U. S. Corps of Engineers' main control plan for the comprehensive development of the Columbia River and tributary system.[3] The plan for comprehensive development as proposed in the Engineers' original plan[4] would provide a system of reservoirs having 26,990,000 acre-feet of storage in order to limit stream flows to 800,000 feet per second at The Dalles—the focal point for the system—under conditions comparable to the 1894 "flood of record." The system of interrelated projects originally proposed is shown in Table 19.

Opposition to the Glacier View project, because of its estimated adverse effect on Glacier National Park, resulted in its elimination from present plans for the main control features of the Columbia tributary system. Proposals for substituting storage at other sites for the deficiency caused by abandoning the Glacier View site call for increasing the storage at Libby from the 4,250,000 acre-feet originally planned to 5,010,000 acre-feet, and for finding suitable alternative storage to eliminate the remaining deficiency. In addition, as a result of the difference in the storage planned for the original High Hells Canyon Dam and the alternate three-dam plan of the Idaho Power Company, approximately 1,300,000 acre-feet will need to be found to maintain the integrity of the main control plan.

It is apparent from the record that control of the flood flows of the Columbia River may be possible under a number of different combinations of projects distributed among the major streams of the Basin. It is not evident nor likely, however, that any combination will provide a system of comparable flood control at costs the same as or less than the main control plan originally proposed.[5] Moreover, the flood control plan represents only one of the interdependent purposes which the multiple purpose Hells Canyon

[2] FPC, *Decision, op. cit.,* p. 23.

[3] *Ibid.,* p. 8, and Finding No. 80, p. 60.

[4] *Columbia River and Tributaries, Northwestern United States,* House Document No. 531, 81st Congress, 2nd Session, March 20, 1950.

[5] FPC, *Transcript of Hearings, op. cit.,* pp. 13,488, 13,496, 13,507, 13,515.

TABLE 19. *Reservoir Projects Included in the Main Control Plan of the Corps of Engineers for Columbia River and Tributaries*

Projects	Usable flood control storage (thousand acre-feet)
Libby	4,250
Hungry Horse	2,980
Glacier View	3,160
Albeni Falls	a
Grand Coulee	5,120
Hells Canyon High Dam	3,280
Palisades	1,200
Anderson Branch ⎫ Arrowrock ⎬	1,000
Lucky Peak ⎭	
Cascade ⎫ Garden Valley ⎭	1,900
Priest Rapids	2,100
John Day	2,000
Total	26,990

a Local flood control only.

site could serve. The proposed High Hells Canyon Dam would have been a monumental, concrete arch structure, 1,733 feet long at the crest and 722 feet in maximum height. This structure also would have developed fully the 602 feet of fall in the Hells Canyon Reach of the Snake, with 800,000 kilowatts of installed capacity initially, and 100,000 to be added subsequently for an ultimate total of 900,000 kilowatts at site. The 3.8 million acre-feet of usable storage, as contemplated in the design for the High Dam, would have warranted installation of 774,000 kilowatts of additional generating capacity at downstream structures on the lower Snake and Columbia rivers. The total of 1.6 million kilowatts was destined for incorporation in the federal hydroelectric system and, upon completion, would have represented about 16 per cent of the system's total.

Against this backdrop, the Idaho Power Company proposal represents, from a financial standpoint, a substitution of private financial resources for investment funds originating in public financing—and the provision without compensation of certain

factor services to be discussed below—in exchange for the opportunity to utilize the water power site for which the federal government is the custodian and has the obligation to require development "best adapted to a comprehensive plan."[6]

The first question to be asked is: Does this form of licensing
arrangement, under conditions similar to those found in the Hells
Canyon Reach of the Snake River, represent the most efficient
method by which to exploit returns awaiting development of this
reach of the tributary system? An answer to this question can be
approached in terms of the principles outlined in preceding
chapters.

We shall evaluate the efficiency of this type of partnership
arrangement by analyzing the extent to which it permits the most
efficient investment or developmental plan. To do this, we compare the costs and gains under the alternative plans of development, as provided in the record of the public hearings preceding
the licensing of Idaho Power Company by the FPC.[7] Since accounting costs differ between private and governmental operations, the
evaluation of alternative plans of development must proceed on
the assumption that the two plans represent alternative investment
opportunities for the same enterprise unit, whether public or
private.

Some uncompensated gains would appear in the operation of
either plan;[8] our interest here centers on economic costs and gains
whether or not they would appear on the financial accounts of the
enterprise. Consequently, we first evaluate the alternative plans
as if they were being considered for investment by a public agency.
Finally, in order to translate the physical characteristics of the

[6] Federal Power Act (Washington: U. S. Government Printing Office, 1955),
Section 10 (a), pp. 10-11.
[7] FPC, *Transcript of Hearings, op. cit.* At the outset of this task, we must
acknowledge that our analysis can provide results no better than the data on
which it is based—and, that the precision, relevance, and accuracy of data which
can be culled from the record of a public hearing often leave something to be
desired. In spite of limitations of this sort, there are a number of illustrative
uses to which our result can be put.
[8] Even under the three-dam plan, a certain amount of storage capacity would
be utilized to control flood flows downstream, provide navigation benefits for
which a private firm would not be compensated, and contribute to increased
prime power output at downstream installations.

alternative plans into their economic counterparts, we employ
benefit-cost comparisons.[9]

*

Costs and Benefits of Federal Development of
a High Dam and Three Low Dams

Consider first the costs under federal development. Because of
the great capital intensity of multiple purpose river structures, the
most significant element of cost is represented by imputed capital
charges. In Chapter IV, two views with respect to capital costs were
considered: (1) the opportunity cost of funds obtained by means
of federal taxation, derived by reference to individual preferences
of members making up the present generation of society; (2) the
typical conservation viewpoint which implicity attempts to take
into account the preferences of individuals comprising future generations of society, and thus seeks a redistribution of income toward
the future. Since the lower interest rate associated with the second
approach is consistent with the traditional practices in evaluating

---

[9] Benefit-cost analysis is useful in providing the correct investment criterion
for evaluating projects, but the criterion may differ depending on the nature
of the specific problem assumed. On the one hand, a correct investment criterion
will assure that the best use is made of federal funds and that no funds are
used in the government sector which would have yielded greater benefits in the
private sector in the applications from which they would be withdrawn.
Several criteria may then be appropriate, depending on the problem at hand.
If it is assumed that the federal budget is limited, a rational allocation of federal funds would require undertaking those projects which have the highest
benefit-cost ratios in descending order until the limited funds were exhausted.
This would involve passing up projects for which estimated benefits exceeded
costs—costs in the sense of alternatives foregone in the private sector, but not
the opportunity costs represented by the better projects in the public sector. On
the other hand, if no budget restraint is imposed, it is assumed that investment is undertaken in the public sector in an amount sufficient to equalize the
social product at the margin in the private and public sectors. In such cases,
all investment opportunities in the public sector which promise benefits sufficient to compensate for alternatives foregone in the private sector are assumed
to be undertaken. If an interest rate equivalent to the opportunity cost of
federal funds is imputed, therefore, all projects (or, more properly, project
increments) with benefit-cost ratios in excess of unity would qualify. The latter
approach underlies the analyses which follow.

public works projects,[10] we first evaluate the comparative efficiency of the alternate plans on the assumption that the conventional rate of 2.5 per cent applies.[11]

A second question involves selecting the appropriate estimate of construction costs for each plan from among the several estimates presented by expert witnesses during the public hearings preceding the issuance of the license. For the High Dam, we accept the construction costs appropriate to the design standards traditionally reflected in structures of the Bureau of Reclamation and other federal agencies; for the three dams, we accept estimates appropriate to the design standards of the private utility. Although the private standards are considerably lower than those employed by the federal agencies,[12] they were judged by the FPC staff to be adequate.[13] Accordingly, the company's relatively lower estimates of construction costs are taken to reflect an appropriate response to economic considerations. In both cases, however, the estimates of the two parties were adjusted by the FPC staff to achieve comparability in terms of estimated unit costs for like items employed in construction.[14]

The relevant cost data are given as annual average equivalents for the two plans in Table 20 on the assumption that the projects would be operated within the context of an integrated system design. Annual costs of the Hells Canyon High Dam ($15.9 million) are shown to exceed the corresponding costs for the three low dams ($9.5 million) by approximately $6.4 million.

---

[10] Discussion of the interest rate used for project evaluation is usually related to the rate at which the federal government can borrow in the open market. Since the risk associated with lending to the federal government is reduced by the taxing authority of the government, such a lower rate of interest in ordering investment opportunities results in a higher rate of investment, and a greater deferment of consumption, thus effecting an income redistribution toward the future.

[11] This is the rate, incidentally, that was actually employed in the analysis of alternative Hells Canyon plans. FPC, *Hearings, op. cit.*

[12] FPC, *Exhibits, op. cit.,* No. 186, pp. 25a-26.

[13] The fact that one of Idaho Power Company's coffer dams subsequently washed out, while the Middle Snake was at flood stage, does not necessarily contradict the FPC staff's judgment. It has been implied by the former FPC chairman to have resulted from a departure from standards, by Idaho Power Company.

[14] FPC, *Staff Brief, op. cit.,* Appendix B, pp. 18-24 and Table 14.

TABLE 20. *Comparative Costs of Hells Canyon High Dam and Three Low Dams, Assuming Federal Development and Imputed Interest Rate of 2.5 Per Cent*

Item	Alternatives ($ thousand)	
	High Dam	Three Low Dams
Investment [a]	399,221	209,451
Interest and amortization [b]	10,898	5,720
Interim replacements [c]	1,545	1,074
Payment in lieu of state and local taxes [d]	1,999	1,047
Operation and maintenance [e]	1,495	1,666
Total average annual costs	15,937	9,507
Increment of average annual costs of High Dam over three low dams	6,430	

[a] The investment figure was obtained as follows: For the High Dam—(1) construction costs at site $310,740,000 (FPC, *Staff Brief,* Table 14); (2) construction costs for downstream generating capacity $58,707,000 (Witness Cotton's estimate, *ibid.,* Appendix B, p. 35); (3) interest during construction at site for a six-year construction period at 2.5 per cent, $23,306,000; (4) interest during construction for downstream installation of generators for two-year construction period at 2.5 per cent interest, $1,468,000; and (5) estimated capital cost of facilities for migratory fish of $5,000,000 (*ibid.,* Appendix B, Table 14). For the three low dams—(1) construction costs at site of $183,941,000 (*ibid.*); (2) construction cost for downstream generators of $13,862,000 (*ibid.,* Witness Cotton's estimate of *capital* costs, p. 31); (3) interest during construction at site for a 2.8-year average construction period at 2.5 per cent, $6,438,000; (4) interest during construction for installation of downstream generators, two-year construction period at 2.5 per cent, $348,000; and (5) estimated capital cost of facilities for migratory fish of $5 million.

[b] Interest at 2.5 per cent and amortization over 100 years. See Otto Eckstein, *Water Resources Development: The Economics of Project Evaluation* (Cambridge: Harvard University Press, 1958).

[c] FPC *Staff Brief, op. cit.,* Appendix B, p. 87.

[d] *Ibid.,* Appendix B, p. 88.

[e] *Ibid.,* Appendix B, pp. 89-90.

Annual benefits will be accounted for predominately by power, although flood control and navigation will contribute modestly to the total. Power output from the development will vary, depending on such factors as the time profile of storage capacity added at different points to the system and the depletion of stream flows associated with irrigation withdrawals upstream. The record thus contains many dissimilar estimates of power output which arise out of differences in assumptions governing the determining variables. In order to achieve comparability among plans of development, we have attempted to obtain estimates based on common assumptions which reflect a consensus of expert witnesses as to reasonableness of technical assumptions, appropriateness of measures used, etc.[15]

Several measures of power output are available. In the Pacific Northwest, served basically by hydroelectricity, estimates of prime power appear to be the most relevant.[16] The amount of prime power from the Hells Canyon development will change over time, however, and different basic assumptions will alter the estimated total power output for both plans of development. Several methods are available. First, we could use an estimated average length of critical period and estimated depletion, generally accepted as reasonable by the expert witnesses. Or we could use an estimated average annual prime power output, based on changes in critical period during the time span. Finally, we could move to a somewhat different method by comparing time streams of estimated input and output. For our purpose, we have employed the first method—largely because this enables us to cull from the record the maximum relevant data, which are both consistent among plans of development, and useful in illustrating some of the significant aspects of the total problem.[17]

At the site of development, annual benefits would be accounted for by 647,000 kilowatts of prime power generated at the High Dam and 585,000 kilowatts at the three dams, as well as a certain amount of navigation service provided on the reservoirs themselves. Downstream benefits would accrue from increased prime power at eight installations (314,000 kilowatts resulting from the

---

[15] Even so, our results should be regarded as useful only in illustrating some of the basic factors underlying efficient multiple purpose development, rather than a definitive determination of the most efficient plan of development for Hells Canyon.

[16] FPC, *Decision, op. cit.,* p. 45.

[17] In general, while different assumptions or approaches in analysis will yield different estimates for *total* power output, this is of little consequence if the *differences* between plans remain relatively unchanged. To the extent that this is not the case, we will provide results obtained by alternative methods for comparative purposes.

High Dam and 117,000 from the three dams), and from flood control and navigation benefits on the Lower Snake and lower reaches of the Columbia. These benefits, or their annual average monetary equivalents, are detailed in Table 21. Total benefits of $42.8 million annually available from development by means of the High Dam would be approximately $12 million more than the annual average available from development of the three-dam alternative.

The more efficient scheme of development is revealed by comparing the added benefits and the added costs of the High Dam over the three-dam alternative. The ratio of incremental benefits to

TABLE 21. *Average Annual Value of Project Services of Hells Canyon High Dam and Three Low Dams, Assuming Public Development*

Item	High Dam	Three Low Dams
	(kilowatts)	(kilowatts)
Prime power [a]:		
At site	647,000	585,000
Downstream	314,000	117,000
Total	961,000	702,000
	($ thousand)	($ thousand)
Value of prime power at $41.58 per kw.[b]:		
At site	26,902	24,324
Downstream	13,056	4,863
Increment to system	39,958	29,187
Value of flood control benefits [c]	2,600	1,400
Value of navigation benefits [c]	250	100
Total average annual value of project services	42,808	30,687
Increment of average annual benefits of High Dam over three low dams	12,121	

[a] FPC, *Staff Brief, op. cit.*, Appendix A, pp. 14, 17; Appendix B, p. 10. Assumes depletion flows associated with 366,650 additional acres to be irrigated, a critical period of thirty-two to thirty-four months, and operation of the facilities under conditions of hydraulic integration.

[b] *Ibid.*, p. 14; FPC, *Decision, op. cit.*, p. 47.

[c] *Exhibits, op. cit.*, No. 372.

incremental costs is about 1.9:1. In short, provided that an interest rate of 2.5 per cent would be acceptable (subject to all of the qualifications implicit in our treatment of the problem in Chapter IV), the High Dam appears more efficient.

In Chapter IV, however, some questions were raised regarding the relevance of the conventional rate used to evaluate projects. Given the preferences of individuals presently making up our society, the structure of taxes relevant to the case, and the probable incidence of the increased income (or of decreased income) of private individuals and enterprises contingent on a tax reduction (or an increase in taxes), an opportunity cost equivalent to 5 or 6 per cent seems appropriate for the funds raised by federal taxation—or the funds which are prevented from being distributed to private parties through a reduction in federal taxes. This implies that a rate of return of this level should be earned at the margin if water resource development projects are to be economically efficient. If the conventional rate of 2.5 per cent is imputed for purposes of project evaluation, accordingly, an incremental benefit-to-cost ratio in excess of 1.9:1, rather than simply in excess of 1:1, would be required to ensure a rate of return to capital that would be equivalent to the opportunity cost of the tax-raised funds. There are certain advantages in using the lower rate as an imputed interest charge coupled with a higher benefit-cost ratio.[18] However, when projects of similar capital intensities are being compared, equivalent results can be approximated in a more straightforward manner by simply imputing an interest rate equivalent to our opportunity cost.

Accordingly, if, for purposes of evaluating the alternative plans of development, we impute an interest rate of 5.5 per cent, the cost data of our previous comparisons will be altered substantially. The results, which appear in Table 22, show an added cost of around $13 million for the High Dam. The added benefit of $12 million no longer justifies on efficiency grounds the added cost; the added benefit-to-cost ratio is only 0.9:1.[19] It is conceivable that

[18] Otto Eckstein, *Water Resources Development: The Economics of Project Evaluation* (Cambridge: Harvard University Press, 1958), Chapter IV.

[19] It must be acknowledged that this conclusion is particularly affected by the set of data which is employed. We have used Witness Cotton's estimate of prime power output, equivalent to 961,000 and 702,000 kilowatts, respectively, for the High and three low dams. This is consistent with an average depletion

higher recreational values (for which there are no adequate estimates of monetary value commensurate with other data employed
in our analysis) would justify the Hells Canyon High Dam. It is
apparent that for any reasonable value of the increased recreational
potentialities attributable to the High Dam, however, the added
$211 million of investment would represent a substantial churning
of economic activity, income redistribution, etc. While there may
be no net loss resulting, there would not be any clearly demonstrable gain. If an opportunity cost of 5.5 per cent is attributed to
the capital funds raised for development of the Hells Canyon
Reach, therefore, there is no clear-cut evidence that the three-dam
scheme is less efficient than the High Dam.

of stream flows associated with an average of 366,650 additional acres of
up-stream irrigation and a critical period of thirty-two to thirty-four months.
Employing Cotton's estimates expressed as average annual prime power, the
output appropriate to the two alternatives would be, respectively, 893,100 and
598,000 kilowatts. Although the total annual benefits ($38,739,000 and $26,365,-
000, respectively) would be smaller than those appearing in the text, the
difference between the High and three low dams ($12.4 million) would be
larger. Even so, the incremental benefit-to-cost ratio would not exceed unity.
   An objection to this result relates to the fact the conclusion is based on data
employing an annual average of fifty years, whereas added depletion of stream
flows may result over the remaining fifty years of the amortization period. As
a rough check, we can use data presented by Witness Riter which are consistent with Cotton's estimates, save for failure to include additional power
output resulting from system integration and an estimated higher rate of
additional irrigated acreages. Riter's estimate for increased acreages under
irrigation (1,140,000 acres by the end of the amortization period, or an average
of 631,000 for the time span) is approximately double that of Cotton's whose
data are based on the commonly accepted estimates of the Columbia Basin
Inter-Agency Committee. Accordingly, we can consider Riter's estimates as
appropriate to the 100-year amortization schedule and approximate results by
the following means: Prime power output is estimated to fall from an initial
amount of 1,108,000 kilowatts to 679,000 kilowatts by the end of the amortization period for the High Dam, and from 660,000 to 509,000 kilowatts for the
three-dam plan. If we assume that the decrements in each case occur in equal
annual amounts, we can infer the time distribution of the total prime power
output and obtain the present value of the stream of benefits when discounted
at 5.5 per cent. Similarly, the annual operating and maintenance costs can be
discounted to the present and added to the original investment. The resulting
difference in present value of the stream of benefits from the High Dam over
the three low dams is about $317.7 million, compared with a difference in cost
of $287 million. This results in a ratio of added benefits to the added costs of
1.3:1 from the High Dam plan over the three dams.

TABLE 22. *Comparative Costs of Hells Canyon High Dam and Three Low Dams, Assuming Federal Development and Imputed Interest Rate of 5.5 per cent*

Item	Alternatives ($ thousand)	
	High Dam	Three Low Dams
Investment [a]	428,943	217,728
Interest and amortization [b]	23,721	12,040
Interim replacements [c]	1,545	1,074
Payment in lieu of state and local taxes [d]	2,145	1,089
Operation and maintenance [e]	1,495	1,666
Total average annual costs	28,906	15,869
Increment of average annual costs of High Dam over three low dams	13,037	

[a] The investment figures were obtained in the same manner as in Table 20, except for the use of an interest rate of 5.5 per cent instead of 2.5 per cent.

[b] Interest at 5.5 per cent over a 100-year amortization period.

[c] FPC, *Staff Brief, op. cit.*, Appendix B, p. 87.

[d] *Ibid.*, Appendix B, p. 88.

[e] *Ibid.*, Appendix B, pp. 89-90.

Feasibility of an Intermediate, Two-Dam Plan

Since the plans for the High Dam and three low dams are so nearly equal in comparative efficiency (when the higher opportunity cost is employed), despite the fact that they are so different in scale, it appears that the resources committed to the development of the incremental opportunities represented by the High Dam would be employed over some range of diminishing total net returns. A plan of development intermediate between the two, therefore, may be economically superior to both.

Details of such a plan of development were prepared by one of the expert witnesses for consideration at the FPC hearings. The plan involved two structures—a dam of medium height (325-foot head) to occupy the site proposed for the High Dam, and a second structure identical in location and characteristics to the Idaho Power Company's proposed Brownlee Dam.[20] Together, the two

[20] FPC. *Staff Brief, op. cit.*, pp. 6-7, and Appendix A, pp. 3-4; also *Exhibits, op. cit.*, No. 186.

dams would provide up to 1.3 million acre-feet of usable storage, develop 602 feet of head, and provide for initial installed capacity at site of 783,400 kilowatts. This plan can be considered intermediate in size in the sense that it would provide more storage than the three-dam plan, and would permit a greater amount of power generation downstream, more flood control, and more improvements to navigation. However, in terms of investment outlays and annual costs, it represents the smallest of the three plans.

The estimated annual average benefits from the intermediate, two-dam plan are shown in Table 23.

TABLE 23. *Average Annual Value of Project Services of Brownlee and Medium-Height Hells Canyon Dams, Assuming Public Development*

Item	Two dams
	(kilowatts)
Prime power [a]:	
At site	566,000
Downstream	145,000
Total	711,000
	($ thousand)
Value of prime power at $41.58 per kw.[b]:	
At site	23,534
Downstream	6,029
Increment to system	29,563
Value of flood control benefits [c]	1,800
Value of navigation benefits [c]	150
Total average annual value of project services	31,513
Increment of average annual benefits of High Dam over two dams	11,295

[a] Estimates of nominal prime power were taken from Witness Meadowcroft's estimate (FPC, *Staff Brief, op. cit.,* Appendix A, p. 16), and adjusted to conform with estimates for the High and three dams (i.e., a critical period of thirty-two to thirty-four months, 366,650 additional acres irrigated and all downstream generation credited to the Hells Canyon Reach) to achieve results based on assumptions consistent among all three plans.

[b] See note b, Table 21.

[c] See note c, Table 21.

TABLE 24. *Comparative Costs of Brownlee and Medium-Height Hells Canyon Dams, Assuming Public Development and Different Interest Rates*

·Item	Costs ($ thousand)	
	Interest at 2.5 per cent	Interest at 5.5 per cent
Investment [a]	204,031	212,461
Interest and amortization [b]	5,386	11,749
Interim replacement [c]	961	961
Payment in lieu of state and local taxes [c]	1,020	1,062
Operation and maintenance [d]	1,625	1,625
Total average annual costs	8,992	15,397
Increment of average annual cost of High Dam over two-dam intermediate plan	6,945	13,509

[a] The investment figure was obtained as follows: (1) construction costs at site of $177,935,000 (FPC, *Staff Brief, op. cit.*, Appendix B, Table 14); (2) construction costs associated with downstream generation, $13,862,000; (3) interest during construction of $6,672,000 at 2.5 per cent and $14,680,000 at 5.5 per cent, respectively, over a three-year construction period; (4) interest of $352,000 at 2.5 per cent and $774,000 at 5.5 per cent, respectively, on downstream installation of generators, two-year installation period; and (5) estimated capital cost of facilities for migratory fish of $5 million.

[b] Computed alternatively at 2.5 and 5.5 per cent annual interest and 100-year amortization.

[c] FPC *Staff Brief*, Appendix B, p. 88.

[d] *Ibid.*, Appendix B, p. 89.

Estimated annual costs, assuming both the 2.5 per cent rate of interest, officially proposed for economic analysis of river basin projects, and the 5.5 per cent, derived by means of our analysis in Chapter IV, are presented in Table 24. The average annual benefits of the two-dam plan exceed the costs by a ratio of 3.5:1, if interest is computed at 2.5 per cent, and by a ratio of 2:1 if we employ 5.5 per cent appropriate to the opportunity cost of capital raised by means of federal taxes.

The added benefits of the Hells Canyon High Dam over the two-dam alternative amount to approximately $11.3 million as an annual average. These benefits would justify the increased investment in terms of the standard procedure (an imputed interest rate of 2.5 per cent and an incremental benefit-cost ratio at least equal to unity). With the opportunity cost estimated at between 5 and 6 per cent, however, the added cost, $13.5 million, would exceed the added benefits. In fact, at any rate exceeding 4.5 per cent, the added benefits would not compensate for the costs of developing the incremental opportunity in the Hells Canyon Reach of the Snake.[21]

Evaluation of these two projects is particularly sensitive to the choice of data, both the physical output and the value per kilowatt of prime power, as well as to the assumed time distribution and the discount factor. To a large extent, the conclusions are conditioned on imponderables; there is no definitive answer as to whether the High Dam or the two dams would be more efficient.

While there may be room for doubt involving comparisons between the High Dam and the two dams, there is a considerably more clear-cut case when the two-dam and three-dam plans are compared. The two-dam plan would provide more power, flood control, and navigation benefits than would the three-dam plan. These benefits are estimated to total around $825,000 more, as an annual average, than the value of output from the three-dam plan. Coupled with this, total investment for the two dams would approximate $5 million less, and annual costs about $472,000 less than the three-dam scheme.

Analysis of Two and Three Dams, Assuming Construction and Operation by Idaho Power Company

In view of the marked economic superiority of the two-dam plan as compared with the Idaho Power Company three-dam plan, the question arises: Why did Idaho Power Company seek a license for construction of the three dams instead of the socially more efficient two-dam alternative? An answer to this question must

---

[21] If we use Riter's estimates for the prime power output of the two-dam scheme, which drops from an original 677,000 to 508,000 kilowatts by the end of the amortization period, we would have to alter our conclusions. Discounting the annual operating and maintenance costs for the two plans, we get a difference in terms of current costs of $284 million between the two plans. The difference in present value of benefits from the two plans of development approximates $307 million when both streams are discounted at 5.5 per cent. The incremental benefits-to-cost ratio, in terms of these data and evaluation methods, would approximate 1.1:1, tending to favor slightly the High Dam.

take into account the relevant factors on which a private enterprise unit must base its investment decisions. It, in some measure, must maximize the difference between costs and returns which appear on its own financial accounts, irrespective of any associated costs and gains which, while appearing on social accounts, are not directly relevant for reaching a private investment decision. The economic superiority of the two-dam alternative partly results from the increased downstream power generation—28,000 kilowatts—for which a private enterprise unit could receive no compensation.[22] The increased storage available for flood control and low-flow regulation to provide navigation services—essentially nonmarketable services—also would not be given much weight in private investment decisions. In short, for Idaho Power Company, only the at-site power generation would be a significant factor in ordering its investment alternatives. Accordingly, if we assume the same at-site value ($41.58 per kilowatt of prime power) for power production in this case as in our analyses of publicly developed plans, the financial returns to Idaho Power Company from the three-dam plan would approximate $24.3 million annually, about $800,000 more than the two-dam alternative. Annual costs for the alternatives, as indicated in Table 25, show that costs for the three dams would be about $794,000 higher than the two-dam plan.

In terms of the costs and returns available to a private enterprise unit considering alternate plans of development, the added financial returns from the three-dam plan would about compensate for the added costs—but without any clearly demonstrable advantage. It is unlikely, therefore, that the decision in favor of the three-dam plan was reached in terms of the factors which we have considered. In fact, several factors facing the private utility would differ substantially from those we have considered as controlling.

---

[22] The hydroelectric potential in river sites along navigable streams belongs to the federal government (see *United States v. Chandler-Dunbar Co.*, 229 U. S. 53, reaffirmed in the recent Supreme Court Opinion, *United States v. Twin City Power Company*, No. 21, October Term, 1955). Hence, increased generation at federal power installations downstream from a private development of storage in the headwaters is considered somewhat as a *quid pro quo* for granting a license to the firm for private development. Thus, while the Federal Power Act requires private licensees who benefit from federal headwater storage development to compensate the federal agency providing the regulation, the reverse is not true.

Our analysis of the comparative efficiency of the alternative Hells Canyon dams employed an estimate of $41.58 as the value of prime power per kilowatt. We also assumed power output consistent with operations under conditions of complete hydraulic and electrical integration for a system of which the Middle Snake is but a part. While both of these assumptions are appropriate for evaluating the different plan under public operation, where social costs and gains are compared at the margin, they are not very useful for analyzing the problem facing a private firm in reaching an investment decision.

TABLE 25. *Comparative Costs of the Two-Dam and Three-Dam Alternatives, Assuming Idaho Power Company Construction and Operation*

Item	Alternatives ($ thousand)	
	Two Dams	Three Dams
Investment [a]	196,280	201,817
Interest and amortization [b]	10,752	11,055
Interim replacement [c]	893	1,074
Federal corporate taxes [d]	6,379	6,559
State and local taxes [e]	2,944	3,027
Operation and maintenance [f]	1,625	1,666
Insurance [g]	196	202
Total average annual costs	22,789	23,583
Increment of average annual costs of three dams over two dams		794

[a] Construction costs taken from FPC *Staff Brief*, Appendix B, Table 14, at 5 per cent interest during construction, and exclusive of provision for downstream generators.

[b] Interest at 5 per cent, amortization period of fifty years (*ibid.*, Appendix B, p. 94).

[c] *Ibid.*, Appendix B, pp. 87-88.

[d] Investment at 3.25 per cent (see note to Chapter V for explanation).

[e] Investment at 1.5 per cent (note to Chapter V).

[f] FPC, *Staff Brief, op. cit.* Appendix B, p. 89.

[g] *Ibid.*, Appendix B, p. 88.

The at-site value of power was derived by the FPC staff by estimating the lowest cost of alternative non-hydroelectric power, on the assumption that the alternative thermal capacity would be built by some public body with investment funds available at 2.5 per cent.[23] While this may be an appropriate estimate for use in comparing the economics of different plans, it has no particular significance for estimating returns on investment by an electric utility. Rates for utility companies are traditionally established by public regulatory agencies by means of a cost-plus formula. The rates at which Idaho Power Company could expect to market its output, within the territory it has been franchised to serve, would be such as to compensate it for all operating expenses plus a reasonable return on prudent investment. However, there is a serious complicating factor involved in this instance.

The market which Idaho Power Company is franchised to serve is very small in relation to the power potential in the Hells Canyon Reach. The 783,400 kilowatts of planned initial generating capacity in the Hells Canyon Reach is more than double the present generating capacity of the Idaho Power Company's total system. Such a large block of new capacity would not be fully utilized for two decades if its use were restricted to servicing the Idaho Power Company's franchised territory.[24] However, the surplus power relative to its marketing area could not be sold in the remainder of the Northwest Power Pool at a rate which would return full costs, in spite of conditions of tight power supply. The Northwest has a public power tradition in which agents of state and local governments can provide supplies of power at lower rates than can a private utility. Largely, this stems from the doctrine of intergovernmental tax immunity, which derives its justification outside of economic considerations. Supplies of power developed by such public bodies, accordingly, would be more attractive to users than the potential Hells Canyon surpluses of Idaho Power Company.[25] Moreover it seems unlikely that the Idaho regulatory authority

[23] FPC, *Decision, op cit.,* pp. 21-22, 25. Whether or not this appears to be the most appropriate manner by which to estimate the value of prime power per kilowatt, the figure of $41.58 appears defensible on other grounds. Power sells for from $17.50 per kilowatt-year in some sub-markets in the Northwest to well over $70.00 for other portions of the regional market. If we assume that this represents discriminatory pricing under a linear demand function, the average value can be approximated by a figure midway between, or somewhat in excess of the $41.58 employed.

[24] *Ibid.,* pp. 23 ff.

[25] *Ibid.,* p. 25, and Finding No. 23, p. 35.

would grant Idaho Power Company the privilege of making up the deficiency on its export power by increased charges on its domestic customers.[26]

The scale of development which Idaho Power Company can undertake profitably, therefore, is restricted by such institutional factors as the more favorable terms under which publicly developed sources can be obtained in the area and the limitation on the marketing territory which Idaho Power Company is franchised to serve exclusively—in conjunction with the sheer amount of hydroelectric potential in the Hells Canyon Reach.

From these cost and marketing considerations alone, it appears that a private firm—choosing between a more efficient two-stage plan which would create surplus power over a longer period, and a three-stage plan in which the capacity could be brought into production more gradually—would select the socially less efficient scheme of development.

A further factor which would influence the private utility's decision is the plan of operation. Our estimates of at-site power generation were predicated on operations consistent with an integrated hydraulic system.[27] The actual at-site generation for both plans when operated by an independent private enterprise unit would be somewhat different from the estimates in Tables 21 and 23. Those estimates assumed that the storage capacity developed in the Hells Canyon Reach of the Snake River would be utilized in the most efficient manner to maximize system output, irrespective of the effect on an isolated installation or set of facilities in a sub-system. Under Idaho Power Company management, the operating rule curve for the reservoir would strive for high at-site generation and peaking capability, irrespective of its influence on the output of other units of the hydraulic system.[28] Neither does Idaho Power Company contemplate the transmission facilities necessary to permit taking full advantage of the technical possibilities for complete hydraulic and electrical integration with the remaining systems in the Northwest.[29] Operation of the reservoir would involve annual drawdown and refilling operations rather

---

[26] *Ibid.*, p. 26.

[27] See Table 21, note *a*.

[28] Testimony of Witness Hogg for Idaho Power Company, FPC, *Transcript of Hearing, op. cit.*, pp. 3494-95, 5658-59, 5710, 5716, 5729-30, 5758, 6130-31.

[29] FPC, *Decision, op. cit.*, Finding No. 139, p. 64.

than storage utilization over the total hydraulic system's critical period of two to three years.[30]

What is the economic significance of this decision in quantitative terms? While it is not possible to obtain a refined estimate of unquestionable precision, at least a crude approximation can be attempted.

First, the annual costs associated with the smaller investment in the two-dam plan of operation would be approximately $472,000 less than under the three-dam set of facilities (see Tables 22 and 24). Increased power generation from the two-dam plan would amount to about $374,000 annually.[31] Furthermore, increases amounting to approximately $400,000 in average annual flood control benefits and $50,000 in average annual navigation benefits would accrue if the two-dam plan of development were undertaken. In sum, an annual economic gain averaging approximately $1.3 million represents the advantage of the two-dam plan over the Idaho Power Company's three-dam alternative.

These estimates relate only to the difference which is assumed in project design, comparing both alternatives under the assumption that they would be operated under a constraint to maximize output of the entire system. This, in turn, would require that all facilities be operated under co-ordinated management. For example, the increase in the total river system's prime hydroelectric power from the three Idaho Power Company dams, operated under hydraulic and electrical integration, would be 702,000 kilowatts, of which 585,000 kilowatts would be generated at site, 104,000 kilowatts generated at eight downstream installations, and 13,000 kilowatts would be attributable to operation under system integration.[32]

---

[30] Testimony of Witness Hogg, *op. cit.*, pp. 5716, 5729-30.

[31] This assumes an increase of about 9,000 kilowatts of prime power valued at $41.58 per kilowatt. The increased downstream generation made possible by the added storage capacity would not require additional facilities downstream for the two-dam as compared with the three-dam plan. See, for example, FPC, *Exhibits, op. cit.*, No. 186, 28a.

[32] *Ibid.*, No. 50, p. 77. These estimates are based on the assumptions that Glacier View Reservoir is replaced in the comprehensive plan by increased storage provided at Libby, as a partial offset; stream flows will be depleted consistent with an assumed increase of irrigated acreages in the upper reaches of the Snake amounting to 366,650 acres, and a critical stream flow period of thirty-two months.

TABLE 26. *Costs and Gains from Integrated Operation of Two-Dam Plan and from Operation of Idaho Power Company Three-Dam Plan as Isolated Sub-System*

Item	Operation of Three Dams in IPC Isolated Sub-System	Operation of Two Dams in Integrated Federal System	Gains from Two Dams over Three Dams
	(kilowatts)	(kilowatts)	(kilowatts)
Average annual generation of prime power	669,000 [a]	711,000 [b]	42,000
	($ thousand)	($ thousand)	($ thousand)
Value of prime power at $41.58 per kw.	27,817	29,563	1,746
Value of flood protection	1,400	1,800	400
Value of navigation services	100	150	50
Total average annual value of added benefits	29,317	31,513	2,196
Total average annual costs [c]	15,869	15,397	472
Total average annual economic gains			2,668

[a] FPC, *Staff Brief, op. cit.,* Appendix A, p. 17, Witness Hogg's estimate appropriate to an eight-month critical period.

[b] Based on Witness Meadowcroft's estimate, *ibid.,* Appendix A, p. 16. See also Table 23, note *a.*

[c] See Tables 22 and 24.

These estimates assume a cyclical storage drawdown in which the stored water would be utilized to meet deficiencies arising over a critical period of thirty-two months. The estimates would be smaller if the facilities in the Hells Canyon Reach were operated independently of the constraint to achieve maximum system output. Assuming annual drawdown—although the following estimate is only a crude approximation [33]—output from the three dams under independent management would approximate 567,000 kilowatts at

[33] Witness Hogg for Idaho Power Company employed reservoir operating assumptions for his estimates of prime power which clearly indicated drawdown and refilling on an annual basis (FPC, *Transcript of Hearing, op. cit.,* pp. 5716, 5730) and operations to maximize output from an isolated development (*ibid.,* pp. 3495, 5658-59). The figures presented in the text, therefore, represent his estimate of prime power, which assumes an eight-month critical period.

site and 102,000 kilowatts downstream.[34] Potential primary power of about 33,000 kilowatts accordingly would be sacrificed by operating the Hells Canyon three-dam plan as an isolated sub-system. A net annual increase amounting to roughly $1.4 million would result from operations directed toward maximum output for the system.

To summarize: Gains to be achieved from integrated operation of the two-dam plan of development over independent operation by Idaho Power Company of its preferred three-dam alternative would approximate the magnitudes shown in Table 26.

A difference between the two plans and probable methods of operation results in a sum approaching $2.7 million annually. This suggests the possibility that an alternative approach to development could have improved the position of some who could out of their gains ($2.7 million annually) compensate the losers and still have a net gain remaining.

Summary and Conclusions

The foregoing analyses suggest a number of conclusions. First, the approach which contemplated the Hells Canyon High Dam appears to be most efficient, if an imputed interest rate of 2.5 per cent is employed. However, at an opportunity cost of capital approaching 5 to 6 per cent, the Hells Canyon High Dam may be inferior to a somewhat small scale of development. The plan of development which appears the more feasible from the standpoint of Idaho Power Company falls short of being best adapted to comprehensive development of the Columbia River and tributary system. In our terminology, the three-dam plan of development is economically less efficient than the two-dam plan—that is, a greater amount of project services could be produced with a smaller expenditure of society's resources were the two-dam plan to be substituted for the Idaho Power Company plan. This remains true under any assumptions governing the level of interest rates. Moreover, the three-dam scheme appears to be as good as the Hells Canyon High Dam only under circumstances which warrant a high imputed interest rate together with other particular conditions. At

---

[34] See FPC, *Staff Brief, op. cit.*, Appendix A, p. 17; and *Transcript of Hearing, op. cit.*, pp. 3544-45.

any rate of interest below 5 per cent, the three-dam plan seems inferior to the High Dam as well as to the two-dam alternative.

It therefore appears that Idaho Power Company preferred the three-dam plan rather than the economically superior two-dam plan primarily because of the relatively small system which Idaho Power Company operates—at least small in comparison with the hydroelectric potential in the Hells Canyon Reach. The more efficient plan represented such an extreme case of indivisibility that Idaho Power found it necessary in coping with the problem to select an economically inferior plan. Part of the superiority of the two-dam alternative, also, is accounted for by the increase in downstream generation through turbines of fiscally independent parties which would result from improved stream regulation, as well as increased output of nonmarketable project services which would escape appropriation by pricing practices.

In view of the relatively inefficient plan of development which was licensed, what alternatives might be considered for achieving more efficient development in similar or related cases? This question must be approached against the backdrop of the recent history of the Hells Canyon case.

One alternative, of course, would be to have the federal government undertake the development under provisions of Section 7 (b) of the Federal Power Act. This could be defended in view of three major considerations: There is the size of the development and the enormous hydroelectric potential in relation to all but the federal system in the Pacific Northwest. Also, significant external economies would appear in the federal installations downstream, for which a private developer of upstream storage could not receive compensation under provisions of the Federal Power Act. Finally, there would be a significant amount of nonmarketable project output. The history of proposed legislation to authorize federal development of the Hells Canyon site, however, reflects a stalemate between the advocates and opponents of federal development. Such legislation has consistently failed of passage in the Congress. Moreover, since 1953, the executive branch of the government has withdrawn support for development under federal auspices. Without forceful support, the prospects for development as a federal undertaking appear very slight.

A second alternative would be development by either a local public body or a combination of two or more such organizations.

This would be consistent with the preference provisions of the Federal Power Act, and also with the realities of financing the development at lower costs to provide power at rates attractive to electro-process industries, thereby improving the prospects for marketing profitably such a large block of new generation.[35] In the Hells Canyon case, however, no acceptable local organizations appear to have been interested, nor did any such organization present a plan to be seriously considered by the FPC.

A third alternative would be to license, under authority of Section 10 (a) of the Federal Power Act, a private developer who had exhibited an intent to develop that reach of river. In this case, the FPC would have the authority, as a condition of the license, to require modification of the plan of development so that it would be best adapted to comprehensive development of the Columbia and tributary system. A private firm could then decide whether or not to undertake the development under conditions which, while representing the most efficient plan from a social viewpoint, might not be financially feasible within a private cost-gain calculus.

If the private firm found that such conditions did not warrant investment, there is a fourth alternative. Development of the Hells Canyon Reach [36] could be deferred until a combination of circumstances altered the prospects for development of the most efficient plan.

The FPC followed the third alternative, without requiring such modification of the applicant's plan as to ensure the most efficient scheme of development. The more efficient two-dam alternative was dismissed from consideration by the Commission on the grounds that it had not been "seriously proposed by any responsible parties," and moreover was "substantially the same as the three-dam plan with respect to economics, benefits, and public purposes." [37] The rationale underlying the FPC presiding examiner's decision not to reserve the Hells Canyon Reach for federal development under Section 7 (b) of the act involved a recognition that, in the

[35] Differences in financing costs under alternative approaches to development will be discussed in Chapter VII in connection with a problem involving the Willamette River Basin.

[36] Four other hydroelectric sites upstream, aggregating a much more modest 215,000 kilowatts, were available to Idaho Power Company (FPC, *Staff Brief, op. cit.,* p. 20).

[37] FPC, *Decision, op. cit.,* Opinion No. 283, p. 3.

light of the congressional stalemate in this regard, such a decision "would serve to freeze the Middle Snake for hydroelectric development for an indeterminate period in the future." [38] Consistent with the intention not to "freeze" developmental opportunities on the Middle Snake, the examiner found in favor of issuing the license for Brownlee project of the Idaho Power Company plans, but denied the propriety of a license covering all three projects. The rationale was expressed as follows:

> Section 13 [of the Federal Power Act] seems to prohibit the tying up of power sites with no real prospect of developing them within the immediate future. It seems pretty clear from the legislative history that one of the things concerning the people who contrived the Act was that some power company might try to stake out a whole river considerably in advance of its needs, thereby preventing someone else from utilizing the same water resources in the meantime, and that such monopolistic activities would be detrimental to the public interest. [39]

Again:

> Even if it [Idaho Power Company] were to accept a license which required the building of the three proposed projects in a minimum of nine years as proposed by the Staff, if the market for the power was not evident, there would be little difficulty under the Act in amending the license to eliminate one or both of the excess and unneeded developments. Neither the Commission nor any other governmental regulatory body could lawfully and effectively require construction of a hydroelectric project, a market for which did not exist.
> Even so it would be clearly not in the public interest to license the three proposed dams when there is only a market reasonably predicted for the production of one of them. [40]

In spite of the presiding examiner's findings, the FPC in effect reversed his decision with respect to preventing a private firm from "tying up" the developmental possibilities in the Middle Snake. Idaho Power Company was licensed by the Commission to undertake all three of the projects for which it made application. In light of the disparity between the plan of development proposed by Idaho Power Company and the economically more efficient plan, it is apparent that the FPC valued private development quite highly.

[38] *Ibid.*, pp. 56-57.
[39] *Ibid.*, p. 29.
[40] *Ibid.*, pp. 27-28. See also FPC, *Decision,* Findings Nos. 46-49, p. 37.

If the value which the Commission attached to private development is shared to the same extent by the body politic, we might say that by "collective choice" efficiency was here sacrificed for "higher criteria." Even so, we may consider what alternatives would achieve such higher values without sacrificing efficiency goals. Needless to say, while development can be both private and efficient, such a combination will involve sacrificing at least some other values.

Because of the direct interdependence among facilities in the system, the indivisibility of the site for efficient storage development, and nonmarketable water derivatives, the enterprise would require access, at least in part, to public revenues to realize the gains inherent in the more efficient development. These gains, to repeat, would accrue at eight downstream federal installations and would involve increases of prime power, average annual flood control benefits, navigation benefits, and a reduction in annual average operating costs. Economic gains approaching $2.7 million annually, therefore, would provide justification for compensating a private firm for any costs which it might incur in a private accounting sense were it to undertake the two-dam plan rather than its preferred private alternative. If there were machinery whereby the beneficiaries from the substitution of the economically more efficient plan could compensate Idaho Power Company, such compensation could approach $2.7 million annually without leaving the beneficiaries any less well off than in the absence of the socially more efficient alternative.

In the absence of such machinery for compensation, the gains could be realized only by resort to revenues arising outside of the pricing practices of a private firm. Under certain circumstances, it is conceivable that the FPC could require the most efficient plan as a condition of the license, or permit the privately preferable plan under penalty of charges sufficiently high to induce the private developer to prefer the socially more efficient plan. This approach may have merit under certain circumstances, but in the case of the Hells Canyon Reach, because of the extreme conditions encountered with reference to development by the relatively small power system, it is doubtful that this would have led to early development of that reach of river. The private developer could refuse the license. The remaining alternative for obtaining private development in the immediate future would involve a public subsidy of the private utility, to achieve the public functions inherent in the most efficient development of that reach of river.

A public subsidy could take several forms. The twin goals of private development by the most efficient plan—if these goals are sufficiently valued—could be promoted by congressional appropriations to subsidize Idaho Power Company in an amount up to the present value of the added annual benefits of the two-dam plan over the company's preferred plan. Or the value of the increased generation at federal power installations downstream conceivably could provide the wherewithal to compensate Idaho Power Company for the storage services it would develop through the most efficient scheme.

Such compensation from downstream installations, however, raises significant policy issues. Consistent with tradition, reaffirmed by several Supreme Court rulings [41] that the hydroelectric potential is a public resource, the Federal Power Act contains numerous provisions to the effect that private developers must incur costs for public purposes as compensation for the privilege of developing a resource that is owned by the public. Accordingly, in order to permit compensation for private headwater storage by downstream federal hydroelectric operations, the application of the Federal Power Act would have to be modified in numerous instances. In turn, this would require major changes in existing law. In light of the wide ramifications of such a change and the conceivable relevance of "higher criteria," a judgment on the desirability of such a change remains outside the scope of this study.[42] Nevertheless, if efficient development under private auspices is sought, arrangements similar in effect to the ones suggested would be needed. The other choice, if efficiency is sufficiently valued, is to continue development of storage sites under federal auspices in those cases where the federal government owns and operates run-of-river downstream installations.

If downstream beneficiaries, whether public or private, were

[41] *United States v. Chandler-Dunbar Co., op. cit.; United States v. Appalachian Power Co.,* 311 U. S., 377; and *United States v. Twin City Power Company, op. cit.*

[42] For a discussion of some of the issues involved, see *Headwater Benefits,* Hearings before the Subcommittee on Irrigation and Reclamation of the Committee on Interior and Insular Affairs, United States Senate, 84th Congress, 1st Session, on S. 1574, May 27, June 29, and July 12, 1955.

required to compensate upstream operators for any services incidentally rendered, and if there were adequate machinery to collect such compensation, one further modification of customary practice would be necessary to achieve efficiency. The most efficient design of installations consistent with integrated system development, while necessary, is not enough to ensure economic efficiency in the management of multiple purpose river basin systems. Operation of all of the interdependent units of the system, irrespective of ownership, must be undertaken so as to maximize system output. This in turn would require that all facilities be operated under unified management. For example, the difference in power output between the identical three-dam facilities operated as an isolated subsystem (669,000 kilowatts) and operated as part of an integrated Columbia system (702,000 kilowatts) is 33,000 kilowatts. A net gain, estimated roughly at $1.4 million, would result annually from operating the facilities in the Hells Canyon Reach under integrated management, along with other units of the interdependent Columbia system. Sharing the gains available under co-ordinated management would represent an incentive to both parties—Idaho Power Company and the federal power system—to transfer the management responsibilities for the reservoirs on the Snake to an agency of system-wide responsibilities. A precedent for such a co-operative arrangement is to be found in the Fontana Agreement negotiated between Tennessee Valley Authority and Aluminum Company of America. The company transferred management responsibility for its reservoirs on the Little Tennessee to the TVA in exchange for sharing equally in the added power (22,000 kilowatts) made available through hydraulic integration.[43]

It seems appropriate to observe that where excellent storage sites exist upstream from federal power installations, partnership arrangements involving private development do not, in the absence of a much greater degree of institutional experimentation, promise the ultimate in efficient development. This is, in part, inherent in the political theory and legal doctrine which interpret hydroelectric sites as public assets with ownership residing in the federal government. If both private development and efficiency are highly valued, however, a happy outcome for development of headwater

[43] Tennessee Valley Authority, *The Fontana Project,* Technical Report No. 12, 1950, p. 7.

storage sites seems unlikely without a significant shift in the community's values. The community would need to sanction the transfer of public assets to private ownership, resulting in establishment of the legal right to exact compensation for factor services rendered downstream, whether to private or federal beneficiaries. This would involve competing values which the legal and political process during the past half century has seemed loath to sacrifice. In the Hells Canyon case, however, these questions of direct interdependence between headwater storage and federal downstream installations were relatively minor considerations, one may infer, as compared with the problem of the sheer size of the development relative to the Idaho Power Company system.

Note to Chapter V

Data on which the analyses of Chapter V were based were obtained from the record of the Federal Power Commission hearings, *In the Matters of Idaho Power Company; Project No. 1971, No. 2132, and No. 2133,* on file with the FPC in Washington, D.C. The voluminous records contain many differing estimates for the same items, because different assumptions were employed in deriving estimated magnitudes. The selection of estimates employed in the analyses in Chapter V was governed by a desire to obtain comparability of data as among the three plans of development reviewed, and to use estimates which enjoyed the sanction of a consensus of expert witnesses. A detailed explanation of data employed for each of the significant categories is given below.

1. INVESTMENT

Construction Costs. Estimates of *at-site* construction costs were taken from FPC *Staff Brief,* Appendix B, Table 14, line 14. These data on construction outlays reflect the adjustments required to make the estimates comparable as among the three plans of development. Since no estimates for construction outlays in connection with downstream generating facilities were made by the FPC staff, the data presented by Witness Cotton were employed; these were consistent with a consensus of expert witnesses as to the anticipated depletion of stream flows resulting from additional irrigated acreages upstream, and the length of critical period appropriate to the analysis. (See FPC *Decision,* p. 45, and *Staff Brief,* Appendix A, p. 6, and Appendix B, pp. 4 and 10.)

Interest During Construction. Estimates of the length of construction period involved for each of the alternative plans were taken from the summary presented in the FPC *Staff Brief,* Appendix B, Table 9. Interest during construction for downstream facilities assumed a construction period of two years as reflected in the FPC *Staff Brief,* Appendix B, p. 29. The interest rate for comparing alternate plans under federal construction was taken at 2.5 per cent and 5.5 per cent, respectively, for Tables 20 and 22 in the text. A rate of 5 per cent was used in analysis of alternate plans assuming construction by Idaho Power Company (see FPC *Staff Brief,* Appendix B, p. 94).

Incidental Capital Outlays. The figure for fish facilities was taken as $5 million, representing the capital costs estimated in only approximate terms by expert witnesses for this item of investment (see FPC *Staff Brief,* Appendix B, Table 14).

2. ANNUAL COSTS

Interest and Amortization. Annual capital charges under federal operation were computed on the assumption of a 100-year sinking fund at 2.5 and 5.5 per cent interest rate, respectively, for analyses given in Tables 20 and 22. A 100-year amortization schedule under federal operation was used in light of the extreme durability and anticipated economic life of this type of project (see Otto Eckstein, *Water Resources Development: The Economics of Project Evaluation* [Cambridge: Harvard University Press, 1958], Chapter IV). An amorization period of fifty years was taken as relevant under the assumption of private operation, in view of the recapture provision in licenses granted private parties under the Federal Power Act.

Interim Replacement Charges. These were computed at 0.387 per cent of investment (in all cases employing a 2.5 per cent rate of interest during construction) for the Hells Canyon High Dam; 0.471 per cent for the two-dam alternate; and 0.513 per cent for the three-dam plan consistent with procedures of the FPC staff's Witness Frogatt (see FPC *Staff Brief,* Appendix B, p. 88).

Payments in Lieu of Taxes. On the assumption that alternate

plans would be operated under federal auspices, these payments
were based on an estimate of 0.5 per cent of investment (see FPC
Staff Brief, Appendix B, p. 88).

Taxes. On the assumption that the alternate plans were operated by a private enterprise unit, taxes were estimated as follows:
It was assumed that 50 per cent of the capital structure would
represent venture capital on which a rate of return after taxes
would be 6.5 per cent. Furthermore, assuming a federal corporate
tax rate of 50 per cent on "before tax" net returns, the corporate
tax rate would be 3.25 per cent of investment. State and local
taxes—which FPC records reveal to approximate 2.5 per cent of
investment on the average for electric utilities—were scaled down to
differentiate between state and local taxes on the average of production and distribution systems and the taxes which could be
anticipated on the generating facilities alone, more relevant to the
current problem. (See John V. Krutilla and John M. Peterson,
"Capital Costs of Private v. Public Power for AEC," *Journal of
Land and Public Utility Economics,* February 1956, p. 18, for a
discussion of the desirability of distinguishing between the generating and distribution stages.)

Insurance. An insurance rate of 0.1 per cent of investment was
assumed in connection with the operating costs under private
ownership consistent with the estimates of the FPC staff. (See *Staff
Brief,* Appendix B, pp. 88-89.)

Operation and Maintenance. Annual costs were taken directly
from the estimate provided by Witness Frogatt of the FPC for
reasons justified in the FPC *Staff Brief,* Appendix B, pp. 89-91.

3. ANNUAL BENEFITS

Prime Power. Estimates of witnesses Cotton and McIntyre were
used in the analyses of prime power of high-dam and three-dam
plans of development because these were based on (a) a critical
period of thirty-two to thirty-four months, which also approximates
the average critical period of thirty-one months employed by Riter
and judged to be the most reasonable average length of critical
period (FPC *Decision,* p. 45); (b) estimated stream flows based on
the most reasonable estimate of additional irrigation acreage,
366, 650, provided by Columbia Basin Interagency Committee (FPC
Staff Brief, Appendix B, p. 4); (c) data directly related to the esti-

mate of downstream generating capacity warranted by the development of the Hells Canyon Reach, and the investment associated with its installation; (d) assumed downstream generation based on eight currently completed or authorized downstream structures, considering the Hells Canyon development as the last added; and (e) an incremental method of estimating the increase in system prime power attributable to the development of the Hells Canyon Reach. (See FPC *Decision,* Finding No. 119, p. 62, and also *Staff Brief,* Appendix A, pp. 14, 17.)

The estimate of nominal prime power for the two-dam plan of development employed in the analyses of Chapter V used the estimate of Witness Meadowcroft, adjusted for differences in length of critical period, additional irrigation acreage, and a transformation to achieve comparability with Cotton's estimated results for the three-dam and high-dam plans. (See FPC *Staff Brief,* Appendix A, p. 16.)

Value of Power. This was taken from the estimates prepared by the FPC appearing in the *Staff Brief,* p. 14, and the examiner's *Decision,* p. 47.

Value of Flood Control and Navigation. The estimates of the U. S. Corps of Engineers for flood control and navigation are given in *Exhibits,* No. 372 in the record of the hearings. These estimates differ from somewhat lower early estimates to reflect subsequent re-evaluation and upward adjustment.

VI   The Alabama–Coosa

River System:

INTEGRATED SYSTEM DEVELOPMENT

BY A SINGLE LICENSEE

The difficulties that have beset efforts to develop the Hells Canyon Reach of the Snake River arise from circumstances that do not necessarily prevail on all river basins. There are conditions under which a river system can be efficiently developed, and the system's output efficiently distributed, even under divided ownership. The Alabama-Coosa river system has characteristics that illustrate these possibilities.

Two of the conditions that impede development of the Hells Canyon Reach are indivisibility and direct interdependence. Both were discussed in Chapter III as factors that prevent an efficient allocation of resources in a pure market economy. Even though the federal government interceded in the interest of efficient development as prescribed by the Federal Power Act, the powers of the government seemingly were not employed to ensure the most efficient plan of development.

Part of the difficulty stems from the indivisibility of an excellent storage site when regarded as part of a hydraulically interdependent system. In the Hells Canyon Reach, the characteristics of the site for storage, coupled with the stream flow and the fall in that reach of river, represent a hydroelectric potential which vastly exceeds the present needs of the most eligible private developer. Such conditions may be more or less typical of many of the storage sites on the tributaries of the Columbia and some of the other western streams. But there are other streams, particularly in eastern United States, in which the hydroelectric potential of remaining sites represents only a fractional increment to the generating capacity of any electrical system of which the hydroelectricity could become a part.

Another problem originates in the direct interdependence between headwater storage and the output of generating units downstream owned by fiscally independent parties. If the ownership of these downstream installations resides with the federal government, the private developer of storage capacity upstream, under present law, cannot recoup from beneficiaries his investment in the extra storage required to provide efficient downstream regulation. However, if the headwater storage reservoirs and the downstream run-of-river installations are integrated into a single system under common ownership—even if exclusively private—incentives will exist to provide the most efficient storage facilities and plan of operation. Integration will not necessarily ensure that an adequate amount of storage will be developed to provide regulation required for economically justified flood control, nor that expenditures will be undertaken for the economical provision of other nonmarketable water derivatives. Even so, integration would seemingly eliminate one of the obstacles to achieving an efficient program design and plan of operation.

The principal conditions necessary for efficient development are these: First, the hydroelectric units making up the river system need to be small in relation to the electrical system of the intended developer. Second, either (a) the headwater storage would have to be provided by the federal government, which under present law could recoup the cost of providing headwater benefits downstream, or (b) if the headwater storage were developed by a nonfederal source, no federal installations could be located downstream, for under present law the developer would be providing factor services for which he could not receive compensation. Third, if a part of the development were undertaken by a private party, the license would have to include conditions that nonmarketable water derivatives be provided if their value exceeds their opportunity costs; such costs would be met by resort to public revenues.

One set of conditions required for an efficient development of a river system under private operation appears to be approximated

in the physical conditions of the Alabama-Coosa river system and
the distribution of existing developments there. In this chapter,
we shall describe the Alabama-Coosa river system and sketch the
development plan of the U. S. Corps of Engineers, along with a
plan for its private development by the Alabama Power Company.
This will provide the materials required for an analysis of the
alternative plans. The data available in the case of the Coosa are
neither as comprehensive, nor as relevant in many instances, as
those for Hells Canyon. Hence, we shall treat some of the un-
answered questions and the side issues they raise, before summariz-
ing our conclusions based on information available in the public
record.

The River System and Alternate Plans for Development

The Coosa River is a major tributary of the Alabama-Coosa
branch of the Mobile River system. It drains an area of approximately 10,250 square miles—4,000 square miles of which are drained
by two headwater streams, the Oostanaula and Etowah. These
rivers join at Rome, Georgia, to form the Coosa, which then
descends about 450 feet, in some 285 miles, while flowing from
Rome generally southwesterly toward the Gulf of Mexico. About
15 miles above Montgomery, Alabama, the Coosa unites with the
Tallapoosa River to form the Alabama River. The Alabama, in
turn, flows approximately 315 miles toward the Gulf through the
coastal plains—dropping about 106 feet in its course—before unit-
ing with the Tombigbee, where it forms the Mobile River about 45
miles above Mobile Bay. Combined, the Alabama-Coosa river
system drains about 22,800 square miles and has an annual average
discharge of approximately 26.8 million acre-feet.

PLAN OF U.S. CORPS OF ENGINEERS

Public interest in the development of the Alabama-Coosa river
system dates back at least to 1870, when Congress requested the
U. S. Corps of Engineers to investigate the feasibility of improving
the Coosa River for navigation. Nothing approaching a study of
the multiple purpose potentialities of the Coosa emerged, however,

prior to the Corps of Engineers' "308 report" of 1934.[1] This report presented a general long-range plan of development intended to reflect possibilities of the stream principally for navigation, but also for flood control and, incidentally, for power.[2] The plan as proposed in the 1934 report contemplated five low-lift dams with locks on the Alabama River; one dam on the Coosa River at Wetumpka, below the already existing dams of the Alabama Power Company; locks in the three Alabama Power Company dams above Wetumpka; and four dams upstream from the Power Company's installations—at Fort William Shoals, Embry Bend, Patlay, and Leesburg. The plan also recognized the need for either storage reservoirs to regulate flow or auxiliary thermal power to firm up the hydroelectric generation. This original multiple purpose plan of development contemplated less than 30,000 kilowatts of primary power in the entire Coosa River.[3]

Partly because of the incidental nature of the power development and the negative findings with respect to economic feasibility of the navigation and flood control features at the time of the 308 report, the Committee on Rivers and Harbors of the House of Representatives instructed[4] the Corps of Engineers to undertake several subsequent reviews of the plan of development. The response was an interim report, dated October 1941,[5] in which six power dams on the Coosa were discussed, along with storage projects on the tributaries. This report recommended congressional authorization for the comprehensive development of the Alabama-Coosa river system. In keeping with this recommendation, approval of at least one power and navigation dam on the Coosa was sought. Such approval for the construction of navigation and power dams on the lower river system was obtained four years later by the Rivers and Harbors Act of March 2, 1945. The language of the authorizing legislation, in Public Law 14, reads as follows:

Initial and ultimate development of the Alabama-Coosa River

---

[1] "Alabama-Coosa Branch of Mobile River System," House Document No. 66, 74th Congress, 1st Session.

[2] *Ibid.*, p. 112. See also Office of the Chief of Engineers, Department of the Army, *Alabama-Coosa River Basin: Report to the President's Water Resources Policy Commission,* 1950, pp. 1-7.

[3] House Document No. 66, *op. cit.,* pp. 113-18.

[4] Dated April 1 and 28, 1936, and January 18, 1939.

[5] House Document No. 414, 77th Congress, 1st Session.

and tributaries for navigation, flood control, power development, and other purposes, as outlined in House Document 414, Seventy-seventh Congress, is hereby authorized substantially in accordance with the plans being prepared by the Chief of Engineers with such modifications thereof from time to time as in the discretion of the Secretary of War and the Chief of Engineers may be advisable for the purpose of increasing the development of hydroelectric power; and that for the initiation and accomplishment of the ultimate plan appropriations are authorized in such amounts as Congress may from time to time determine to be advisable, the total of such appropriations not to exceed the sum of $60,000,000.

In the period following World War II, there were numerous modifications of the original multiple purpose plan. By 1950, the evolving plan contemplated a low-lift lock and dam for navigation, and two higher dams with locks and power installations on the Alabama River; a flight of locks in the Jordan, Mitchell, and Lay dams of the Alabama Power Company; four dams on the Coosa River above Lay Dam; and some twenty reservoirs on the tributaries, some of which would be available for flood control storage as well as regulation for the generation of power.[6] Meanwhile, the

TABLE 27. *Principal Corps of Engineers' Structures Proposed for Alabama-Coosa River: Main Stem Only*

Project	Stream	Power capacity (kw)		Estimated investment (thousand 1949 dollars)	
		Initial	Ultimate	Initial	Ultimate
Allatoona	Etowah	74,000	110,000	—	—
Leesburg	Coosa	57,300	57,300	49,000	49,000
Patlay	Coosa	55,500	55,500	27,000	27,000
Howell Mill Shoals..	Coosa	84,000	105,000	28,700	41,722
Ft. William Shoals ..	Coosa	40,900	40,900	28,000	28,000
Jones Bluff	Alabama	51,000	68,000	36,701	43,701
Millers Ferry	Alabama	57,000	76,000	36,807	38,307
Claiborne Project ..	Alabama	—	—	12,612	12,612

Source: Office of the Chief of Engineers, Department of the Army, *Alabama-Coosa River Basin: Report to the President's Water Resources Policy Commission,* 1950, Table I.

[6] *Alabama-Coosa River Basin: Report to the President's Water Resources Policy Commission, op. cit.,* pp. 1-10.

construction of the Allatoona project on the Etowah, authorized under separate legislation in the Flood Control Act of 1941, was begun after the war ended. This project was completed, for all practical purposes, by 1950. The main structures of the comprehensive plan of development for the main stem of the Alabama-Coosa and the Etowah rivers, as of 1950, is shown in Table 27.

Since 1950, the Corps of Engineers' plan for the development of the Coosa River has undergone some modification, account of which will be taken below. However, the general outlines of the comprehensive plan made available to the President's Water Resources Policy Commission are available as a frame of reference within which to compare and contrast an alternate plan of private development proposed in response to legislation rescinding the authorization for the Corps to develop power on the Coosa.[7]

PLAN OF THE ALABAMA POWER COMPANY

In November, 1953, the Alabama Power Company had applied for a preliminary permit to undertake the necessary engineering studies preparatory to applying for a license to develop the Coosa River. When, in June 1954, Congress passed Public Law 436 withdrawing authorization for developing the power potential of the Coosa under federal auspices, it required that certain specific results which would have attended development by the federal government be provided for by the alternate developer.[8] A preliminary permit, issued soon after enactment of Public Law 436, authorized the Alabama Power Company to begin engineering studies looking toward application for a license.

The Alabama Power Company is one of four operating companies making up the Southern Company; the others are the Georgia, Gulf, and Mississippi power companies. This integrated electric system consists of more than 3 million kilowatts of installed generator capacity, over a million and a third of which is accounted for by the Alabama Power Company.[9] Six hydroelectric generating stations are owned and operated by Alabama Power Company.

[7] Public Law 436, Chapter 408, 83rd Congress, 2nd Session, H.R. No. 8923.
[8] *Ibid.*, Sections 1, 3, 4, and 5.
[9] See "Prospectus, The Southern Company," The First Boston Corporation *et al.*, November 1, 1955, p. 12.

These, with a rated installed capacity of 489,700 kilowatts, consist of the Mitchell, Jordan, and Lay dams on the Coosa, developing approximately 233 feet of head, and the Thurlow, Yates, and Martin dams on the Tallapoosa, whose rated generator capacities are shown in Table 28. In addition to its hydroelectric capacity, Alabama Power Company has 890,000 kilowatts of installed generator capacity in thermal plants in Alabama, at Gadsden and Gorgas and one near Mobile. As of December 1955, the total rated capacity of its system was 1,379,700 kilowatts existing, and approximately 321,250 kilowatts of steam electricity under construction.

TABLE 28. *Alabama Power Company's Existing Hydroelectric Facilities on the Coosa-Tallapoosa Tributaries of the Alabama River System*

Project	Stream	Rated installed generator capacity (kw.)
Lay	Coosa	81,000
Mitchell	Coosa	72,500
Jordan	Coosa	100,000
Martin	Tallapoosa	154,200
Yates	Tallapoosa	32,000
Thurlow	Tallapoosa	50,000
Total hydroelectric capacity		489,700

Source: *Alabama Power Company, Application to the Federal Power Commission for a License for the Development of the Coosa River, Project No. 2146,* December 1954.

Alabama Power Company's application for a preliminary permit contemplated development consisting of four dams, roughly corresponding to the plans evolved by the Corps of Engineers, above the company's existing plants on the Coosa, and an additional structure and powerhouse below the existing plants at Wetumpka, for a total of from 240,000 to 360,000 kilowatts in river structures.[10]

[10] See Federal Power Commission, *Order Issuing Preliminary Permit, In the Matter of Alabama Power Company, Project No. 2146,* 1954. Also compare *Coosa River Power Development,* Hearings before the Committee on Public Works, House of Representatives, 83rd Congress, 2nd Session, May 18, 1954, p. 49; and "Providing for the Development of the Coosa River, Ala. and Ga. [sic]," House Report No. 1682, 83rd Congress, 2nd Session, p. 3.

Original estimates of the number, type, and size of structures in the Alabama Power Company's plan were modified as a result of engineering studies undertaken following issue of the preliminary permit. The structures initially contemplated at Fort William Shoals, Drake Island, and Lock 2, were supplanted, by plans for increasing the height of the existing Lay Dam and developing alternate structures at Kelly Creek and Lock 3. The total complement appears in Table 29.

TABLE 29. *Projects of the Alabama Power Company Plan of Development for the Coosa River*

Project	Contemplated generating capacity (kw.)		Estimated investment (thousand 1956 dollars)	
	Initial	Ultimate	Initial	Ultimate
Leesburg	56,000	84,000	27,520	30,198
Lock 3	48,400	72,600	18,561	21,406
Kelly Creek	83,400	125,100	27,877	31,135
Lay (modified)	48,000	96,000	21,552	24,577
Subtotals [a]	235,800	377,700	95,510	107,316
Wetumpka	44,000	44,000	13,645	13,645
Total	279,800	421,700	109,155	120,961

Source: Alabama Power Company, Application, op. cit., Exhibit I as revised May 15, 1956.

[a] Corresponds to the Corps of Engineers' complement of facilities above the existing Alabama Power Company dams.

The proposed Leesburg reservoir at full power pool would have an area of 27,400 acres and would extend upstream approximately 50 miles. A power drawdown of six feet would provide 135,000 acre-feet of storage for regulating the river flows and would increase the generation of energy at downstream plants. A controlled surcharge storage above full power pool would be made to afford additional regulation in the control of floods. The power rule curve for the operation of Kelly Creek Reservoir calls for a drawdown to elevation 455 by January 1 of each year; maintaining the pool at this level throughout the first three months, subject to fluctuations caused by floods; and permitting the pool level to rise to elevation 460 by the first of April. The drawdown from elevation 460 to 455 would begin in September of each year and would be completed by the beginning of the flood season at the start of the following year.[11] The proposal to modify the existing Lay Dam would increase the height some fourteen feet and provide for two additional generating units. At normal power pool, the reservoir would have an area of 12,000 acres and extend nearly 47 miles upstream to Kelly Creek Dam, thereby eliminating the originally contemplated Fort William Shoals site from consideration as a reservoir possibility.

The four proposed structures and reservoirs would develop the reach of river between Rome, Georgia, and the first existing Alabama Power Company dam—roughly the same reach of river proposed for development by the Corps of Engineers' Leesburg, Patlay, Howell Mill Shoals, and Fort William Shoals facilities. In addition to the applicant's four projects in this reach of river, the Wetumpka site is proposed for a reservoir covering 1,200 acres and extending about seven and a half miles upstream to the existing Jordan Dam.

The Alabama Power Company's proposal is for multiple purpose development, consisting ultimately of more than 400,000 kilowatts of capacity, some 688,000 acre-feet of controlled surcharge storage available for flood control in addition to 191,000 acre-feet of storage in the power pool available seasonally for flood control. And there is provision for installation of locks in the event navigation becomes economically feasible on the Coosa River.

It is significant that all of the structures proposed by the company are on the main stem and downstream from the only storage project built by the federal government. Furthermore, the storage provided by the power pools in the Leesburg and Kelly Creek reservoirs would increase generation at proposed or existing installations owned and operated by the same company. Moreover, the possibility of complete co-ordination of water releases is enhanced by the Alabama Power Company's ownership of the Thurlow, Yates, and Martin dams on the Coosa's sister tributary, the Tallapoosa (see Figure 16), and the concurrent application to develop

[11] *Alabama Power Company, Application to the Federal Power Commission for a License for the Development of the Coosa River, Project No. 2146*, Exhibit H, Figure 2.

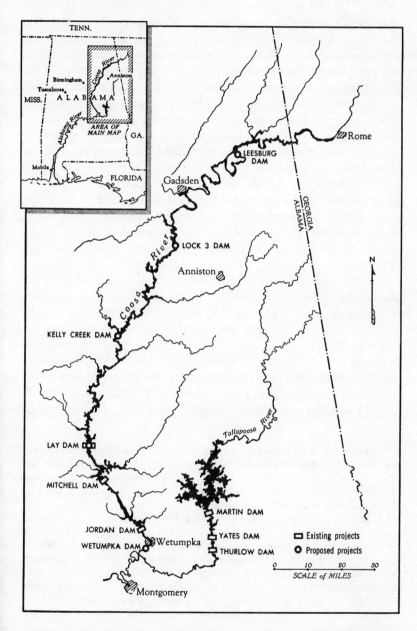

FIGURE 16. *Alabama Power Company Proposed Projects and Existing Dams on the Coosa and Tallapoosa Rivers*

under seperate license a site on the Warrior-Tombigbee.[12] The
plan of development, therefore, envisages an almost completely
integrated hydraulic plan under a single management unit. The
sole exception is the federal government's Allatoona project in the
headwaters of the Coosa. The cost of storage at Allatoona, which
benefits generation at Alabama Power Company's downstream
plants, however, can be recouped under existing law by the federal
government which provides the headwaiter benefits.[13] But none of
the storage for stream regulation provided by Alabama Power Company under proposed plans would benefit any party which is
fiscally independent of the Alabama Power Company.[14] In short,
all problems associated with direct interdependence in this case
would be solved by means of integrating all interdependent units
of the hydraulic system into a single enterprise unit, or by the
relative location along the stream of federal and private headwater
and run-of-river plants.

Nor does the problem of the relative size of the hydroelectric
potential and the electrical system of the developer pose any problems akin to those encountered in the development of the Middle
Snake. Table 30 presents data which highlight the contrast.
Whereas the Brownlee project—the initial development proposed
by Idaho Power Company in the Middle Snake—would approximately double the system's total capacity, the largest project in the
Alabama Power Company's complement of facilities (Kelly Creek,
83,400 kilowatts) would represent only about a 5.5 per cent increase

[12] A relatively small development is in prospect on the Warrior tributary of
the Tombigbee. Alabama Power Company proposes to construct a dam and
power house at Upper New Hope on the Sipsey Fork of the Warrior River and
to install electrical generating capacity at the existing navigation dam of the
federal government at Lock 17 on the Warrior.

[13] Contribution to generation at Alabama Power Company's Lay, Mitchell,
and Jordan plants by the Allatoona storage is computed to be 38.1 million
kw-h during 1953, 52.9 million during 1954, and 26.3 million during 1955. For
this energy, Alabama Power Company was assessed $57,955, $66,375, and $32,120,
respectively, to defray the "equitable proportion of the annual charges for
interest, maintenance, and depreciations" on the Allatoona project. See Federal
Power Commission, *Determination of Proportion of Annual Charges for Headwater Benefits, In the Matter of Alabama Power Company*, Docket No. E-6700,
August 1956.

[14] This will remain true only so long as the Millers Ferry and Jones Bluff
projects, authorized for federal construction, remain unbuilt.

in system capacity. The very serious problem of indivisibility encountered in the development of the Snake River is avoided here.

TABLE 30. *Comparative Data on Coosa and Snake Rivers and Associated Private Developer*

	Coosa River	Snake River
Drainage area (sq. mi.)	[a] 10,200	[b] 73,500
Average annual flow (cu. ft. per sec.)	[a] 16,150	[b] 16,640
Fall in relevant reach of river (ft.)	210	602
Hydroelectric potential (installed generator capacity in kw.)	421,700	900,000
Current installed generator capacity of intended developer (kw.)	1,529,950	374,000

Source: The Report of the President's Water Resources Policy Commission, Vol. 2, *Ten Rivers in America's Future*, 1950, Part 1, No. 1; Part 3, No. 7.

[a] U. S. Geological Survey, *Water Supply Paper 1334,* 1954, p. 234.

[b] House Document No. 531, 81st Congress, 2nd Session, Vol. IV, p. 1446.

Finally, provisions in the legislation suspending the authorization for federal development of power on the Coosa require that a definite amount of one potentially significant collective good—flood control—be provided as a condition of the license. On *a priori* grounds, therefore, none of the necessary conditions for an efficient design and plan of operation is lacking. It is desirable, however, to evaluate a number of considerations more carefully.

Comparative Efficiency of Alternative Development Plans

Neither the plans for the development of the Coosa nor the process of licensing the applicant for developing the river are final at the time of this writing. For this and other reasons,[15] the data for analysis of the Alabama Power Company plan of development

[15] In the Hells Canyon case, expert witnesses with conflicting interests not only defended their positions under cross examination, but also were required to make explicit the controlling assumptions governing all major conclusions. In the case of the Coosa, the application for license is not being contested with respect to matters involving comparative efficiency. Under the circumstances, the paucity of data usable for analysis of the Coosa is in marked contrast with that available in connection with the Hells Canyon development.

lack the completeness and relevance essential to answering the question: "Is the proposed plan of development the most efficient plan?" However, there are sufficient data to permit rather loose comparisons which, while not answering the question posed above, suggest an answer to another question: "Is the plan of development more or less efficient than some alternatives available for comparison?" Inferences drawn from such data can be used to supplement our conclusions, which are based largely on *a priori* propositions.

First, Alabama Power Company's plan of development may be compared with the U. S. Corps of Engineers' plan for the same reach of the Coosa River. The applicant's four proposed river structures above its existing dams on the Coosa are roughly equivalent to the Corps' proposed structures in the reach between Alabama Power Company's existing Lay Dam and the confluence of the Etowah and Oostanaula rivers. To make this comparison, however, several adjustments must be made.

First, the data relevant to the Corps' plan were presented in terms of 1949 cost levels and must be adjusted to take account of rising costs. Because of improvements in construction engineering, we increase the investment given for 1949 by only 17.5 per cent, despite the increase in construction materials and wage rates of 35 to 40 per cent. Secondly, the Corps' plans included the estimated cost of navigation locks,[16] whereas the Alabama Power plan does not include such costs, even though provision is made in the design of structures for their inclusion if locks become justified at some subsequent time. However, the Alabama Power Company's plans do provide for approximately 688,000 acre-feet of controlled surcharge storage for flood control purposes, whereas the 1950 version of the Corps' plan has only 268,200 acre-feet of live storage, none of which is provided for flood control, but only for power generation.[17] Accordingly, to analyze alternate plans in terms of a com-

---

[16] The originally estimated costs of the navigation locks for Leesburg, Patlay, Howell Mill Shoals, and Fort Williams Shoals were respectively 9 million, 6 million, 12 million, and 5 million dollars in terms of 1949 price levels. Adjusted upward by 17.5 per cent they would appear as 10.8 million, 7.1 million, 14.1 million, and 5.9 million dollars respectively. Source: Letter from the Office of the Chief of Engineers, dated March 28, 1957.

[17] *Alabama-Coosa River Basin: Report to the President's Water Resources Policy Commission, op. cit.,* Table i.

parable standard, the costs involved in providing the 688,000 acre-feet of controlled surcharge storage in the Alabama Power Company plan should be removed from the estimated total. Since the incremental costs of flood control storage do not appear in the public record, if they have been determined, we must compare the alternate plans without benefit of this relevant information. The data available for analysis of the alternative plans, with the adjustments described above, are presented in Table 31.

The plan of the Alabama Power Company promises approximately 45 per cent more installed generator capacity than the proposal for development embodied in the Corps' report to the President's Water Resources Policy Commission. Actually, it does not follow that the Alabama Power Company's plan will provide for more electrical energy merely because it will provide more installed capacity. The four projects under the Corps' plan would provide for something like 977 million kilowatt-hours annually, on the average, compared to an estimated 1,024 million kilowatt-hours under Alabama Power Company development. The greater capacity under the company's plan does suggest, however, that it would be used for peaking purposes. Since energy used for peaking purposes will have a higher value than the equivalent amount used for base load, to that extent, the hydroelectric potential would be more efficiently utilized. Aside from the difference in the amount of energy and its purpose in the system, the estimated cost under the Alabama Power Company plan would be approximately 80 per cent as great as under the 1950 version of the Corps' plan. Despite the incidental costs incurred for the controlled surcharge storage for flood management, it is apparent that Alabama Power Company's plan for power development is substantially more efficient; it provides more economic services than does the Corps' plan, at a smaller expenditure of society's resources.

Although we can feel reasonably sure that an economically efficient plan of development for power has been proposed—or would be undertaken—by the Alabama Power Company,[18] another con-

---

[18] In reviewing the evolution of the Alabama Power Company plan, one becomes aware of the alternatives which were analyzed by Alabama Power Company, presumably, exclusively in terms of the calculus of private costs and gains. At any rate, the plan which is advanced in the applicant's license application shows numerous modifications over the plan which was originally contemplated, as indicated in its application for preliminary permit.

TABLE 31. *Multiple Purpose Structures, Estimated Generating Capacity and Cost of Alternate Plans of Development for the Undeveloped Reach of the Coosa*

Corps of Engineers Plan (as of 1950)

| | | Estimated Investment ($ thousand) | |
Project	Ultimate capacity (kw.)	Original estimates including locks	Adjusted estimates excluding locks (1955 prices)
Leesburg	57,300	49,000	47,000
Patlay	55,500	27,000	24,675
Howell Mill Shoals ..	105,000	41,722	34,923
Fort William Shoals .	40,900	28,000	27,025
Total	258,700	145,722	133,623

Alabama Power Company Plan

Project	Ultimate capacity (kw.)	Estimated investment including undetermined cost of flood control storage ($ thousand)
Leesburg	84,000	30,198
Lock No. 3	72,600	21,406
Kelly Creek	125,100	31,135
Lay (modified)	96,000	24,577
Total	377,700	107,316

Sources: Alabama-Coosa River Basin: Report to the President's Water Resources Policy Commission, op cit., Table I; Office of the Chief of Engineers, *op. cit.,* Exhibits I and N as revised, May 15, 1956. *Alabama Power Company Application, op. cit.*

sideration requires attention. The provision of certain nonmarketable services is required, both by projects best adapted to a comprehensive plan of development, and the conditions stipulated in the legislation suspending authorization for public development. These services are not provided voluntarily by private firms acting consistently with our rationality assumption (as described in Chapter II). Potentially, the most significant of these services relate to flood control. Section 5 of the legislation suspending authorization of public development of the power has three relevant requirements: (1) the maximum flood control storage which is economically feasible shall be provided. (2) In no event shall the flood control storage be less than that required to compensate for the effects of valley storage displaced by the proposed reservoirs. (3) The storage shall not be less in quantity and effectiveness than the amount of flood control storage which could feasibly be provided by the currently authorized federal multiple purpose project at Howell Mill Shoals, constructed to elevation 490 with surcharge storage to elevation 495.[19]

The applicant's engineering plans show that adequate storage is being provided to compensate for the effect of valley storage displaced.[20] The U. S. Corps of Engineers, reviewing these plans for the FPC, concludes:

> The applicant's plans would provide substantial flood control for minor and moderate floods and would not make major floods of record any greater in peak discharge downstream from the Kelly Creek development. Therefore, it can be stated that the applicant's project would compensate for Valley Storage displaced by the reservoirs, if properly operated.[21]

With respect to the development of the maximum amount of flood control which is economically feasible, the Corps' judgment is expressed as follows:

> . . . the plan of development as described in the application would provide the maximum economical storage at the Kelly Creek development. Incremental storage at this development above that in the application was studied and the incremental flood control equivalent to that at the authorized Howell Mill Shoals site would have a benefit cost ratio of 0.59. The cost of providing additional storage at the Leesburg development would be expensive.[22]

To understand the third provision of the law relating to flood control, we need to review the evolution of the Corps' planning for the Coosa in the period following submission of its report to the President's Water Resources Policy Commission. Detailed plans for the Howell Mill Shoals site were presented in 1952,[23] and

---

[19] Public Law 436, *op. cit.*

[20] *Alabama Power Company, Application, op. cit.*, Exhibit H, Figures 3, 4, 5, 8, 9 and 10.

[21] Letter from Major General E. C. Itschner, Assistant Chief of Engineers for Civil Works, to FPC Chairman, dated May 18, 1956.

[22] *Ibid.*

[23] Corps of Engineers, U. S. Army, Mobile, Alabama, *Definite Project Report on Howell Mill Shoals Dam, Alabama-Coosa River,* March 1952.

further refined through studies analyzing alternative sizes of structures proposed for the site.[24]

The recommended structure for the Howell Mill Shoals site was approximately 100 feet in height with spillway crest at elevation 490. Storage for flood control contemplated 271,500 acre-feet in the power pool between elevations 480 and 490, to be shared according to the seasonal rule curve. That is, the power pool would be drawn down from normal pool level at elevation 490 to elevation 480 uniformly during the period from September 1 to January 1. It would then be permitted to rise uniformly to the normal power pool level between January 1 and May 1, and held at elevation 490 until September 1 signalled again the time for the seasonal drawdown. In addition, 180,100 acre-feet of surcharge storage between elevations 490 and 495 would be available to provide a total of 451,600 acre-feet.[25] This total is exceeded considerably by the amount of controlled storage (688,000 acre-feet of controlled surcharge storage and 191,000 acre-feet seasonally available in the power pool) contemplated originally in the Alabama Power Company's proposal. The storage in the company's plan, however, is located at three sites along a 100-mile reach of river, and has been judged to be "less effective" than the amount of controlled storage to be concentrated at the one site in the Corps' Howell Mill Shoals plan of development.[26] The Corps of Engineers has estimated that in order to be as effective as the Howell Mill Shoals plan, the flood control storage would have to be augmented in the proposed Kelly Creek reservoir by about 65,000 acre-feet.[27] This would require increasing the height of the spillway gate about three feet and obtaining flowage easements on perhaps five or six thousand additional acres behind the Kelly Creek Dam.[28]

A curious result emerges from analysis of the effects of Section 5 of Public Law 436. On the one hand, the Corps of Engineers'

---

[24] Corps of Engineers, U. S. Army, Mobile, Alabama, *Howell Mill Shoals Dam, Report on Preliminary Height of Dam Study,* August 1954.

[25] Between elevations 495 and 518.1, however, there would be an additional 1,397,000 acre-feet of surcharge storage for partial flood control regulations in the Corps of Engineers' proposed structure.

[26] Itschner letter, *op. cit.*

[27] *Ibid.*

[28] *Alabama Power Company, Application, op. cit.,* Exhibit H, Figure 5.

analysis reveals that the added cost of incremental storage at Kelly Creek exceeds the value of the storage for flood control (a benefit-to-cost ratio of 0.59:1). On the other hand, additional storage for flood control is recommended by the Corps, consistent with provisions of Section 5, to ensure realization of benefits equivalent in amount to those provided by the plan of development for Howell Mill Shoals. The inference seems plain: The incremental benefits from the authorized federal Howell Mills Shoals flood control storage, above the amount provided in the Alabama Power Company proposal for Kelly Creek development, do not justify the cost. If this is true, the last provision of Section 5 requires a less efficient plan of development than is consistent with rational economic behavior.

Some explanation of this conclusion is possible when we reflect how imprecisely the variables in the analysis above have been defined. Unlike conditions implicit in our competitive model in Chapter II, two quite different estimates of costs were employed in evaluating the incremental costs and gains under the federally authorized plan and the applicant's plan of development. The different manner in which those making investment decisions in the public and private sectors of the economy perceive the relevant cost of capital can be illustrated concretely.

Let us assume two alternate scales of development for the Howell Mill Shoals site. Plan I contemplates a maximum power pool elevation at 470 feet, a rated power head of 59 feet, and 119,000 kilowatts of installed capacity with no provision for flood control storage. The plan is assumed to cost $68.8 million if interest is computed at 2.5 per cent on an average of one-half the construction cost during a construction period of five years.[29] Plan II contemplates a maximum power pool elevation of 490 feet, a 71-foot head, 200,000 kilowatts of installed capacity, and a controlled surcharge storage for flood control of 180,000 acre-feet in addition to 272,000 acre-feet seasonally available in the power pool. The second plan is assumed to be available at a net investment of $97.7 million, if interest during construction also is charged at 2.5 per cent on an average of one-half the construction cost during a five-year construction period.

---

[29] A rate of 2.5 is assumed since it has been used, and recommended for use, in evaluating river basin projects undertaken by the federal government.

Given these alternatives, the estimated annual costs and benefits under federal operation would appear as shown in Table 32. As between the two alternatives, Plan II is shown to be economically justified, as the increment of over $2 million in annual benefits more than compensates for the increment in cost, when costs are based on an imputed interest rate of 2.5 per cent.

TABLE 32. *Assumed Alternative Plans of Public Development for Howell Mill Shoals, Assuming Interest Rate of 2.5 Per Cent*

	Plan I ($ thousand)	Plan II ($ thousand)
Investment	68,872	97,772
Annual costs:		
Interest and amortization	1,881	2,670
Interim replacements	112	146
Payment in lieu of taxes	344	489
Operation and maintenance	174	188
Total	2,511	3,493
Increment in costs of II over I		982
Annual benefits:		
Power	2,677	4,310
Flood control		424
Total	2,677	4,734
Increment in benefits of II over I		2,057
Incremental benefit—cost ratio	2.09:1	

Source: Data contained above is based on Corps of Engineers, U. S. Army, Mobile, Alabama, *Howell Mill Shoals Dam, Report on Preliminary Height of Dam Study,* August 1954.

We know, however, that investment funds are not available to a private utility at 2.5 per cent. A certain proportion of the investment funds can be obtained from borrowing at long-term rates of about 3.5 per cent; some funds will be available in exchange for preferred equity shares at rates of between 4 and 5 per cent; and the remainder will have to come from common stock and earnings retained in the enterprise. Since the latter bear the risk in the enterprise, funds available from venture sources will require a higher rate of return than the preferred stock or bonds. It then is reasonable to assume a higher effective rate as the cost of investment funds for a private firm than was employed in the example above. Moreover, a private firm will face other elements of cost—not faced by a public undertaking—which have implications for the effective cost of capital, and the resulting benefit-to-cost ratio of the incremental capacity. If we assume, as in Table 33, that an effective rate of 5.5 per cent represents the cost of investment funds for a private utility,[30] and that structures will be identical with those envisaged under Plans I and II of Table 32, we obtain a substantially different impression of the relative economy of the incremental development. The development of the Howell Mill Shoals site by a private enterprise unit would result in a larger increment in annual costs than in public benefits. Under the relevant conditions governing private investment decisions, therefore, the added costs of $3.5 million attending Plan II exceed the added benefits of $2.1 million. The ratio of the annual added benefits to costs (private) is only 0.59:1.[31]

What is the meaning of this seeming paradox—that under public development one alternative appears to be the more efficient, whereas under private development the other seems to be so?

In a market economy under perfect competition such a paradox could not arise. The value of every factor would have to be the same at the margin in every application for efficiency conditions to be met. It follows, therefore, that the cost of the services of capital in a competitive economy would be the same at the margin, not only as among uses but also as among users. In the workaday economy, however, the model's conditions assumed in specifying efficiency conditions are not realized. Of particular significance in the actual case is the fact that federal taxation in lieu of competitive bidding in the capital market is the more likely alternative in financing federal water resource projects. One approach to resolv-

---

[30] A rate of 5.5 per cent is suggested by the FPC's staff for evaluating power costs. See Federal Power Commission, Bureau of Power, *Information for Staff Use in Estimating Electric Power Costs and Values*, Technical Memorandum No. 1, November 1955, p. 31.

[31] No particular significance attaches to the coincidentally identical ratio in the example above with the ratio (0.59:1) referred to in Itschner's letter, *op. cit.*

ing the paradox, therefore, is to impute to the project a money cost that corresponds to the social cost of tax-raised funds.

Consider then the alternatives on the assumption that the opportunity cost of tax-raised funds is employed. The relevant data for the two plans are then shown in Table 34. We observe that while the incremental benefits exceed the incremental costs, total benefits under either scale of plant are less than the corresponding total costs.[32] Accordingly, we must conclude that if the opportunity cost

TABLE 33. *Assumed Alternative Plans of Private Development for Howell Mill Shoals, Assuming Interest Rate of 5.5 Per Cent*

	Plan I ($ thousand)	Plan II ($ thousand)
Investment [a]	73,037	104,804
Annual costs:		
Interest and amortization [b]	4,314	6,189
Interim replacements [c]	112	146
Federal corporation tax [d]	2,477	3,555
State and local taxes [e]	1,095	1,572
Insurance	73	105
Operation and maintenance [c]	174	188
Total	8,245	11,755
Increment in costs of II over I		3,510
Increment in benefits of II over I		2,057
Incremental benefit-cost ratio	0.59:1	

[a] Interest during construction computed at 5.5 per cent over a five-year period on one-half of construction costs.

[b] Interest at 5.5 per cent with a fifty-year amortization schedule consistent with fifty-year life of FPC license.

[c] Based on *Report on Preliminary Height of Dam Study, op. cit.*

[d] Assumes 45 per cent of investment funds raised by equity on which a rate of return of 16.5 per cent before taxes was earned, and on which a federal income tax of 45 per cent was carried. See Alabama Power Company, *Annual Report for the Year Ending December 31, 1955.*

[e] State and local taxes of 1.5 per cent of investment consistent with rationale underlying similar computations in Chapter V.

[32] In the more usual case, the comparison of incremental costs and gains takes place over the range of diminishing incremental returns; hence, the appropriate criterion is the comparison of incremental costs and gains. In this instance, the

of tax-raised funds is reflected in the benefit-cost analysis, the Howell Mill Shoals project as of the Corps' 1954 design is not economically justified.[33] This casts doubts on the economic justification for the

TABLE 34. *Alternative Plans of Public Development for Howell Mill Shoals Imputing the Opportunity Cost of 5.5 Per Cent for Federal Tax-Raised Investment Funds*

	Plan I ($ thousand)	Plan II ($ thousand)
Investment [a]	73,037	104,804
Annual costs:		
Interest and amortization [b]	4,036	5,792
Interim replacement	112	146
Payment in lieu of taxes	365	534
Operation and maintenance	174	188
Total	4,687	6,660
Total annual benefits	2,677	4,734
Average benefit-cost ratio:		
Plan I	0.57:1	
Plan II	0.71:1	
Increment in costs of II over I		1,973
Increment in benefits of II over I		2,057
Incremental benefit-cost ratio	1.04:1	

[a] Interest during construction computed at 5.5 per cent over a five-year period on an average of one-half of the total construction cost.

[b] Interest at 5.5 per cent with a 100-year amortization schedule.

comparison is made within the range of increasing returns; hence, despite the excess of incremental gains over incremental costs, total gains fall short of total costs and a net social loss would result. There is a discontinuity in the relation between scale and net gains, however, for beyond the scale corresponding to Plan II, the reservoir would inundate large industrial tracts in the city of Gadsden, Alabama, so that a sharp rise in costs would attend any much larger scale of plant.

[33] The Howell Mill Shoals Dam, representing an investment of $104.8 million and providing close to 200,000 kilowatts of installed generator capacity, as well as flood control valued at $424,000 annually, can be contrasted with Alabama Power Company's total complement of structures in that reach of river. The latter represents an investment of $103.7 million and provides for about 422,000

requirement that Alabama Power Company provide for flood protection equal in amount and effectiveness to the Howell Mill Shoals project.

Side Issues and Unanswered Questions

Whether or not the amount of flood control storage required by Public Law 436 is economically efficient, other questions of significance remain. If the amount of flood control storage proposed by Alabama Power Company exceeds the amount necessary to offset the effects of natural storage displaced by its reservoirs, issues arise in connection with (1) efficiency in the distribution of project output, (2) consistency with some other provisions of the legislation, and (3) equity in sharing the nonreimbursable portion of the project's costs.

Unless Alabama Power Company is compensated for the extra cost it incurs (either directly by the beneficiaries in the flood plain or by some public body for undertaking what would be a public responsibility), the flood control costs will be embedded in the investment that makes up its power rate base. The electric utility industry, as a franchised monopoly, is permitted a rate structure calculated to recover the original investment as well as to provide a reasonable rate of return. Power rates would have to average higher if Alabama Power Company were required to absorb the cost of flood protection. Unless the flood control costs could be grafted on to the inframarginal ranges of a set of discriminatory rate schedules, the added price on power to cover these costs would be similar to an excise on power and would adversely affect the marginal conditions for efficient distribution.[34]

It is not clear from Public Law 436 what is intended in connec-

kilowatts of installed generator capacity, as well as some flood control. If we capitalize the annual flood control benefits of the Howell Mill Shoals project ($7.8 million) and deduct this from the investment, the generator capacity costs will exceed $450 per kilowatt, as compared with about $250 for the Alabama Power Company. This much more favorable relation between factor inputs and project output for the Alabama Power Company plan suggests why it can undertake such a development with money costs exceeding 5 per cent, whereas the Corps' Howell Mill Shoals project is unable to show economic justification.

[34] See our discussion of market mechanics and efficiency criteria in Chapter II.

tion with covering the costs of flood protection. On the one hand, Section 1 of the Act requires:

> That the power from such development shall be considered primarily for the benefit of the people of the section as a whole and shall be sold to assure the widest possible use particularly by domestic and rural consumers, and at the lowest possible cost.

Consistent with the requirement that power be provided at the lowest possible cost, provisions in Sections 10 and 11 appear as follows:

> Section 10. An allocation of cost of flood control provided in addition to that required to compensate for displaced valley storage and of cost of navigation shall be approved by the Federal Power Commission taking into consideration recommendations of the Chief of Engineers, based upon flood control and navigation benefits estimated by the Chief of Engineers.
>
> Section 11. . . . In the event the Congress by legislative enactment adopts a policy of compensating such licensees for navigation and flood control costs, any such allocated navigation and flood control costs are hereby authorized to be compensated through annual contributions by the United States.

Furthermore, analysis by the Public Works Subcommittee in making its report to the Committee of the whole [35] provides an interpretation of the intent of Section 3 of the Act, which is quoted below in full:

> This section requires that the series of dams to be built by the licensee, together with the existing hydroelectric power dams on the Coosa River, be, in the judgment of the Federal Power Commission, best adapted to the comprehensive plan for the development of such river—a requirement found in section 10 (a) of the Federal Power Act. One purpose of this section is to require that the ratio of costs incurred by the licensee to the benefits which it obtains from the development shall be such as will attract the investment of private capital.

The last sentence of this analysis of Section 3 appears to place a most unusual interpretation on Section 10 (a) of the Federal Power Act, which nevertheless is concurred in by the Alabama Power Company in its letter to the Commission dated June 27, 1956, which repeats the concept that "the ratio of costs incurred by the licensee to the benefits which it obtains from the development shall be such as will attract the investment of private capital."

[35] House Report No. 1682, *op. cit.*

It appears, therefore, that provisions of Sections 1,3,10, and 11 of Public Law 436 would be consistent with compensating Alabama Power Company for the flood control benefits it will provide, and thus make possible the sale of power "at the lowest possible cost." On the other hand, F. C. Weiss, vice president in the company, testifying before the Committee on Public Works, asserted that flood control would be provided "at substantial cost," and without "any burden being imposed upon the Federal Treasury." [36] The latter part of the statement makes for a somewhat ambiguous position and reflects some evidence which suggests that Alabama Power Company seeks no compensation from the federal government.

In keeping with the latter interpretation is the testimony of Thomas W. Martin, chairman of the board of Alabama Power Company. The following colloquy between Congressman Jones of the Subcommittee and Mr. Martin gives the flavor of the latter's views on the matter:

> MR. JONES: Is that section [Section 11] inserted for the purpose of leaving the door open for the power company subsequently to come to the Congress and say, "We either are going to have to raise the rates under the general law as it now exists, or we are going to have to ask the Congress to compensate us for the flood-control work that is done on this river?"
>
> MR. MARTIN: I am glad you asked the question, Mr. Jones. Frankly, we are not the authors of that section.
>
> MR. JONES: Is the Corps of Engineers the author?
>
> MR. MARTIN: Perhaps the Corps of Engineers, or perhaps Senator Hill. I am not clear myself. We did not propose that section. We say to you again: We will carry out the financial burden which is put at $100 million or more. We will meet our financial burden. We are not asking the Congress through the device of this section for an appropriation, Mr. Jones.
>
> MR. JONES: As I understand it, under existing law, . . . that in establishing a rate before the Federal Power Commission, if, by the construction of these dams you were to make a flood control contribution, then that contribution that you made to flood control would. be reflected in the rates of the electricity which you sell.
>
> MR. MARTIN: Of course, the investment of our company goes into the ratemaking base.[37]

---

[36] *Coosa River Power Development,* Hearings before the Committee on Public Works, *op. cit.,* pp. 46, 48, 51.

[37] *Ibid.,* p. 39.

Consistent with this interpretation of the intent of Public Law 436 on the matter of sharing costs for flood control, Chairman Dondero obtained the following view from Colonel Whipple of the Corps of Engineers:

CHAIRMAN DONDERO: As you understand the language at the bottom of page 4—and at least it is my interpretation that the Alabama Power Company really takes the risk of expending that money for providing for flood control or navigation, and they could include it in the rate-making application in the State of Alabama unless some time in the future Congress should enact legislation to change that.

COLONEL WHIPPLE: Yes.

CHAIRMAN DONDERO: Is that not about the picture?

COLONEL WHIPPLE: Yes, Sir. That would be part of their capital expenses. There is no question about it.

CHAIRMAN DONDERO: It would be part of the hazard in taking over the power features on this river?

COLONEL WHIPPLE: Yes, sir.

CHAIRMAN DONDERO: At least that is the way I understand that language.

COLONEL WHIPPLE: Yes, sir.

CHAIRMAN DONDERO: Mr. Rains.

MR. RAINS: [one of the co-sponsors of the legislation]: I think that is correct and I think it is a proper interpretation.[38]

The record then is not clear as to who ultimately will bear the cost of flood protection in excess of that required to compensate for the effects of valley storage displaced. Chairman Martin speaks emphatically against the notion that the Alabama Power Company intends to approach the Congress for an appropriation. On the other hand, a letter from the Alabama Power Company to the Federal Power Commission dated March 5, 1956, reflects the view that the former regards the suspension of payments assessed by the Federal Power Commission for the headwater benefits provided by the Federal Allatoona storage project as a legitimate *quid pro quo* for the flood control benefits Alabama Power Company would provide under terms of Public Law 436. The two expressions of opinion are not necessarily inconsistent. In order to obtain compensation for costs it incurs for flood control, the company would not have to employ "the device of this section [Section 11] for an appropriation," in Mr. Martin's words. Instead, it could use Section 11 as a device to get compensation through the medium of another agency's decision to dispense with the requirements that Alabama Power Company compensate the federal government for headwater benefits from Allatoona. The fact that Section 11 is phrased in terms of annual compensation in lieu of an appropriation suggests that some parties instrumental in drafting the legislation may have considered this possibility.

Be this as it may, it is not consistent with Mr. Weiss' testimony that the development was being planned "without any burden being imposed on the Federal Treasury," and it therefore remains unclear whether the electric customers of Alabama Power Company, the Federal Government, or conceivably some other parties will carry the burden of flood protection. Perhaps the question will be answered by the terms of whatever federal license may be issued. In any case, this is not primarily an issue of "efficiency," as defined in Chapter II, but rather the co-ordinate consideration "equity" which is involved when differences in policies have different consequences for income distribution.

Summary and Conclusions

A review of the record in the case of the Alabama-Coosa deauthorizing legislation and Alabama Power Company's application for license, along with economic analysis of the problems, suggests several general conclusions.

There is nothing in the physical characteristics of the Coosa—the relation between the hydroelectric potential and the size of the Alabama Power Company's system, nor in the locational relationship between the federal project and the intended private development—to prevent the efficient development of the Coosa under private auspices. Furthermore, the legislation suspending authorization of federal development of the Coosa for power provides for the inclusion of nonmarketable project services, or "collective goods," which normally would not be undertaken by private enterprise. All the necessary conditions, both physical and institutional, for the development of a river basin in the most efficient manner under private auspices, therefore, are present in the circumstances surrounding the Alabama-Coosa.

Still, not all of the information required to determine the most efficient plan of development—or, in the words of the Federal Power Act, "project . . . best adapted to a comprehensive plan . . . including beneficial public uses"—has been developed for the public record. This may be accounted for partly by the ambiguity of Public Law 436 in numerous particulars. Under one interpretation of this legislation, some provisions require that a private developer assume a public responsibility—that is, the provision of a nonmarketable project service, flood control, at "substantial cost" directly to himself and indirectly to customers toward whom he has responsibility as a public utility. Under another interpretation for which there is support, the Act intends that a plan of development be undertaken such that "the ratio of costs incurred by the licensee to the benefits which it obtains from the development shall be such as to attract the investment of private capital." Such an interpretation of the benefit-cost investment criterion, in cases where there are possibilities for the provision of economically justified nonmarketable project services, would substitute the calculus of private costs and gains in an area where divergence exists between the private and social marginal productivity of capital. This interpretation of the criterion clearly defeats the purpose of benefit-cost analysis and the possibility of defining the most efficient plan of development. The fact that Alabama Power Company has apparently tested out a number of alternative plans—as indicated by the several modifications made to its originally suggested plan of development—does not necessarily mean that it has evolved the most efficient plan of development. For given the perversion of the benefit-cost criterion, comparisons of private costs and gains are substituted for the relevant social costs and gains. The benefit-cost criterion which emerges from this case would require river basin developments inconsistent with provisions of Section 10 (a) of the Federal Power Act.

In spite of the lack of the sort of information required for a determination of the most efficient plan, the record supports the conclusion that Alabama Power Company's plan is more efficient than the alternative plans proposed under public development. Under the plan indicated by its application for a license, Alabama Power Company would develop more power capacity and less flood protection—both changes in the direction of economic efficiency—than a combination of (1) an alternate set of plans proposed by the Corps of Engineers and (2) requirements of Section 5 of Public Law 436.

Finally, the record does not make clear the anticipated amount of public benefits to be provided, what they will cost, and who is ultimately going to bear these costs. If Alabama Power Company is required to provide flood control storage in an amount and effectiveness called for by Section 5 of Public Law 436, it has two conceivable ways of recouping its costs from such privately unprofitable undertakings. On the one hand, Alabama Power Company may be compensated in the future by the federal government, through the Treasury or another of its agents, for costs incurred in the provision of public benefits. This possibility is already apparent in the legislation. Another, and perhaps independent, possibility exists in the proposal by Alabama Power Company to trade flood control benefits for headwater benefits provided by the federal upstream project. There is nothing in the record, however, which would permit one to determine if this were appropriate compensation, too little, or too much. On the other hand, if it should never become the policy of the Congress to provide for compensation in connection with the provision of public benefits by Alabama Power Company, the burden of these costs will be shifted to the power consumers in the company's system. Recouping of costs by resort to the federal Treasury would be consistent with practices throughout the remainder of the country, and with our efficiency criteria. But only by coincidence or by a theoretical special case would the recouping of investment outlays for public benefits from trading benefits or by shifting the burden to the electricity consumers be consistent with our efficiency criteria.

The Willamette River Case:

ANALYSIS OF THE

DISTRIBUTION OF COSTS

Our previous case studies dealt with co-operative arrangements in which a complete project or set of projects was planned by a non-governmental unit under federal license. In the case of Hells Canyon, it became apparent that problems of indivisibility and direct interdependence impede efficient development as a private venture in the absence of extra-market incentives. For the Coosa River, where the circumstances are significantly different, there appears to be a much more promising prospect for efficient development under private auspices. There, complete hydraulic integration under unified management is possible, and the relatively modest contributions to power output from the river system can be readily absorbed into the developer's electrical system. But even in the case of the Coosa, there remain some problems of providing the project services which do not produce revenue. Although the legislation enabling the Federal Power Commission to license Alabama Power Company for developing the Coosa required provision of a specified amount of nonmarketable project services, some difficulties are encountered in the distribution of the costs and gains; and there is a question of propriety in the method advanced to solve that problem.

As a practical matter, however, the problems of the Coosa are of a much lower order of magnitude than those of Hells Canyon, since they concern a relatively small system from which the predominant share of project services are of the revenue-producing, investment-reimbursing type. This factor must figure prominently in undertaking the development of streams by co-operative arrangements; it may not be present in all such relatively small river systems.

In this chapter, we identify one relatively small stream to analyze an approach to problems that arise in such circumstances. We first detail the background material pertinent to development of Willamette River Basin sites and assess the implication of alternative approaches to efficient development. In this case, we conclude that the differences in efficiency between alternative approaches to development are likely to be small; we, therefore, select the distribution of costs and gains as the major problem for analysis in connection with co-operative arrangements of this type. We then analyze the difference in accounting costs [1] occasioned by different methods of developing a hypothetical site, before analyzing the differences in the distribution of those costs that correspond to the various approaches that have been suggested.

The object of all this is to provide better understanding of the income redistributive consequences of public policies. To complete the picture, it is necessary to consider gains as well as costs. Chapter VIII analyzes, to the extent possible, the differences in the distribution of gains associated with different approaches to development in similar cases.

The significance of these two companion chapters is this: although we have concentrated on questions of economic efficiency, we cannot ignore the redistributive consequences and the issues which these raise in terms of equity. Ideally, analyses such as those which follow should have been undertaken along with our efficiency analysis to provide the significant information relevant to a policy decision in each case. Since our main purpose has been to illustrate efficiency relationships and clarify issues, rather than to exhaust the possibilities for fruitful analysis for each case study, we have reserved the analysis of income redistribution for treatment in connection only with the present case.

The Willamette River System and Proposals for Development

The Willamette River drains an area of 11,200 square miles, approximately the size of the Coosa River's drainage area. This

---

[1] The term "accounting" cost is used to distinguish the costs appearing in the financial accounts of the enterprise unit from the "opportunity" or "social" costs used where we are concerned with economic efficiency.

TABLE 35. *Proposed Structures and Reservoirs of the Willamette River Sub-Basin*

Reservoir	Stream	Acre-feet of storage				
		Flood control	Power	Joint	Conservation	Total
Cottage Grove	Coast Fork Willamette	30,000	—	—	3,000	33,000
Dorena	Row	70,000	—	—	6,000	76,000
Hills Creek	Middle Fork Willamette	145,000	21,000	55,000	59,000	280,000
Waldo Lake	Middle Fork Willamette	—	220,000	—	—	220,000
Meridian	Middle Fork Willamette	230,000	28,000	110,000	88,000	456,000
Dexter	Middle Fork Willamette	—	3,650	—	23,850	27,000
Fall Creek	Fall Creek	105,000	—	10,000	10,000	125,000
Cougar	South Fork McKenzie	125,000	27,000	30,000	28,000	210,000
Blue River	Blue River	75,000	—	10,000	5,000	90,000
Gate Creek	Gate Creek	43,000	—	7,000	5,000	55,000
Fern Ridge	Long Tom River	95,000	—	15,000	7,000	117,000
Tumtum	Tumtum River	24,000	—	—	4,000	28,000
Holley	Calapooya River	80,000	—	10,000	7,000	97,000
Cascadia	South Santiam River	115,000	—	30,000	15,000	160,000
Green Peter	Middle Santiam	200,000	52,000	70,000	38,000	360,000
White Bridge	Middle Santiam	—	1,850	—	6,650	8,500
Wiley Creek	Wiley Creek	38,000	—	5,000	4,000	47,000
Detroit	North Santiam	235,000	40,000	65,000	115,000	455,000
Big Cliff	North Santiam	—	1,800	—	1,950	3,750
Lewisville	Little Luckiamute	34,000	—	6,000	5,000	65,000
Total		1,664,000	395,300	423,000	431,450	2,913,750

Source: Columbia River and Tributaries, Northwestern United States, House Document No. 531, 81st Congress, 2nd Session, March 20, 1950, Vol. I, Table IV-53, p. 244.

Oregon stream is formed by its Coast Fork and Middle Fork which join in the vicinity of Springfield, Oregon—some 188 river miles above the confluence of the Willamette and Columbia rivers at Portland. (See Figure 17.) The major tributaries which feed into the Willamette rise in the Cascade Range at elevations that in some cases exceed 6,000 feet. Among the major tributaries, the McKenzie, draining approximately 1,300 square miles, and the Santiam, servicing a watershed of about 1,800 square miles, are among the most important.

The comprehensive plan of development prepared by the U. S. Corps of Engineers involves nearly three million acre-feet of storage distributed among twenty reservoir sites, as shown in Table 35. Of the approximately 800,000 acre-feet of power and joint storage, 395,300 would be available for power primarily, while 423,000 would serve jointly the purposes of flood control, power, and conservation. The storage thus provided will justify the installation of power in the amount of approximately 387,000 kilowatts distributed among the reservoirs as indicated in Table 36.

TABLE 36. *Proposed Power Installations, Willamette River Sub-Basin*

Reservoir site	Installed capacity (kilowatts)
Middle Fork, Willamette:	
Hills Creek	20,000
Waldo Lake [a]	—
Meridian	115,000
Dexter [b]	15,000
McKenzie River:	
Cougar	25,000
Middle Santiam River:	
Green Peter	81,000
White Bridge [b]	15,000
North Santiam:	
Detroit	100,000
Big Cliff [b]	16,000
Total	387,000

Source: House Document 531, *op. cit.*, Vol. I, Table IV-54, p. 246.

[a] Holdover storage project without power installation.
[b] Re-regulating reservoir with power installation.

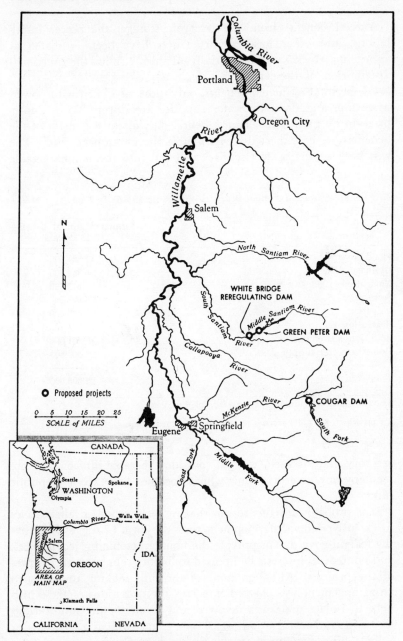

FIGURE 17. *The Willamette River Sub-Basin and
Selected Project Sites*

Annual benefits from the reservoir storage, the power installations, and other local appurtenances have been estimated at approximately $27 million initially. Table 37 shows the functional distribution of these benefits.

Of the total estimated benefits, only those associated with power, irrigation, and domestic water supplies are susceptible of appropriation by pricing mechanics; hence, only about a quarter of the benefits can be expected to reimburse the developer's costs. The vast bulk of the project services will fall into the nonmarketable

TABLE 37. *Estimated Annual Benefits, Willamette Sub-Basin Plan*

Feature	Estimated annual benefits (1948 dollars)
Flood control	11,881,400
Drainage	6,354,300
Navigation	813,500
Power	a 4,922,800
Irrigation	1,665,000
Recreation	361,400
Pollution abatement	701,800
Domestic water supply	307,800
Total	27,008,000

Source: House Document 531, *op. cit.,* Vol. I, p. 248.

a Of which $114,800 accrues to installations downstream.

category and, as such, will fall outside the capability of development by any enterprise unit which does not have access to public funds.

It is probably for this reason that recently proposed alternatives to exclusive federal development took the form of suggestions that the federal government provide the nonmarketable project services, and nonfederal interests be licensed to finance reimbursable features of the projects. Although none of the bills looking toward such an arrangement was enacted into law, the provisions of these bills help to isolate the issues involved and to clarify the implications for the twin considerations of efficiency and equity.

Two bills introduced in the Eighty-third Congress would have affected the manner in which three of the twenty structures listed in Table 35 were undertaken.[2] One of these, H.R. 7815, would have modified the authorization to construct the Cougar Dam by providing that the city of Eugene finance and own the power-generating facilities and share in the proportionate cost of the dam and reservoir which could be appropriately allocated to power development. Section 1 of the proposed legislation made provision for the construction, operation, and maintenance of Cougar Dam substantially in accordance with the plans contained in the comprehensive plan. Similarly, H.R. 8661 provided for authorizing the construction of the Green Peter and White Bridge dams and reservoirs consistent with the plans proposed in the Corps' 308 report, as amended; but it provided further that the power facilities be undertaken by the proposed licensee—in this case, the Pacific Power and Light Company. Also, the licensee would have been granted ownership in the power-generating facilities,[3] although the dam and reservoirs would have remained in the possession of the federal government.

After these measures failed of passage, another attempt was made.[4] The separate pieces of legislation for the Cougar, Green Peter, and White Bridge reservoirs were combined into a single bill with certain provisions modified. In this version of the proposed co-operative arrangement, the nonfederal parties to the agreement would have built the power facilities directly, or advanced funds for their construction, and would have borne a proportionate share of the joint cost of the reservoirs. They would not have gained possession of the facilities,[5] however. Moreover, Section 4 of the proposed legislation authorized the Chief of Engineers "to enter into agreements with the respective licensees for the operation of the dams and reservoirs insofar as such operation affects the production of power *so as to secure the maximum multiple benefits from the operation of the dams and reservoirs as set out in the comprehensive plan of improvement for the Willamette. . . . "* [Italics added.]

The proposed legislation would have permitted implementation

[2] H.R. 7815, 83rd Congress, 2nd Session; and H.R. 8661, 83rd Congress, 2nd Session.

[3] H.R. 8661, Section 2.

[4] H.R. 4662, 84th Congress, 1st Session.

[5] Compare Sections 3 and 2 of H.R. 8661 and H.R. 7185, Section 2 of H.R. 4662, *op. cit.*

of the identical physical plan contemplated in the Corps of Engineers' comprehensive plan for the Willamette. In the area of reservoir operation or management, it would have required an operating plan consistent with maximizing economic, rather than only financial, returns. In the physical aspects, therefore, the contemplated development would be the same as the fully integrated plan of development and operation that was originally proposed under federal auspices. The one modification consisted in permitting those features associated with marketable services to be financed by nonfederal enterprise units which could recoup their investments through sale of the marketable output. It therefore appears that from an efficiency viewpoint results of development under this proposal would be identical with development exclusively by the federal government. The same quantity and quality of resources would be committed, and the entire complement of facilities would be managed in the same manner for maximizing economic returns as if development and operation were integrated under federal auspices. This result would hold on two assumptions: In the practical situation, the need to accommodate any differing points of view among co-operators would not compromise the integrity of the comprehensive plan.[6] The social cost of investment funds would not differ for the sources tapped for investment purposes under the two proposals. If it is assumed that any differences which might exist would be small, this type of co-operative arrangement would not seem to involve any changes in the level of real costs and gains from the plan as initially proposed.

While there would be no *a priori* bases for anticipating any

[6] In some cases, of course, the proposed federal development and the nonfederal development would not necessarily be physically the same. Even in the case of the Willamette River plants, where it has been proposed that the government build the dams and nonfederal utilities supply the generators, there might be different installations in the two cases. It has been brought to our attention that the city of Eugene proposed to install more peaking capability at Cougar Dam than the Corps of Engineers. The city, able to purchase at least part of its requirements at Bonneville Power Administration kilowatt-year rates, would find it economical to install additional peaking capacity at Cougar Dam to meet its load, whereas the federal government might find it more economical to install the peaking capacity at other sites in its system. Eugene would not have as wide a range of possibilities as are open to the integrated federal system. While this is doubtless true, the sacrifice of efficiency in this case would be of a different order of magnitude from that treated in Chapter v.

differences in economic efficiency were this method of undertaking river basin projects employed, there are substantial reasons for believing that there would be differences in the distribution of income resulting from the project.

Differences in Costs Under Public and Private Development

If the reimbursable features of a multiple purpose project are financed by nonfederal participants in the development, two major differences in income redistributive effects become probable. First, the accounting costs will differ as among the alternative ways of financing the reimbursable feature; moreover, these costs will exhibit differences in their incidence. Second, there are possibilities of differences in the distribution of gains as well as costs, if the reimbursable feature is financed by other than a public nonfederal participant; this is caused, at least in part, by the suspension of the preference provision in the distribution of the project's electrical output.

In looking at the differences in accounting costs, we assume alternatively that the reimbursable feature is financed by the federal government, a nonfederal public body, and a private utility. Accounting costs associated with each alternative are shown in Table 38.[7] Here we assume that the separable and common costs of the hydroelectric features of a multiple purpose project would approximate $280 per kilowatt of capacity. We assume a relatively small-scale development—80,000 kilowatts—which is not unrealistic for a Willamette River Basin hydroelectric site. Construction costs are assumed to be the same, irrespective of the means by which the investment funds for the power feature are provided. Total investment differs among the three alternatives, however, because of assumed differences in relevant rates of interest over the construction period. The differences in investment outlays, however, are not very significant for a project which would require a relatively short time to build.

[7] These estimates are only approximations of the magnitudes which would appear for corresponding items in any particular case, as there will be considerable variability both in accounting practice and financial characteristics among particular installations. The estimates, however, represent reasonable approximations based on either average data or recommended practices as referenced in notes to Table 38.

TABLE 38. *Construction, Investment, and Annual Costs of Hydroelectric Development at a Willamette River Site, Assuming Federal, Nonfederal Public, and Private Construction and Operation*

	Federal	Nonfederal public	Private utility
Construction costs	$22,400,000	$22,400,000	$22,400,000
Interest during Construction [a]	560,000	638,400	1,008,000
Investment	22,960,000	23,038,400	23,408,000
Capital charges:			
Interest on bonds [b]	—	—	376,869
Dividends on preferred stock [b]	—	—	149,226
Dividends on common stock [b]	—	—	380,965
Depreciation [c]	—	—	468,160
Interest and amortization	[d] 809,525	[e] 870,178	—
Taxes:			
Federal income [f]	—	—	681,758
Other federal [g]	—	—	23,408
State and local (or in lieu of tax payments)	[g] 114,800	[h] 287,980	[g] 533,702
Interim replacements [g]	46,816	46,816	46,816
Insurance [g]	22,960	23,038	23,408
Operation and maintenance [g]	160,000	160,000	160,000
Administrative [g]	48,000	48,000	48,000
Total annual costs	1,202,101	1,436,012	2,892,312
Undistributed profits added to surplus [i]	352,301	435,089	151,567
Total annual charges to customers	1,554,402	1,871,101	3,043,879

[a] Assumes interest for federal at 2.5; nonfederal public, 2.85; and private utility, 4.5 per cent, on an average of one-half the total construction cost over a two-year construction period.

[b] Capitalization assumes 50 per cent in bonds bearing 3.22 per cent; 15 per cent in preferred stock bearing 4.25 per cent; and 35 per cent in common stock paying 4.65 per cent, but also having an earnings-price ratio of 6.5 per cent. (See *Electric Utility Industry in the United States,* Statistical Bulletin for the Year 1955, Edison Electric Institute, May 1956.)

[c] Assumes straight line depreciation over the fifty-year license period.

[d] Assumes fifty equal annual payments, including interest at 2.5 per cent on debt outstanding.

[e] Assumes fifty equal annual payments, including interest at 2.85 per cent on outstanding obligation, consistent with revenue bond rates for local public bodies during 1955.

[f] Assumes federal income tax of 50 per cent on $1,365,516 returns before taxes, leaving an earnings-price ratio of 6.5 per cent on common stock and a preferred dividend rate of 4.25.

ᵍ See Federal Power Commission, Bureau of Power, *Information for Staff Use in Estimating Electric Power Costs and Values*, Technical Memorandum No. 1, November 1955.

ʰ See annual reports of Northwest publicly owned utilities to FPC, 1955.

ⁱ Assumes power rates set by the federal establishment to return 4.5 per cent on investment; for nonfederal public, assumes power rates set to earn 1.5 times annual debt service; and for private utility, additional net returns required to supplement dividends on common stock to provide the 6.5 per cent earnings-price ratio. (See Edison Electric Institute Statistical Bulletin, *op. cit.*)

Examination of the annual charges to customers reveals marked differences in the accounting costs. Annual costs for the private undertaking range from 60 to 90 per cent greater than for the local public and federally undertaken alternatives.

Part of the differences in annual costs can be attributed to the differences in money costs. That is, the rate of interest imputed to the federal undertaking is only 2.5 per cent[8] as compared, for example, to the earnings-price ratio of 6.5 per cent on common stock of the utility. But these differences in so-called money costs might appear greater than they are. For example, a private utility can use a variety of kinds of securities which it seeks to arrange in the least cost combination. In our example, the weighted average of interest on bonds, dividends on preferred equity securities, and the earnings-price ratio on common stock is only 4.5 cent—or an over-all rate of return approximately equal to that rate which is often achieved by federal agencies in their power operations. Federal agencies often follow a conservative practice in their power rate schedules to ensure a rate of return substantially in excess of their interest requirements.[9]

The extremely favorable rates on revenue bonds of local units of government also are, to some extent, more apparent than real. Partly, they are accounted for by the tax-exempt status of the securities themselves and to this extent represent a substantial advantage to municipal and other local governments. But a low interest rate is largely accounted for by stipulations in the bond contract requiring that returns be sufficiently high to exceed debt

---

[8] Since this is an analysis of accounting cost only, the rate used in actual accounting practice is applicable, rather than approximation of the rate reflecting social cost derived in Chapter IV.

[9] See, for example, the annual reports of the Tennessee Valley Authority or the Bonneville Power Administration.

service charges by some considerable margin. Thus, while the interest rate as such can be less because of the reduction of risks for the investor, actual power charges to customers will be greater than those necessary only to return costs. In our illustration, although we employed a rate of 2.85 per cent appropriate to revenue bonds of public bodies during 1955,[10] we assumed that the resulting debt service charges would have to be earned one and a half times to enable so favorable a rate in the actual disposition of the revenue bonds.

To a significant extent, however, the private undertaking will follow a more conservative policy with respect to depreciation. And this will increase the accounting costs that appear in the annual charges to power customers. Even so, the resulting differences are only partially accounted for by the money costs given for capital charges and undistributed profits added to surplus in Table 38. The differences in annual money costs are $143,441 more for the nonfederal public undertaking than for the federal; $364,961 more for the private than for the federal, and $221,520 more for the private than for the nonfederal public undertaking.

The remaining part of the difference is accounted for by taxes, as given in Table 38. Money costs account for less than a quarter of the difference in facilities under federal and private operation, whereas differences in taxes account for over three-quarters of the total. In the case of the nonfederal public and the private operation, less than 20 per cent of the total differences in costs is attributable to money costs, and more than 80 per cent to tax liabilities. As between federal and nonfederal public operation, the somewhat higher cost under the local public operation is accounted for much more nearly equally by the differences in money costs and tax liabilities.

We have earlier sought to show that in an economy where markets were perfectly competitive and market organization sufficiently comprehensive to preclude anything of economic value from being enjoyed except through the intermediary of the market, no such differences in accounting costs could arise, given *facilities of identical characteristics*.[11] In the actual world, of course, the

[10] See Board of Governors, Federal Reserve System, *Federal Reserve Bulletin*, March 1956, p. 253.

[11] This, of course, does not hold for facilities of inherently different characteristics. The costs of TVA power, for example, abstracting from problems of interest

theoretical prerequisites for the competitive model are not realized. Market institutions, although sophisticated and in large measure comprehensive, still do not permit all of our economic wants to be satisfied individualistically through market choices. Various instruments of group decisions and collective choice enter the resource allocation process. Thus, public bodies of various kinds are organized to assist in meeting the requirements of our society. Laws, customs, and traditions governing these intergovernmental relations emerge. And there is no particular reason to believe that the practices—for example, those imbedded in the doctrine of intergovernmental tax immunity—are consciously inspired by the economists' conception of efficiency. It is more appropriate to our interests here, however, to seek some understanding of the income redistribution resulting from differences in accounting costs which arise from different means of undertaking the same development, and from different tax policies and traditions implicit in those means.

Distribution of Costs by Income Classes

The differences in annual costs of operating basically the same set of physical facilities will be reflected in the rates charged to power consumers. It is here that the redistributive effects of these alternative approaches to development of reimbursable project features begin to appear.

As a first consideration, we must recognize that power customers will pay the costs of the development if rates on power provide revenues equal to the costs, and if the accounting costs thus met are equal to the true social costs.

Beginning with the case of federal development, we must consider the problem in terms of our findings on social costs. In Chapter IV, we concluded that unless the level of total (rather than hydroelectric only) investment is raised by collective choice to the point where all investment opportunities promising returns over 2.5 per cent are exhausted, a rate of return of only 2.5 per cent for water

rates and taxes, will approximate only a half of the average for the private electric utility industry. These differences are readily accountable for by inherently different physical and locational characteristics of the TVA system. See *Distributors of TVA Power, 1953 Annual Report,* prepared by the Tennessee Valley Authority, November 1953, pp. 12-13.

resources development involved some unmet opportunity costs.[12] In fact, given the probable way in which federal funds would be raised, the incidence of the tax on different income classes and productive enterprise sectors, and the time preference or rates of return earned by investments made by these individuals or enterprises, a more realistic social cost of the investment funds, we found, would approximate 5 to 6 per cent.

In Table 38, however, an imputed interest rate of 2.5 per cent was used, consistent with federal practices. This might suggest an element of subsidy close to 3 per cent, or a shifting of costs to that extent from power customers to others; but this view is not tenable, for several reasons.

The 5.5 per cent in our computation has been coupled for purposes of project evaluation with an amortization period of a hundred years. That is, we have argued that it is not meaningful to discount benefits from water development projects completely after fifty years; therefore, the higher discount factor (5.5 per cent) used in combination with a longer amortization schedule more accurately reflects the real economic costs.[13] In Table 38, however, the accounting costs shown (for interest and amortization, and undistributed profits added to surplus) include an annual sum equivalent to 4.5 per cent coupled with an amortization schedule of fifty years. The difference between an imputed rate of 5.5 per cent employing a 100-year amortization schedule (annual charges of $55,261 per million of invested capital) and 4.5 per cent with a fifty-year amortization schedule (annual charges of $50,602 per million of invested capital)[14] amounts to only 0.446 per cent on the investment. In absolute terms, annual charges for the federal operation would fall short of those necessary to cover opportunity costs by only about $144,000 on an investment totaling $23.6

[12] In Chapter III, however, we pointed out how in the case of decreasing-cost industries, financial returns insufficient to cover full costs need not imply an inefficient investment. However, we are not concerned here with the problem of efficiency, but rather with the redistributive consequences of alternative policies.

[13] See Otto Eckstein, *Water Resources Development: The Economics of Project Evaluation* (Cambridge: Harvard University Press, 1958), Chapter IV.

[14] Consult any standard set of financial tables—for example, Justin H. Moore, *Handbook of Financial Mathematics* (New York: Prentice-Hall, Inc., 1947), Table VIII, annuity which $1.00 will buy.

million.[15] This annual sum, if not met by power consumers, would be shifted to others.

We have argued that where identical physical facilities are being operated alternatively by the three possible developers, the costs of money and differential tax liabilities mainly account for the differences in charges to customers. The next problem is to determine how best to handle the distributive effects of the tax liabilities. Two approaches to this question may be advanced.

On the one hand, tax liabilities can be viewed as the result of governmental policy directed toward a redistribution of wealth. We can argue, for example, that in terms of the prevailing value system there is some notion of an "equitable" distribution of income and wealth; that individual and corporate tax liabilities are merely consistent with a governmental responsibility to see that income and wealth—and with these, influence and power—do not become so concentrated as to infringe on democratic processes and contradict prevailing sentiments of justice and equity. If taxes were motivated exclusively by these considerations, we would not be concerned by greater tax liabilities under one method of development and operation than another, and we might properly ignore the question of the distribution of the costs under alternative approaches. The question would be raised, if at all, only in terms of whether the intended objectives were in fact realized.

But, there is another view of the proper accounting for tax liabilities. This holds that the federal government is committed to a certain level of public services because specific needs (such as national defense and similar collective goods or services) cannot be obtained by members of the community acting individualistically through market choices.[16] If we assume that the federal government is committed to perform such services, and that tax liabilities arise out of the need for their financing, we have a somewhat different rationale for comparing the differences in costs stemming from tax differentials and their distribution.

In this study, we adopt the second alternative, and assume that a certain amount of public revenue is required to perform the

[15] This would represent construction costs of $22.4 million at an interest rate of 5.5 per cent on an average of one-half of the construction costs over a two-year construction period.

[16] See William J. Baumol, *Welfare Economics and the Theory of the State* (Cambridge: Harvard University Press, 1952).

necessary services. These revenues appear in one form as tax liabilities of individuals and corporate bodies. In short, the tax liabilities
in Table 38 are viewed as arising out of a need for revenues to support generally desired governmental services. We assume that
neither more nor less of these essential services would be provided
were the reimbursable features of our multiple purpose project
undertaken by a body subject to federal taxation. The presence
or absence of federal tax liabilities under the alternative column
headings in Table 38 in no way implies any differences in the
amount of public services the federal government would provide.

If we assume that present federal tax revenues are adequate to
provide a generally acceptable amount of services and that the
Willamette project is undertaken by a private enterprise unit subject to federal taxation, a tax reduction (of the nature suggested
in Model A and Model B of Chapter IV) could take place. In
contrast, let us assume that the level of public services generally
accepted as adequate could not be provided without increased
revenues equivalent to the federal tax liabilities for the private
undertaking. Under this assumption, a general increase in taxation
would be needed if the reimbursable features were undertaken by
either a federal agency or by a nonfederal public body enjoying
intergovernmental tax immunity.

In the quantitative analysis of the distribution of costs, it is necessary to have clearly in mind just what costs or income transfers
we are interested in. We are not concerned ultimately with learn-
ing who has supplied the investment funds for the development
of the reimbursable feature in any of the alternatives. In the sale
of corporate securities or local government revenue bonds the
purchasers of these evidences of wealth supply the funds used in the
development. The voluntary surrender of funds in exchange for
securities is accompanied by the prospect of an income stream in
the form of interest or dividends, or of capital gains. There is full
compensation for the sacrifice associated with surrendering liquid
wealth in exchange for securities, if the transaction is entered into
voluntarily in response to the anticipation of financial returns. In
these circumstances, there will be no unmet costs whose incidence
we are seeking to locate.

This particular analysis also concerns only an aspect of funds
raised by federal taxation. Our interest here is neither ultimately
associated with the fact that funds are supplied nor uniquely

related to the amount of such funds. It is true that when funds are raised by taxation, they are not supplied voluntarily, but rather in response to the implicit threat of coercion embodied in taxing authority. A certain marginal sacrifice is faced by the taxpayer, whether measured by his time preference (if he borrows for consumption purposes) or the alternative opportunities for returns (if he invests his savings). But not even these rates are determinative in the final analysis of the cost with which we are concerned here.

The center of attention is rather the *difference* between these rates (average of 5.5 per cent in our computations) and the rate of return to the investment for which the taxes were raised. As an extreme example: If a small amount of funds raised by taxation were invested by the federal government in some enormously high-return opportunity open only to it, and these returns were adequate to provide in perpetuity for all of the public services normally required of the government, it would be difficult to argue that elimination of all future taxes would not compensate for supplying in the current year the small sum necessary to accomplish this objective. Similarly, if the rate of return to the federal investment exceeded the opportunity cost of the funds raised, periodic repayment of investment funds with interest to the U. S. Treasury would justify, under our assumptions, an equivalent reduction in taxes. Costs would arise only if the returns to the federal investment were less than the opportunity costs of funds raised by taxation.[17]

Except for the purely local question of probable shifts in tax burdens, we are primarily interested here in the incidence of costs on two fronts. First is the difference between the opportunity costs of capital raised by taxation and the assumed financial rate of return to federal hydroelectric power development—corrected for the difference between the fifty-year and the ideal term of amortization discussed above. Second is the effect of shifts in the incidence of federal tax liabilities.

The problem may be stated thus: With public development taxes would have to be increased (or could not be reduced), and

---

[17] If we are concerned with efficiency alone, economic returns must equal opportunity costs, whether financial returns do or not. But if no shifting of tax burdens is to be experienced, financial returns, and corresponding repayments to the Treasury, will have to be equivalent to the opportunity costs.

with private development taxes would not need to be increased (or could be reduced). Under these circumstances, who bears the burdens not borne by power customers when public development is undertaken?

With federal development of the reimbursable feature, a certain amount of tax shifting from the power customer to others results from the need to finance essential public services. In addition, there is a shifting of that part of the opportunity cost of factor services which remains uncompensated by receipts from power sales. The shifting of the federal tax liability would amount to something like $705,000 annually; the shifting of costs, on the other hand, would be on the order of $144,000 annually.

Discovering the incidence of the shifted burdens by income classes is similar to the problem addressed in Chapter IV, where the incidence of the change in taxes had to be discovered in order to determine an opportunity cost for funds raised by federal taxation. The distribution of the shifted tax burdens by income class, assuming the two tax models employed previously, is shown in Tables 39 and 40.

TABLE 39. *Incidence by Income Class of Shifted Tax Burden,*
           Assuming Tax Model A

Income classes ($ thousand)	Change in personal exemption [a] (per cent)	Change in excises [b] (per cent)	Weighted average incidence (per cent)
0 to 3	19.5	9.0	17.4
3 to 5	40.6	21.0	36.7
5 to 7.5	23.6	28.0	24.5
7.5 to 10	6.1	16.0	8.1
10 to 15	4.2	10.0	5.4
Over 15	6.0	16.0	8.0
Total	100.0	100.0	[c] 100.1

[a] Distribution of 80 per cent of total tax change assumed in Model A; obtained from Table 4.

[b] Distribution of 20 per cent of total change; obtained from Table 9.

[c] Discrepancy in total caused by rounding.

A comparison of the incidence of the tax shift reveals sharp variations in the two tax models. Assuming a reduction in taxes consistent with tax Model A, the burden would be skewed toward the low-income groups; 54.1 per cent of the total would be borne by those earning $5,000 or less annually. If we assume the appropriate model to be the one favoring high-income groups and investment, the two low-income groups would bear only 20 per cent of the total, while those in families earning $10,000 and over would bear approximately 47 per cent of the total.

A similar approach could be employed, in principle, in connection with the differential state and local tax liabilities. However, because of the complexity of questions involving an appropriate tax model for state and local bodies, and the paucity of published data useful for quantitative analysis, we do not attempt to analyze the intra-regional incidence.

In the case of the nonfederal public body, funds would be raised through voluntary subscription to revenue bonds; thus, there is less reason to question the correspondence between the interest rate and the marginal sacrifice of savers subscribing to the bonds.[18] In one particular, however, the interest on these bonds overstates their price relative to similar securities whose yields are not exempted from federal taxes. Thus, the rate of 2.85 per cent used in our analysis may be understated relative to securities which enjoy no advantages conferred by public policy. However, our assumption of power rates set to return revenues adequate to cover debt service charges one and a half times should compensate for a tendency to diverge on the low side in estimating the appropriate annual capital charges.[19] The only significant difference in incidence involves the shifting of federal tax liabilities; that is possible because of the doctrine of intergovernmental tax immunity. This shifting of tax incidence from power customers to others is of the same order of magnitude, $705,000 annually, as in the case of federal development of the reimbursable project features. The incidence of shifted tax burdens from power consumers to the general public is symmetrical with that shown for the federal case and can be obtained from Tables 39 and 40.

---

[18] Voluntary subscription to bonds promising a specified yield distinguishes the case from that in which the coercive powers of a public body are employed to raise funds through taxation.

[19] Annual capital charges imputed to the operation ($1.3 million) actually approximate the level which is indicated to be necessary to cover opportunity costs in the case of federal development. Where funds are raised through taxation, rather than subscribed to voluntarily, social costs will probably be higher, and we may actually have erred on the high side in our estimate in this case.

TABLE 40. Incidence by Income Class of Shifted Tax Burden, Assuming Tax Model B

	Proportionate change in personal tax liabilities [a]	Change in corporate income tax liabilities			Weighted average incidence of total tax change (per cent)
		Wages and salaries [b]	Consumption [b]	Dividend receipts [c]	
Per cent distribution of total tax change	50	6	16.5	27.5	
Per cent distribution, by family personal income, of change in each tax category ($ thousand):					
0 to 3	3.6	15	12	4	
3 to 5	13.2	33	24	6	
5 to 7.5	24.0	29	29	8	
7.5 to 10	14.4	11	15	7	
10 to 15	10.3	5	9	11	
Over 15	34.5	7	11	64	
Total	100.0	100	100	100	100

personal income, of total tax change[d] ($ thousand):				
0 to 3	1.8	0.9	2.0	1.1	5.8
3 to 5	6.6	2.0	4.0	1.7	14.3
5 to 7.5	12.0	1.7	4.8	2.2	20.7
7.5 to 10	7.2	0.7	2.5	1.9	12.3
10 to 15	5.1	0.3	1.5	3.0	9.9
Over 15	17.7	0.4	1.8	17.6	37.5
Total[e]	50.4	6.0	16.6	27.5	100.5

[a] Distribution of 50 per cent of total tax change assumed in Model B; see Table 10.

[b] Distribution to wages and salaries is 12 per cent of total change in corporate income tax; that to consumption is 33 per cent; see Table 16.

[c] Distribution to dividend recipients is 55 per cent of total change in corporate income tax; see Table 17.

[d] Weighted by per cent distribution of change in each tax category.

[e] Discrepancies caused by rounding.

Finally, in the case of private development of the reimbursable feature, the costs appear to fall exclusively on the consumers of electricity.[20] However, utilities have on occasion been regarded as a fruitful source of local governmental revenues which otherwise would have been obtained from levies against property owners or from other tax sources. One reason for this is that utilities have been granted their monopoly privileges by the local bodies and thus are often expected to provide a substantial part of the tax requirements in compensation. Another reason is the irreversible demand related to the monopolistic nature of the utility's services. Accordingly, state and local taxes which are levied against utilities, and indirectly borne by their customers, sometimes may be excessive. In view of the monopoly conditions under which utility services are provided, the political context in which utility rates are set and tax levies against utilities justified, and other considerations, it is likely that charges to electric customers of private utilities in many cases exceed opportunity costs. While we can treat this problem qualitatively in passing, it is not readily amenable to quantitative analysis.

There are, however, the special circumstances that arise in connection with accelerated amortization. Since the need to accelerate additions to electrical capacity was recognized after Korea, private electric utilities have been permitted to depreciate an average of about 45 per cent of their investment involving additions to capacity over a period of five years in computing their federal tax liabilities.[21] In the case of the Pacific Power and Light Company (in whose behalf the bills, H.R. 8661 and H.R. 4662, were introduced to promote co-operative development of the Willamette sites), certificates of necessity for accelerated amortization on from 65 to 75 per cent of the investment in new facilities have been granted.[22] This has the effect of shifting federal corporate tax liabilities from the utility to the general public.

[20] There are special circumstances involving the privilege of accelerated amortization in which the costs in part appear to be doubly borne, i.e., by both the consumers of electricity and also partly in addition by the taxpayers. Such a case will be discussed below.

[21] Staff of the Joint Committee on Internal Revenue Taxation, *A Report on 5-Year Amortization of Emergency Facilities under Section 168 of the Internal Revenue Code of 1954, 1956*, pp. 23 ff.

[22] Pacific Power and Light Company, *Annual Report, 1955*, pp. 7, 10, 21.

For example: Assume that 70 per cent of the $23.4 million investment in our hypothetical Willamette River hydroelectric facilities was adjudged to be defense-supporting under private development. If so, $16.4 million would be eligible for complete depreciation, for purposes of tax conputation, during the first five years. Depreciation charges are deductible from income, for tax purposes; hence, there would be a tax saving to the private utility. Since we have assumed a marginal corporate tax rate of 50 per cent, this saving during the first five years of operation would amount to one-half the difference between depreciation charges computed under rapid amortization schedules and the charges which would be appropriate under normal depreciation. In our particular example, the $16.4 million, if depreciated by means of straight-line depreciation schedules [23] over a fifty-year period, would require depreciation charges of $327,712 per year. If rapid amortization schedules are assumed, reduction of the write-off period to a tenth (from fifty to five years) would increase annual depreciation charges tenfold—from $327,712 to $3,277,120, or a difference of $2,949,408. Half of this, $1,474,704, would represent the amount of tax liability that would be avoided by the private utility each year during the first five years.

During the following forty-five years, having that part of its investment eligible for rapid amortization completely depreciated, the utility's annual depreciation charges would run $327,712 less than in the absence of accelerated amortization. Its annual income would be correspondingly overstated. This would result in an annual increased tax liability of $163,856 over the next forty-five years of its operation under the federal license.

Under rapid amortization, the tax savings during the first five years would be compensated for by increased tax burdens on the utility during its next forty-five years of operation, provided only that the marginal corporate tax rate remained constant.[24] Over the first five years, tax liabilities amounting to $1,474,704 per year would be shifted from the utility to the general public; during the remainder of the license period, the shift, in the amount of

[23] *Ibid.*, "Notes to Financial Statements," Note 3, p. 21.

[24] For a treatment of a related case in which the effects of changing marginal tax rates are taken into account, see John V. Krutilla, "Locational Factors Influencing Recent Aluminum Expansion," *The Southern Economic Journal*, January 1955, Appendix IV.

$163,856 annually, would reverse, moving from the general tax-payers to the private utility. Since there is a difference in the time distribution of receipts and disbursements, the effect is similar to the provision of a loan in five annual installments, the principal of which is repaid without interest during the next forty-five years in equal annual installments. This becomes clearer as we analyze the problem further.

First, when a private utility is permitted to enjoy a reduction in tax liability during the first five years, consistent with the effects of rapid tax amortization, by our method of approach, others are assumed to be burdened with an equivalent increase in tax liabil-ities. We have previously estimated that the social cost of this change in tax burden is on the order of 5.5 per cent. Consider the results, then, as a loan to the utility in the amount of $1,474,704 annually for five consecutive years, which bears an opportunity cost of 5.5 per cent per year by the remaining taxpayers. After five years, at 5.5 per cent compounded annually, this sum would be equivalent to $8,230,457. If left unattended for the remaining forty-five years, it would accumulate to $91,576,250. Actually, it would not be left unattended; for part of this otherwise accumulat-ing burden would be liquidated by the utility's increased tax liabilities, beginning with the sixth year. These increased liabilities, by our line of argument, would reduce the taxes required from others, on which we assume an average marginal rate of 5.5 per cent. Accordingly, the increased tax payments of $163,856 per year, beginning with the sixth year at 5.5 per cent compounded annually, would be equivalent to an accumulation of $30,169,030 by the fiftieth year. This would leave a deficit, or shifted tax burden, of $61,407,220 over the entire fifty-year period of the license.

Now, since we are interested in the annual burden which is shifted to the general public, we must ask what amount set aside each year, and earning 5.5 per cent compounded annually over a fifty-year period, would equal the accumulated deficit. This would be approximately $249,000—the annual amount of the tax shifted from the utility to the remaining taxpayers.

One aspect of tax shifting remains. When the reimbursable fea-ture was assumed to be publicly developed—and therefore exempt from federal taxes—we observed that power charges to consumers of electricity would be lower and therefore assumed a shift in tax burdens from power users to the general public. In the present case, however, the problem is complicated by the fact that the rapid amortization is computed for tax purposes only. It is not carried over to reduce the rate base on which a utility is permitted to schedule its power charges to customers. It has been used, rather, to serve as an added incentive to investors to encourage more rapid expansion of hydroelectric facilities than could be anticipated in the absence of the accelerated amortization privileges.[25] It is the equity shareholder, in this case, rather than the power consumer who is the beneficiary of the shifted tax burden.

Here, as in the case of the nonfederal public body, the incidence of the shifted tax burden by income classes is symmetrical with that involving federal tax avoidance under public development and can be similarly observed from Tables 39 and 40, depending upon which of the tax models is assumed to apply.[26]

Distribution of Costs by Regions

Our analyses to this point have been principally concerned with identifying the direction of the shift and the incidence of the shifted tax burdens by income classes. It is also desirable to analyze the shifted incidence in terms of the geographical dimension, since regional income redistribution is a significant phenomenon of resource development expenditures.

REGIONAL INCIDENCE, ASSUMING TAX MODEL A

In our consumption model of Chapter IV, we assumed that 80 per cent of the reduction in taxes would come from an increase in personal income exemptions and 20 per cent from a reduction in

---

[25] For the administrative ruling as to how the deductions under rapid amortization are to be handled, see Federal Power Commission, *Opinion No. 264, In the Matter of Treatment of Federal Income Taxes as Affected by Accelerated Amortization,* Docket No. R-126, December 1954, pp. 5-6.

[26] It is recognized that the relevant costs and gains involved in tax shifting where rapid amortization is concerned are only indirectly related to the differences in approach as to whether the reimbursable project features are to be privately or publicly developed. They are more immediately related to the associated policy of using accelerated amortization as an instrument of economic policy to accelerate expansion of electrical capacity.

excise taxes. These were employed as weights to determine the distribution of the total change in taxes by income classes. If next we observe what proportion of the total income within each class is accounted for by each region, we can determine the regional incidence of the tax change corresponding to our Model A.[27] This is illustrated in Table 41. And, finally, to carry through with the distinction between the incidence of the change in taxes and the incidence of total power costs, we apply the data of Table 39 as weights to the portion of the total power costs which annual charges to customers did not meet. We observe from Table 38 that total power charges for the federal operation would approximate $1.5 million per year. We concluded that, in addition, a certain amount of cost shifting was inherent in the fact that opportunity costs of funds raised by federal taxation would not be met. This was on the order of $144,000. Moreover, we concluded that there would be a shifting of the incidence of tax liabilities in the amount of about $705,000 annually. In the case of federal development, approximately $849,000 annually would not be recouped by power charges. The incidence of costs can be seen in Table 42.

From Table 42, we conclude that approximately 69 per cent of the total costs would be borne by the Pacific Coast region, in which the Willamette River hydroelectric site is situated. Approximately 31 per cent of the total costs, however, would fall on regions other than the one in which the development is centered.

In the case of the nonfederal public development, a somewhat larger proportion of the total would be borne within the region and a somewhat smaller proportion, correspondingly, by others outside the region. Because of the doctrine of intergovernmental tax immunity, however, a portion of the tax liability ($705,000 annually) would be shifted to the general public, as in the case of federal development. This is shown in Table 43. Given this alternative for the development of the reimbursable feature of the Willamette site, we note that more than three-quarters of the total of costs would be borne by the Pacific Coast region, whereas less than a quarter would be carried by other regions.

In the usual case of private development, we have noted that all

[27] Census regions were arbitrarily chosen to illustrate the regional redistributive effects because of the more readily available data on this geographic breakdown.

TABLE 41. *Regional Incidence of the Change in Taxes, Assuming Tax Model A*

Income class [a] ($ thousand)	Per cent distribution by region									Weighted incidence by income class (per cent)
	New England	Middle Atlantic	South Atlantic	East South Central	East North Central	West North Central	West South Central	Mountain	Pacific Coast	
0 to 3	1.58	4.38	2.05	0.70	3.79	1.60	1.03	0.49	1.74	17.4
3 to 5	2.64	8.88	3.60	1.25	9.54	2.94	2.28	1.06	4.51	36.7
5 to 10	1.98	7.54	2.96	1.04	9.17	2.34	2.04	0.94	4.49	32.5
10 to 15	0.31	1.32	0.56	0.18	1.27	0.45	0.39	0.18	0.73	5.4
Over 15	0.54	2.23	0.79	0.25	1.76	0.53	0.66	0.22	1.02	8.0
Regional incidence of total tax change [b]	7.05	24.35	9.96	3.42	25.53	7.86	6.40	2.89	12.49	100

Sources: Tables 20 and 25; U. S. Treasury Department, *Statistics of Income for 1951*, Part 1, 1955, Table 13, pp. 81-87.

[a] The finer breakdown employed in Chapter IV and earlier in this chapter had to be abandoned in some cases and a consolidated class used to replace these, because the breakdowns for income classes for which regional data are available are significantly broader.

[b] Total is off .05 per cent because of rounding.

TABLE 42. *Regional Incidence of the Cost of Federal Development of the Hypothetical Willamette River Power Site, Assuming Tax Model A*

Regions	Costs covered by power charges ($ thousand)	Unmet opportunity costs and shifted incidence of taxes ($ thousand)	Total costs ($ thousand)	Per cent distribution of total cost
New England	—	59.9	59.9	2.5
Middle Atlantic	—	206.7	206.7	8.6
South Atlantic	—	84.6	84.6	3.5
East South Central	—	29.0	29.0	1.2
East North Central	—	216.7	216.7	9.0
West North Central	—	66.7	66.7	2.8
West South Central	—	54.3	54.3	2.3
Mountain	—	25.5	25.5	1.1
Pacific Coast	1,554.4	106.0	1,660.4	69.1
Total	1,554.4	[a] 849.4	2,403.8	[a] 100.1

[a] Discrepancies in totals caused by rounding.

TABLE 43. *Regional Incidence of the Cost of Local Public Development of the Hypothetical Willamette River Power Site, Assuming Tax Model A*

Regions	Costs covered by power charges ($ thousand)	Federal tax avoided or shifted ($ thousand)	Total of combined power and public service costs ($ thousand)	Per cent distribution of combined costs
New England	—	49.7	49.7	1.9
Middle Atlantic	—	171.7	171.7	6.7
South Atlantic	—	70.2	70.2	2.7
East South Central	—	24.1	24.1	0.9
East North Central	—	180.0	180.0	7.0
West North Central	—	55.4	55.4	2.2
West South Central	—	45.1	45.1	1.8
Mountain	—	20.4	20.4	0.8
Pacific Coast	1,871.1	88.0	1,959.2	76.1
Total	1,871.1	[a] 704.6	2,575.8	[a] 100.1

[a] Discrepancy in totals caused by rounding.

of the costs will be borne by the customers of the private electric utility. In the special case of accelerated tax amortization, however, there will be additional costs—costs arising in connection with the provision of financial incentives to equity shareholders in the enterprise, with the general public providing the inducements through taxes. We have already estimated the amount of the shifted tax burden to approximate a quarter of a million dollars annually. Table 44 shows the incidence of the shifted burden, by regions.

TABLE 44. *Regional Incidence of Shifted Tax Liabilities Associated with Rapid Amortization, Assuming Tax Model A*

Regions	Distribution of the change in tax liabilities (per cent)	Distribution of annual amount of changed tax liabilities ($ thousand)
New England	7.05	17.6
Middle Atlantic	24.35	60.7
South Atlantic	9.96	24.8
East South Central	3.42	8.5
East North Central	25.53	63.7
West North Central	7.86	19.6
West South Central	6.40	16.0
Mountain	2.89	7.2
Pacific Coast	12.49	31.2
Total	ª 99.33	ª 249.3

ª Discrepancy in totals caused by rounding.

REGIONAL INCIDENCE, ASSUMING TAX MODEL B

Tax Model B, mainly affecting upper-income families and investment, assumed that 50 per cent of the change in taxes would result from a proportionate reduction of personal tax liability and 50 per cent would be distributed among enterprises in proportion to their tax liabilities. In this instance also we adopted Musgrave's assumption that 55 per cent of the tax on corporate earnings would fall on profits, 33 per cent would be shifted to consumers, and 12

per cent would be passed on to wage and salary earners.[28] Our
estimates of the regional incidence of the change in taxes, given
the characteristics of this tax model, are given in Table 45.

Starting with that half of the change in taxes which is assumed
to be distributed among corporations, what proportion of the
affected profits accrues to the residents of each region? To determine this, we assume that profits either are distributed as dividends
or, if retained in the enterprise as undistributed profits, will contribute commensurately to the value of the enterprise and, accordingly, will appear as gains to equity shareholders. Therefore, we
assume that the distribution of total dividend receipts in the
property income component of regional personal income reflects
the distribution by regions of the profits affected by this tax change.
Using the per cent distribution of total dividends among regions
as weights,[29] we determine the change in taxes for 55 per cent of
that half of the tax change which affects corporate profits.

Next, we consider the distribution of that part of the change in
corporate taxes which is passed on to consumers. We assume that
the incidence of this part of the change is proportional to consumption by regions, and that the latter is proportional to income.
This may appear to imply a uniform average propensity to consume among regions, irrespective of the differences in regional per
capita income. Actually, this is more apparent than real, as the
change in taxes affecting consumers via the corporate profit route
has both an income and a price effect, which operate to offset in
part some of the objections to the proportionality assumptions.[30]

---

[28] R. A. Musgrave, J. J. Carroll, L. D. Cook, and L. Frane "Distribution of
Tax Payments by Income Groups: A Case Study for 1948," *National Tax
Journal*, March 1951, p. 16.

[29] The dividend component of property income by states was obtained from
unpublished data provided by the National Income Division, U. S. Department
of Commerce.

[30] Although this assumption may not seem realistic at first blush, it is nonetheless a useful working assumption. A reduction (or an increase) in prices
effects an increase (or a decrease) in real income proportional to consumption.
With a national average propensity to save of about 7.5 per cent, an average
propensity to consume of 95 per cent in the lower-income regions and 90 per
cent in the higher-income regions would appear to mark the outer boundary
of the regional variation. A variation of five over ninety would produce a
discrepancy of only about 5.5 per cent. And this percentage of that one-third
of the half of the change in taxes, related to the shifting of corporate profits

Using the per cent distribution of personal income among regions as weights, we can estimate the regional incidence of that part of the corporate tax change which is shifted to consumers.

Finally, we determine the regional incidence of that part of the change in corporate taxes assumed to be passed on to wage and salary earners. First, we observe the distribution of corporate tax liabilities among major industry divisions.[31] Next, we determine the distribution of wages and salaries within each major industry division by regions.[32] Since we assume that the incidence of the change in taxes regionally will be proportional to the regional distribution of wages and salaries, we combine these coefficients to obtain the distribution of the total corporate tax liability shifted to wage and salary earners by major industry division and region. Summing these by regions, we get the per cent distribution of this change in corporate taxes by regions only.[33] We now employ these coefficients as weights to that part (50 per cent) of the total change in tax liabilities under Model B affecting corporate profits which is shifted to wage and salary earners (12 per cent). The results represent estimates of the regional incidence of 6 per cent of the total change in taxes consistent with our Model B.

As a last step in estimating the regional incidence of the 50 per cent of the total change in taxes which results from a proportionate change in personal income tax liability, we turn, in Table 45, to considering what proportion of the total change in taxes is borne by each income class and the per cent distribution of the tax liability within each income class among regions, as we did in Table 41.

taxes to consumption, would affect our ultimate results by less than 1 per cent. For this reason alone, while the assumption of proportionality appears unrealistic, the practical value of refining our working assumption is negligible.

[31] These are: farming, 0.52 per cent; mining, 2.72 per cent; construction, 1.34 per cent; manufacturing, 61.6 per cent; wholesale and retail trade, 4.91 per cent; finance, insurance, and real estate, 6.65 per cent; transportation, 13.03 per cent; communication and public utilities, 7.62 per cent; and services, 1.56 per cent. See U. S. Treasury Department, *Statistics of Income for 1951*, Part 2, 1955, Basic Table II, pp. 46-51.

[32] U. S. Department of Commerce, *Survey of Current Business*, September 1955, Table 4, "Major Sources of Personal Income by States and Regions," pp. 20-21.

[33] These are: New England, 7.27; Middle Atlantic, 25.56; East North Central, 27.41; West North Central, 6.94; South Atlantic, 9.55; East South Central, 3.97; West South Central, 6.36; Mountain, 2.33; and Pacific Coast, 10.44.

TABLE 45. *Regional Incidence of the Change in Taxes, Assuming Tax Model B*

				Per cent distribution by region					Per cent distribution of total tax change
	New England	Middle Atlantic	South Atlantic	East South Central	East North Central	West North Central	West South Central	Mountain	Pacific Coast	
Change in corporate income tax liabilities by functional class:										
Effects on profits[a]	2.75	8.80	3.03	0.83	5.50	1.65	1.38	0.55	3.03	27.5
Effects on consumer[b]	1.09	3.79	1.90	0.74	3.79	1.39	1.27	0.52	2.01	16.5
Effects on wages and salaries[c]	0.44	1.53	1.57	0.24	1.64	0.42	0.38	0.14	0.63	6.0
										50.0

...come tax liabilities
by income classes [d]
($ thousands):

0 to 3	0.16	0.45	0.21	0.07	0.39	0.17	0.11	0.05	0.18	1.8
3 to 5	0.48	1.60	0.65	0.22	1.72	0.53	0.41	0.19	0.81	6.6
5 to 10	1.17	4.45	1.75	0.61	5.41	1.38	1.21	0.56	2.65	19.2
10 to 15	0.29	1.26	0.54	0.17	1.22	0.43	0.38	0.17	0.70	5.15
Over 15	1.16	4.81	1.71	0.53	3.81	1.14	1.43	0.48	2.19	17.25
										50.00
Regional incidence of total tax change	7.54	26.69	10.36	3.41	23.48	7.11	6.57	2.66	12.20	100.0

[a] Per cent distribution of dividend component of income supplied from unpublished state personal income data, the U. S. Department of Commerce, National Income Division.

[b] Per cent distribution corresponds to per cent distribution of personal income, U. S. Department of Commerce, *Survey of Current Business*, Sept. 1955, pp. 14-16.

[c] Derived from data published in *Statistics of Income for 1951, op. cit.,* Part 2, Table II, and *Survey of Current Business*, Sept. 1955, pp. 20-21.

[d] *Statistics of Income for 1951, op. cit.,* Part 1, and Chapter IV, Table 10.

The foregoing analysis of the regional incidence of the change in taxes under Model B suggests results not dissimilar from those shown under Model A. To preserve the symmetry in exposition, however, we will apply these results regarding tax incidence to the problem of determining the regional incidence of costs, as we did with the results of our tax Model A.

Keeping all elements of the problem the same except for the incidence of the unmet opportunity costs and shifted tax incidence, we show, in Table 46, the regional incidence of the cost of federal development under tax Model B.

TABLE 46. *Regional Incidence of the Cost of Federal Development of the Hypothetical Willamette River Power Site, Assuming Tax Model B*

Regions	Costs covered by power charges ($ thousand)	Unmet opportunity costs and shifted incidence of taxes ($ thousand)	Total costs ($ thousand)	Per cent distribution of total cost
New England	—	64.0	64.0	2.7
Middle Atlantic	—	226.6	226.6	9.4
South Atlantic	—	88.0	88.0	3.7
East South Central	—	29.0	29.0	1.2
East North Central	—	199.3	199.3	8.3
West North Central	—	60.4	60.4	2.5
West South Central	—	55.8	55.8	2.3
Mountain	—	22.6	22.6	0.9
Pacific Coast	1,554.4	103.6	1,658.0	69.0
Total	1,554.4	a 849.3	a 2,403.7	100.0

a Discrepancies in total caused by rounding.

The regional incidence of cost associated with federal development of this hypothetical Willamette River hydroelectric site—when our tax model assumes an emphasis on upper income and investment—is not too unlike the results obtained from use of consumption Model A, in Table 42. Essentially the same proportion of the total cost is borne by the Pacific Coast region under either assumption with respect to the functional sectors from which the tax funds will be raised or to which tax savings would otherwise accrue. But not every other region would participate in financing to the same extent under the two models. Under investment Model B, for example, the Middle Atlantic states would contribute about 10 per cent more than they would under the assumptions governing the consumption model, whereas the East North Central states would experience opposite effects. However, since no region other than the one in which the project is centered contributes as much as 10 per cent toward meeting the costs, even variations of 10 per cent between the two models for any region do not affect its participation in the total costs by as much as 1 per cent.

Since comments relative to the regional incidence of costs assuming nonfederal public or private development, based on the investment tax model, are symmetrical with those made in discussion of the consumption tax model, they will not be repeated here.

VIII The Willamette River Case:

ANALYSIS OF THE

DISTRIBUTION OF GAINS

In the last chapter, we examined the differences in accounting costs that would result from different methods of undertaking the reimbursable feature of the Willamette River project and estimated the distribution of these costs by income classes and by regions. We shall now look at the other side of the coin—the distribution of the gains—to complete the picture of the income redistributive consequences of different ways of financing the project's reimbursable feature.

The first need is to discover the probable distribution of project output, assuming the three potential developers: federal, nonfederal public, and a private utility. This will involve taking account of the "preference clause," which is a feature of power marketing policy governing the distribution of federally developed hydro-electricity. From this, we can approach an understanding of the "first-round" effects in the distribution of gains under alternative approaches to the undertaking.

The more complicated, and doubtless the more interesting, problem relates to the second and successive rounds of effects. Here the complexity of the problem, as well as the relative scarcity of relevant quantitative information, restricts the effort to rough approximations only, in contrast with our quantitative analysis in connection with the distribution of costs. It is hoped, however, that important insights may come from this type of analysis in spite of the crudeness of the numerical inferences we draw for illustrative purposes.

Analysis of First-Round Effects

The most immediate gains from development of a hydroelectric site go to customers who receive power at less cost than would be possible from the next most attractive alternative. The federal power agencies do not engage in retail distribution of electrical energy; the immediate beneficiaries of federally developed hydroelectricity are either the institutions which obtain the power for sale directly or those which use such enormous quantities of energy in their operations that they purchase it only at the wholesale level. Sales to these buyers represent the first-round effects in our case involving federal development. If the site were developed as a nonfederal undertaking, the savings at retail of either the local public or the private undertaking would constitute the first-round effects. In view of this difference, a preliminary analysis of the wholesaling activities of the federal power agency is a starting point for comparing alternative approaches.

When the federal government develops a total project, the distribution of gains from the project's reimbursable hydroelectric feature will be influenced by the operation of the preference clause. The preference clause that would apply to the hypothetical Willamette River site relates to provisions of Section 4-A of the Bonneville Act. This requires that public bodies and co-operatives be given preference in the distribution of electric energy from federally developed projects "for benefit of the general public and particularly of domestic and rural consumers." [1] If the federal government were to finance as well as build all of the features of the multiple purpose 80,000-kw. hydroelectric feature used as an example in the previous chapter, the power would be distributed in conformance with this preference clause. Municipalities, public utility districts (PUD's), and rural electric co-operatives would receive first consideration in the meeting of area requirements. Only after their needs were met would any surplus be available for disposal to private electric utilities in the Bonneville Power Administration's marketing territory.

Insight into the probable distribution of the power from our hypothetical Willamette River site developed as a federal under-

[1] Bonneville Act, as amended, Public Law No. 329, 75th Congress.

taking is provided by the distribution of recent additions of power to the Bonneville system. Between June 1954 and June 1955, total BPA sales increased from 18 billion to 21 billion kilowatt-hours. Of the total increase, an estimated 37.5 per cent was sold to municipalities, PUD's, and rural electric co-operatives; 34.4 per cent was sold to private electric utilities for distribution to their customers; another 5.8 per cent was provided for use of the federal agencies in the area, most of it for activities related to national defense. Finally, 22.3 per cent of the total increase in sales was accounted for by increased deliveries to electro-chemical and electro-metallurgical industries, a substantial portion of whose output is also related to defense production.

Conceivably there would be circumstances under which all of the output in our hypothetical illustration could be distributed to public bodies or rural co-operatives. At the other extreme, if the requirements of all of these preference customers were already met, the total conceivably could be made available to private utilities. So while the preference clause requires that first choice should go to public bodies and rural electric co-operatives, private utilities in the Northwest have in practice relied to a considerable extent on the federally developed hydroelectricity as a source of supply.

Given the enormous hydroelectric potential in the sites on Northwest streams in which the federal government has a paramount interest, it appears likely that an economically efficient rate of development could provide adequate energy to meet all of the requirements of preference customers as well as a substantial portion of the private utilities' needs. Hence, for purposes of the following analysis, we will assume that the distribution of project output from our hypothetical Willamette River site would conform closely to the distribution of the increment added during the fiscal year 1955.

Distribution of project output by a federal agency involves the wholesaling of most of its power for resale by the public or private distributors. In BPA's marketing territory, there are close to 90 of these retail distributors of which 17 are municipalities, 25 are public utility districts, 37 are rural electric co-operatives, and 10 are private electric utilities. In order to get an idea of the distribution of gains, or the ultimate distribution of project output to customers, we need to learn something about the sales patterns of these distributors. The sales of the municipalities, PUD's, and private electric utilities [2] to domestic-residential and commercial-industrial customers—which virtually exhaust total sales to ultimate customers [3]—will indicate any significant differences in distribution patterns. Table 47 provides the breakdown for each type of distributor among the two categories of sales.[4]

The data from Table 47 also can be used in combination with the information on BPA's energy sales to determine what proportions of the latter's sales end up in industrial and domestic uses.

TABLE 47. *Per cent Distribution of Kilowatt-Hour Sales by Type of Use in the Bonneville Power Administration Marketing Area*

Class of distributor	Domestic-residential [a]	Commercial-industrial [a]
Municipalities	57.3	36.6
Public utility districts	52.6	42.5
Private electric utilities	44.3	51.2

[a] Failure of the figures for each class of distributor to total 100 per cent is accounted for by miscellaneous sales not included in our categories.

[2] The sales of rural electric co-operatives have not been broken down for two reasons. First, they are not required to report annually to the Federal Power Commission, and therefore the data on their distribution are not readily available. Second, despite their number, they account for only about 3 per cent of the total of BPA's power sales (4 per cent of the increment between 1954 and 1955) and therefore do not appear to justify the added effort required to obtain data from them comparable to that available for the other distributors.

[3] Interchange transactions with other utilities are excluded in the analysis.

[4] The data on which these statistics are based were taken from those annual reports of distributors in the BPA area to the FPC which were available for analysis during the first week of December 1956. These represent 82 per cent of the annual reports from municipalities, 96 per cent of the PUD reports, and 78 per cent of the total from private utilities. In this sense, we can regard the data as a relatively complete enumeration of the total statistical population. It may be of interest, however, to regard these data as samples from a possibly larger universe of municipalities, PUD's, and private utilities which conceivably could be supplied with power for resale by BPA. In that case, we would wish to know whether or not the differences among our summary statistics were statistically significant. We have thus analyzed the variances about the means for each group and have determined that the variance among group means exceeds the variance within groups indicating that the differences which are shown to exist in Table 47 can be regarded as significant at the 1 per cent level.

Using the distribution between residential and industrial customers among the three classes of distributors as weights to apply to the federal sales to these distributors, we get an idea of the distribution of federally developed energy between sales for final consumption and sales of energy to be used as factor services in commercial operations. This is shown in Table 48.

TABLE 48. *Per Cent Distribution of Kilowatt Hours Sold from Federal Power Development by Bonneville Power Administration*

Wholesale customers of BPA	Per cent of total purchased	Per cent distribution between final uses	
		Consumption	Factor service
Municipalities	18.27	10.47	6.69
Public utility districts	15.21	8.00	6.46
Co-operatives [a]	4.01	4.01	—
Private utilities	34.38	15.23	17.60
Federal agencies	5.79	—	5.79
Electro-process firms	22.34	—	22.34
Total distribution by end-uses		37.71	58.88

[a] For the sake of convenience, we have assumed that all of the deliveries to rural electric co-operatives end up as final consumption; even though we recognize that some of this energy must be used as a factor input in commercial farming.

What now can be said regarding the distribution of gains from the development of our hypothetical Willamette River hydroelectric site? Table 48 shows that the distribution of power from a federally developed source favors factor services over final consumption by a considerable margin—about 59 per cent compared to 38 per cent. This is accounted for only partially by the priority given to federal agencies in the distribution of federally developed hydroelectricity. To a much greater extent, the use of energy for production, rather than final consumption, is accounted for by the provision of energy directly to electro-process industries. These industries receive close to 40 per cent of the total allocated to customers which use the energy as a factor input.

The fact that distribution of federally developed power favors industrial uses can be explained in terms of the enormous potential of low-cost hydroelectricity in the region—and, consistent with this, the rate of investment in its development. Thus, while preference uses are granted priority, a rate of development which has appeared justified in the past has provided for a growth in output sufficient to meet all of the preference customers' requirements (37.5 per cent of the increment added during fiscal year 1955); an almost equivalent amount for the private utilities (34.4 per cent); and, in addition, more than a quarter of the total for federal defense and defense-supporting private electro-process industries.

Alternatively, if the development of the reimbursable feature were undertaken by a municipality—and the average figures for the distribution of municipalities' energy sales were used as an indication—about 57 per cent of the project's output would end up in final consumption whereas about 37 per cent would end up as factor services in commercial and industrial operations.

Finally, if we take the average for the private electric utilities' distribution of power as between final demand and factor services, more of the energy (51 per cent) would be sold to commercial and industrial enterprises, and a smaller proportion (44 per cent) would be sold to residential and domestic consumers.

The above data present only statistical summaries of the probable distribution of project output under alternative approaches to undertaking the reimbursable project feature. For a more meaningful picture of the distribution of gains, we must look to the second and successive rounds of consequences.

Successive Rounds of Effects Under Federal Development

Consider first the distribution of output on the assumption that the hypothetical site is developed under federal auspices. Purchasers of federally developed power for resale in their own power marketing operations will be treated first.

GAINS FROM SALES BY PREFERENCE CUSTOMERS

The savings from a supply of lower-priced federal power would be passed on to customers by the municipalities, public utility districts, and rural electric co-operatives. This follows, since the federal agency is a sole supplier in most instances and hence is in a position to monitor the resale provisions and other contract terms governing power rates, the level of returns to investment in the distributors' operations, and similar resale contract provisions. If we assume that most of the rural co-operatives' distribution ends up as rural domestic consumption, close to 60 per cent—as a weighted average—of federally developed power sold to local public bodies ends up in uses to satisfy final demand. Accordingly, the regional incidence of the corresponding portion can be fairly accurately estimated. Since these gains represent increases in real income without any corresponding increases in money income, there will be no partially offsetting increases in federal income tax liability of the beneficiaries in the region. Thus, the income gains associated with final consumption remain in the region. Since about 22.5 per cent of such sales to public bodies was estimated to end up in final consumption (Table 48), the real income gains would amount to about 22.5 per cent of the difference in annual operating costs under the three alternative approaches. Comparing the federal and local private operations, the gain would amount to approximately $335,000 annually.

The ultimate distribution of gains associated with that part of preference customers' purchases which are sold to commercial and industrial establishments cannot be as easily located. Doubtless some of these gains will appear as increased profits and, therefore, factor returns to the capital invested in these enterprises. Consider this to be on the order of 55 per cent.[5] The regional distribution of that part of these gains that does not represent increased federal income tax liabilities depends on whether these firms are "home-owned" or represent corporate enterprises whose equity shares are distributed largely outside the region. We will assume that such enterprises are predominantly home-owned, and that the proportion of extra-regional ownership is only on the order of a quarter of the total equity shares. If these assumptions are reasonable for purposes of illustration, what can we say about the distribution of gains associated with the resale of federal power to regional estab-

---

[5] We employ for this purpose the assumption that the shares of the gains would be similar to the 55, 12, and 33 per cent distribution respectively to capital, labor, and the consumers as in Chapters IV and VII. See R. A. Musgrave, J. J. Carroll, L. D. Cook, and L. Frane, "Distribution of Tax Payments by Income Groups: A Case Study for 1948," *National Tax Journal*, March 1951.

lishments of a commercial or industrial character? On that part of the total federal sales which ends up in factor services via the public distributors (13.15 per cent), the differences in operating costs in which capital factor services share would be approximately $195,900 (item B-2 of Table 49). If we assume that 55 per cent of this is retained as rewards to capital, the before-tax share going to capital would amount to approximately $107,800. Assuming a marginal tax rate on corporate income of 50 per cent, only half of this would be retained as rewards to capital and the remainder would appear, granted our approach, as a reduction to an equivalent amount in tax liabilities of the general taxpayers (items D and E-1 and E-2, of Table 49). Furthermore, if we assume that a quarter of the equity shares of these regional enterprises are held outside the region, the final distribution of gains which originally went to capital ($107,800) would be divided between the Pacific Coast region and other regions in the proportion of about 44 and 56 per cent respectively.

A part of the gains to commercial enterprise from resale of federal power by public bodies may be absorbed by complementary factor services. Corresponding to capital's share, labor in the enterprises is assumed to obtain 12 per cent of the gain from less expensive power. In this case, its share of the $195,900 would be about $23,500, most of which would accrue to households in the region.

We assume that the remaining 33 per cent of the difference in costs of federally developed power resold through public distributors is passed on to customers in the form of lower prices for commodities and services. So consumers would share in the gains to the extent of about $64,600. The locus of the ultimate distribution of these gains will be governed by the extent to which the commodities in question enter into the export trade of the region. Since the Northwest is a producer of primary commodities—exporting a large proportion of its timber and products of fisheries and farms—we assume that 33 per cent of the output for which the power is used would be exported. On this basis, residents of the region would enjoy two-thirds of the gain to consumers ($43,000), while a third ($21,500) would accrue to the regional enterprises' customers who are outside the Pacific Coast region.

Table 50 summarizes the distribution of regional gains, to the extent that we can do so.

TABLE 49. *Derivation of Regional Distribution of the Gains from
Federal Power Sold by Preference Customers
for Use as Factor Inputs*

		Per cent
A.	1. Total federal sales to preference customers	37.5
	2. Total resold to commercial establishments	13.2

		Dollars
B.	1. Difference in federal-private costs	$1,489,500
	2. Difference corresponding to 13.2 per cent sold as factor inputs	195,900
C.	Retained originally as capital's share (55 per cent)	107,800
D.	After-tax rewards to capital	53,900
E.	Reduction in otherwise required general federal taxes [a]	
	1. In the Pacific Coast region	6,700
	2. Other regions	47,200
F.	Dividend gains	
	1. In the Pacific Coast region	40,400
	2. In other regions	13,500
G.	Combined dividend gains and tax reductions	
	1. In the Pacific Coast region	47,200
	2. In other regions	60,600

[a] Using weight derived from tax Model A.

TABLE 50. *Summary of Regional Distribution of Gains from Federal
Power Sold by Preference Customers*

	Regional gains ($ thousand)	Extra-regional gains ($ thousand)
Final demand	335.0	—
Use as factor input:		
After-tax returns to owners of capital ..	40.4	13.5
Reduction of otherwise required federal taxes	[a] 6.7	[a] 47.2
Rewards to complementary factor services	23.5	—
Consumers' share through commodity price reduction	43.0	21.5
Total [a]	448.6	74.2

[a] Using weights derived from tax Model A.

The locus of gains associated with that portion of the federally developed power distributed through private electric utilities follows a somewhat different pattern. Since power is made available to these utilities only after the power requirements of the local public distributors are met, the available federal power may be in surplus. The bargaining position of the federal agency is not so great vis-à-vis the private distributors, when it has power in surplus, as vis-à-vis the public distributors. Moreover, the federal agency lacks comparable justification for monitoring the operations of the private utility. As a result, there is greater likelihood that relatively more of the savings associated with purchases from the federal power sources will be retained by the utility than that they will be passed on to residential and rural customers. Several reasons may be advanced for this. The rates approved by regulatory commissions are calculated to provide an established rate of return to the private utility's investment on its relatively higher cost generation, transmission, and distribution facilities. The resale of lower cost federal power at prevailing rate schedules involves only small and incidental investment in distribution facilities. This permits a margin of profit not only substantially in excess of that allowed under the resale clauses negotiated by the federal agency with its preference customers, but also larger than the margin the utility earns on the distribution of the power it generates.

The larger margins make it possible, however, for some part of the energy purchased from the federal power agency—or power which it displaces in the system—to be sold under rate schedules favorable to commercial and industrial customers. We have seen, for example, that private utilities have a significantly different distribution of total energy deliveries to domestic and commercial uses than do local public distributors of electric energy. If this results primarily from pricing practices which favor the commercial-industrial customers, there is likely to be a substantially different regional incidence in the gains to power consumers attributable to lower purchase costs. Stated differently, if the private utility resells the federally developed power to domestic consumers at the same rate as for power from its own sources, the second-round effects do not result in any gains to households in the region. The regional distribution of gains will then be significantly influenced by the distribution of the equity shares in the utility undertaking. We can work this through for illustrative purposes.

Look at a case in which a private utility would retain 50 per cent of the gains as increased profits and pass on the remainder in lower commercial and industrial rates to business establishments. If the utility obtained 34.4 per cent of the output of the federal project, this would represent a saving amounting to about $512,000 annually, compared with annual operating costs if such power were provided by its own financing of the reimbursable project feature.[6] Taking up, first, the gains associated with that part of the savings which appears as increased profits to the private electric utility ($256,000, of which $128,000 is shared with the Internal Revenue Service), what can we say about their distribution?

To obtain an estimate of the regional locus of these gains, we need some idea of the distribution of the utility's common stock ownership. Although such information is seldom a matter of public record, the regional distribution of common stock ownership for a utility in the Northwest has been made public and can be used here as the basis of an approximation.[7] The distribution of junior equity securities by regions indicates the distribution of that part of the after-tax gains to the private electric utility retained from the savings in costs of power supplied through federal development. This is shown in Table 51, along with the distribution of gains from the assumed reduction in the general tax burden associated with the utility's increased tax liability.

The distribution of both forms of gains from the profits earned by the private utility appears to be about $32,700 in the region and $222,300 among residents of other parts of the country.

Next, consider the distribution of gains relating to that part of the savings in cost of power passed on to the utility's commercial and industrial customers. We assume that the before-tax gains will be about 55 per cent of the total savings, or $140,800; and, of this, that 50 per cent will be absorbed by an increase in the enterprise's federal tax liabilities. On the assumption that this permits an

[6] See Tables 48 and 38.

[7] The data employed in the following analysis appear as insert sheets 8a and 8b of the Idaho Power Company's *Annual Report to the Federal Power Commission* for the year 1955, adjusted to represent a Willamette Basin development by transposing the data for the states of Idaho and Oregon.

TABLE 51. *Regional Distribution of Gains to Utility Equity Owners from Federal Power Sold by Private Utilities*

Regions	Distribution of common stock (per cent)	Annual gains to shareholders ($ thousand)	Distribution of reduced tax liabilities (per cent)	Annual reduced tax liabilities ($ thousand)
New England	32.92	42.1	7.05	9.0
Middle Atlantic	29.97	38.7	24.35	31.2
South Atlantic	3.87	5.0	9.96	12.7
East South Central ...	1.70	2.2	3.42	4.4
East North Central ...	10.47	13.4	25.53	32.7
West North Central ..	4.32	5.5	7.86	10.1
West South Central ..	0.45	0.6	6.40	8.2
Mountain	2.55	3.3	2.89	3.7
Pacific Coast	13.08	16.7	12.49	16.0
Total [a]	99.33	127.5	[b] 99.95	128.0

[a] Discrepancy in totals caused by rounding.
[b] Weights derived from tax Model A.

equivalent reduction in tax burdens of other taxpayers, about $8,800 of this gain would accrue to residents of the Pacific Coast region, whereas $61,600 would go to households in the rest of the country. The other half, or $70,200 after taxes, would accrue to equity owners in the commercial and industrial establishments. We assume, as in the case of the preference customers' sales to business establishments, that three-quarters of the equity securities are owned by residents of the Pacific Coast region, while a quarter are held by residents in other parts of the country. Accordingly, in the case of after-tax rewards to venture capital, residents of the region would receive about $52,800, and those in other regions about $17,600.

Using the same assumptions as for the commercial sales of the public distributors, $30,700 would be labor's share and $56,300 the consumers' share in the region; and $28,400 would be enjoyed by consumers outside the region.

The regional distribution of these total gains from the federally developed power supplied to private electric utilities for resale is summarized in Table 52.

TABLE 52. *Summary of Regional Distribution of Gains from Federal Power Sold by Private Utilities*

	Regional gains ($ thousand)	Extra-regional gains ($ thousand)
Final demand	—	—
From before-tax rewards to capital on resale of federal power:		
Dividends or increased net worth	16.7	110.3
Reduction in general tax liabilities	16.0	112.0
From derived-demand uses:		
Dividends or increased net worth	52.8	17.6
Reduction in general tax liabilities	8.8	61.6
Labor's gains	30.7	—
Consumers' gains	56.3	28.4
Total	a 181.3	a 329.9

a Discrepancy in totals caused by rounding.

GAINS FROM SALES TO FEDERAL AGENCIES

Of the two remaining classes of purchasers from BPA, federal agencies absorbed 5.79 per cent of the increment added during fiscal year 1955. To a very large extent, such sales are to defense or defense-supporting agencies, such as the Atomic Energy Commission. There were some sales to the Bureau of Reclamation for pumping associated with the irrigation projects in the area; to a very large extent these represent sales for use as factor inputs.

When federal agencies such as the Atomic Energy Commission can meet their energy requirements at less cost than from an alternative source of power, the gains will be reflected in a reduced operating budget. The ultimate gainers will be those whose tax liabilities support the federal agencies, and the regional locus of gains will be similar to those given by our tax models in Chapter VII.

If we assume that the alternate source of supply would have been energy from a privately developed reimbursable project feature, the annual savings would amount to about $86,200 annually. The regional distribution of gains for the two previously used tax models is given in Table 53.

TABLE 53. *Regional Distribution of Gains from Federal Power
Sold to Federal Agencies*

Regions	Distribution Model A		Distribution Model B	
	(Per cent)	($ thousand)	(Per cent)	($ thousand)
New England	7.05	6.1	7.54	6.5
Middle Atlantic	24.35	21.0	26.69	23.0
South Atlantic	9.96	8.6	10.36	8.9
East South Central ..	3.42	2.9	3.41	2.9
East North Central ...	25.53	22.0	23.48	20.2
West North Central ...	7.86	6.8	7.11	6.1
West South Central ...	6.40	5.5	6.57	5.7
Mountain	2.89	2.5	2.66	2.3
Pacific Coast	12.49	10.8	12.20	10.0
Total	ᵃ 99.95	86.2	ᵃ 100.02	ᵃ 85.6

ᵃ Discrepancies in totals caused by rounding.

GAINS FROM SALES TO ELECTRO-PROCESS INDUSTRIES

Finally, and perhaps most complicated, is the case of gains from
sales of part of the federal power to the electro-process industries.
Although only thirteen firms in all were involved during the fiscal
year ending June 1954, these firms accounted for over 47 per cent
of all BPA sales. During the next fiscal year, BPA sales to these
firms accounted for a little over 22 per cent of the year's increment;
but their proportion of the total dropped to about 44 per cent.
For some time in the future, as in the past, these electro-process
industries will participate in the gains incident on federal development of hydroelectric sites in the Pacific Northwest.[8] With so large
a proportion of the total of federal sales going to the electro-process

[8] There has been some change in policy in making available large blocks of
hydroelectricity from federal power development to the electro-process industries.
Power for these industries is less likely to be forthcoming from federal development in the immediate future than it has in the not too distant past. Despite
this fact, contracts with electro-process firms have been negotiated for long
terms; hence they will continue to participate in the associated gains, at least
until the expiration of their current contracts. Because of the enormous
quantity of energy taken by these industries, we feel justified in treating the
distribution of gains from their purchases of federal power, despite the uncertainty that they will gain from additional increments to BPA's supply.

industries, it becomes necessary to explore the locus of gains associated with this power.

In order to simplify the analysis somewhat, we can confine our attention to only that part of the BPA's industrial sales which goes to the aluminum industry. This will cover the bulk of the sales to directly served customers since the aluminum industry in the Northwest has accounted for upwards of 85 per cent of the total of such sales.

Our analysis of the distribution of gains by the aluminum industry differs somewhat from that of the cases involving industrial sales by local distributors of Bonneville power. In most of the commercial or industrial operations served by the local distributors, the power bill represents a relatively small proportion of total costs. Accordingly, changes in relative rates for power do not create large new investment opportunities in the region, or particular incentives for capital to flow into or out of the region. That is our reason for assuming that the gains for these enterprises can be taken as the difference between rates for power supplied from federal sources and the next most inexpensive alternative in the same region. This is not true of the aluminum industry.

Because of the enormous quantities of electrical energy required to produce aluminum,[9] relatively small differentials in power rates represent large differences in total mill costs at the aluminum reduction level. Even small differences in regional power rates, therefore, may influence the location of aluminum reduction facilities. In the aluminum industry, however, the gains are not determined simply by comparing power rates from alternative sources in the same region. These enterprises must compare differences in total assembly, processing, and transfer costs attending production in the region having lower power rates with the total costs in other regions, where power may be somewhat higher but the cost of complementary resources or transportation charges may bulk less. In short, the gains from the less expensive power supply in the Northwest will only partly increase the returns to the aluminum industry. Part of the gains will accrue to complementary resources used in production and in providing the increased transportation services required if production is undertaken in that relatively more remote region.

[9] The requirement is on the order of 18,000 kilowatt-hours per ton of metallic aluminum.

As an example, assume that our hypothetical 80,000-kilowatt hydroelectric development is available to support 40,000 tons of annual aluminum reduction in the Northwest. At annual costs of about $1.5 million, this federally developed power would be available at the bus bar for about 2.25 mills per kilowatt-hour; an additional half mill may be considered an appropriate transmission charge. An alternative source might conceivably be a privately developed thermal source in the coal-rich Ohio Valley, available to the aluminum industry at about 4 mills per kilowatt-hour.[10] For an aluminum producer turning out 40,000 tons of metallic aluminum annually, there would be a difference in the power bill amounting to about $900,000. Only part of this difference would accrue to the aluminum producer, however, for transport costs involved in assembling his raw materials would reduce the amount of his gains. Delivered prices on alumina drawn from Gulf Coast refining operations for the Northwest reduction plant would exceed corresponding costs for assembling supplies for an Ohio Valley reduction mill.[11] For 80,000 tons of alumina required for 40,000 tons of annual aluminum reduction, there would be a $258,400 difference in freight charges. Assembly costs of carbon requirements would also differ. Approximately a half ton of petroleum coke and 252 pounds of binding material are required per ton of aluminum. An Ohio reduction mill could draw on a Chicago source of supply for petroleum coke and obtain the required coal tar pitch from Ironton, Ohio, at considerable savings in freight charges over drawing on a Wilmington, California, source for petroleum coke and on St. Paul for the binding material—the sources of supply for a Northwest reduction plant.[12] Taking the

---

[10] This abstracts from the possibility that these Ohio plants may be undertaken with the aid of certificates of necessity, which would permit more favorable rates for power associated with the gains from rapid amortization privileges.

[11] Rates on alumina from Gulf Coast to Northwest points are taken at $9.73 per ton, while rates on movements from Gulf Coast to Ohio Valley points are estimated to be in the neighborhood of $6.50 per ton. See *Railway Tariffs*, T.C. 1-A and S.F.A. 817-A.

[12] Petroleum coke used by the aluminum industry is produced by the Great Lakes Carbon Corporation's plants in Chicago; Port Arthur, Texas; and Wilmington, California. Binding material for the coke comes principally from the Allied Chemical and Dye Corporation and the Koppers Company plants. Plants of the two firms producing coal tar pitch binding materials are located in

carbon requirements of a reduction mill of 40,000 tons of annual capacity, the differences in transport costs would approximate $103,600 annually between the alternative locations.[13]

Finally, differences between the freight bills of the two locations would appear in connection with moving the metallic aluminum from reduction mills to markets, or to fabricating centers located with reference to major markets. Only a relatively small amount of fabricating capacity is in the Northwest—at Spokane and Vancouver in Washington. A small amount of additional capacity is located in Vernon and Los Angeles in California. Some capacity exists in other parts of the West, such as Phoenix, Arizona. But rail rates to these locations are roughly comparable to those on movements all the way to the Midwest.[14] Much of the metal produced in the Northwest actually will move to the eastern part of the United States at freight rates greatly in excess of those for an Ohio Valley location.[15] Consider then, freight rates on metal produced in the Northwest to average about $20 per ton as compared with an estimated $10 per ton on metal produced in the Ohio Valley. A difference in the annual freight bill on aluminum pigs and ingot shipments would amount to about $400,000.

If we assume no differences in processing costs, the sum of increased transfer costs—involving both assembly of raw materials and distribution of processed output to markets—would approximate $762,000 annually, leaving the Northwest reduction mill a net locational advantage of only $138,000 of the original $900,000 savings on power costs. Taking this into account, what is the regional locus of the ultimate gains from the federally developed hydroelectric feature of the project?

The proportion of the total output assumed to be available from the hydroelectric site for sale to the electro-process industries would

Detroit; Woodward and Fairfield, Alabama; Ironton, Ohio; and St. Paul, Minnesota.

[13] These estimates assume a transport rate of $8.50 per ton on petroleum coke from Wilmington to the Northwest reduction mill, and $6.85 per ton from Chicago to the Ohio Valley destination. Transport charges on coal tar pitch are assumed to be $1.10 per hundredweight on movements from St. Paul to the Northwest plant as compared with 40¢ per hundredweight on movements from Ironton to the Ohio Valley location.

[14] See *Railway Tariffs*, P.S.C. F.T. 1-S, T.C. 2-R, and P.S.C. 1-S.

[15] Cross-country rates for shipments of 80,000 pounds minimum car-load lots have been $27.96 per ton in recent years. *Railway Tariff*, T.C. 2-R.

not support the scale of aluminum reduction operations assumed in our example immediately above.. We can assume, however, that this amount of power (22.34 per cent of the total 80,000 kilowatts) is allocated, along with power from other federally developed sources, to the production of aluminum. Given the difference in annual power costs between a federal Northwest and a private Ohio Valley plant of $900,000, we reduce the amount to only 22.34 per cent, or $201,100. This is the amount of the gains with which we are concerned.

This gain of $201,100 next is divided between the aluminum industry and the railroads providing complementary services, and further broken down in Table 54. First, we treat the regional locus of gains associated with the share going originally to the aluminum industry.

The increase in the before-tax share of the aluminum industry's gains would amount to about $30,800 (22.34 per cent of $138,000). Again, assume that the industry retains 55 per cent of the total out of which to reward the owners of capital services and distributes 12 per cent to labor and 33 per cent to consumers. This would leave the industry with a before-tax gain of $16,900, shared equally with the Internal Revenue Service on our assumption of a 50 per cent marginal corporate profit tax rate. We further assume that only 10 per cent of the shareholders in the industry reside in the Pacific Coast region, with the remainder of the shares owned by residents of other regions. Gains to labor are taken to be regionally oriented, whereas the distribution of gains to consumers, in the light of the national market served by the aluminum industry, are restricted to only 10 per cent in the Pacific Coast region.

We now take up the regional locus of gains associated with the share going to the railways. We have assumed that approximately 85 per cent of the gains to the aluminum industry from lower cost power would be disbursed for increased transport services. This would amount to approximately $170,300 of the total. If we assume that 75 per cent of the increased receipts of the railways must be deducted to cover marginal costs,[16] about $42,600 would remain

---

[16] *Railway Freight Service Costs in the Various Rate Territories of the United States,* Senate Document No. 63, 78th Congress, 1st Session, 1943, pp. 41-44, 63-70; and G. H. Borts, "Increasing Returns in the Railway Industry," *Journal of Political Economy,* August 1954, p. 323.

as the net gains from the railways' share of the savings. We divide these gains functionally as before—55 per cent representing the before-tax share of capital, 12 per cent labor's gains, and 33 per cent the share of general consumers of railway services. To determine the locus of these gains, we assume that 50 per cent of the total before-tax gains to capital appears as reductions in general tax liabilities, distributed regionally for convenience by the weights given by tax Model A; the other 50 per cent appears as dividend payments or increased net worth of shareholders in the railways. We assume that 10 per cent of these are distributed in the Pacific Coast region, the remainder in other regions. Moreover, we assume that the gains going to labor are distributed about equally between the Pacific Coast and all other regions; while the gains to general consumers of railway services are assumed to share 10 per cent in the Pacific Coast region and 90 per cent in the remainder of the nation.

Table 54 presents in schematic fashion the distribution of gains by regions to provide a rough approximation of relative magnitudes. The assumptions employed in this model do not have a carefully grounded empirical basis, but were selected rather on the basis of rough judgment as to realistic possibilities to provide some insight into the nature of the regional locus of gains.[17]

To locate the gains beyond the point at which they first come to rest as gains to households, we would have to embark on an inordinately complex piece of empirical and institutional analysis. For example, an increased demand in the Northwest for labor in aluminum reduction would represent a relative decline in the labor market from which the firm would have drawn in the Ohio Valley. Labor in the Northwest would gain, whereas in the Ohio Valley it would suffer relative losses. Increased orders for petroleum coke from the Wilmington, California, plant of the Great Lakes Carbon Cor-

---

[17] We hold no brief for the model employed here. Students of regional economics in the Northwest more intimately familiar with the structure of Northwest industry, the interregional commodity flows, rates of return to different industrial undertakings, the participation of co-operating factors in the shares of gains, and the regional distribution of equity securities in Northwest business enterprises may improve on the assumptions to provide a more refined model. The regional distribution of gains resulting from such a model, however, on balance is not likely to differ in any startling degree from those summarized in Table 55.

TABLE 54. *Regional Distribution of Gains from Federal Power Sold to Electro-Process Industries*

	Pacific Coast	Other regions
Difference in annual power bill, Northwest federal vs. Ohio Valley private $900,000		
Relevant share (22.34 per cent) of total going originally to aluminum industry 201,100		
Division of relevant share between:		
Aluminum industry retained gains 30,800		
Increase in transport costs 170,300		
Division of aluminum industry's share of before-tax gains:		
55 per cent before-tax returns to capital:		
After-tax rewards to venture capital	$ 800	$ 7,600
Reduction in general tax liabilities [a]	1,100	7,400
12 per cent as labor's share	3,700	—
33 per cent as consumers' share	1,000	9,200
Total aluminum industry retained gains	$ 6,600	$24,200
Division of railways' share of before-tax gains:		
55 per cent before-tax returns to capital:		
After-tax rewards to venture capital	$ 1,200	$10,500
Reduction in general tax liabilities [a]	1,500	10,200
12 per cent as labor's share	2,500	2,500
33 per cent as general railway consumers' share	1,400	12,600
Total railways' share ($170,300) less marginal costs	$ 6,600	$35,800
Regional locus of total gains shared by aluminum and railway industries	[b] $13,200	[b] $60,000

[a] Using weights derived from tax Model A.
[b] Discrepancies in totals caused by rounding.

poration would represent an increase in the demand for factor serv-ices in the Pacific Coast region, and a relative decline in the demand for such services in the regional markets from which the Chicago plant draws its factors. The coastal railways would gain, whereas the transcontinental railroads would lose in the petroleum coke movements. The St. Paul plant of the Koppers Chemical Company would gain from the increased orders for coal tar pitch; the Iron-ton, Ohio, plant of Allied Chemical and Dye Company would suffer relative decline. Where one firm with a given regional distribution of equity is substituted for another firm located elsewhere and with a different regional distribution of ownership shares, there will be a different regional distribution of gains and losses among the owners of capital services as well as among labor.

Accepting our limited analytical techniques, and the state of present knowledge in relation to the complexity of the problems involved, it is not possible to detail the ultimate regional locus of gains, in a dynamic context, in connection with the federally developed sources of hydroelectric power in the Northwest. We can present only in schematic fashion for illustrative purposes a summary of the effects of a hypothetical case to provide a rough notion of the diffusion of consequences beyond the locus of original impact. Such a summary is provided in Table 55, which is drawn from the previous tables in this section.

TABLE 55. *Summary of Regional Locus of Gains from Federally Developed Sources of Hydroelectricity in the Pacific Northwest*

	Pacific Coast	Other regions
Locus of gains distributed via preference customers:		
Final-demand uses	$335,000	—
Derived-demand uses	113,600	$ 74,200
Locus of gains distributed via private utilities:		
Final-demand uses	—	—
Derived-demand uses	181,300	329,900
Locus of gains distributed via federal agencies:		
Final-demand uses	—	—
Derived-demand uses	10,800	75,400
Locus of gains distributed via electro-process industries:		
Final-demand uses	—	—
Derived-demand uses	13,200	60,000
Total	$653,900	$539,500

Tracing the locus of gains in each instance to the point at which they appear as either money or real income to households, we note that the regional distribution of gains would be about 55-45 as between the Northwest region in which the federal hydroelectric project is located and the remainder of the nation.[18] Accordingly, in considering the regional income redistributive consequences, we find that the Pacific Coast region would share in the total opportunity costs of the development and the cost of supporting federal public services (through increased regional tax liabilities by both power consumers and others in the region), to the extent of close to 70 per cent of the total, under either tax model. On the other hand, we find that gains from lower power rates would be shared more equally as between the Pacific Coast region and the remainder of the nation. Even so, we must recognize that the federal development of hydroelectric sites in the Northwest would result in a net income redistribution in favor of the Pacific Northwest when successive rounds of effects terminating with households, in each case, are taken into account. In our illustration, estimated gains to regional households as a result of the difference in annual power bills between the federal and private power operations amounted to approximately $654,000 (Table 55). To infer the *net* gain to the region we must deduct the increase in federal tax liabilities of regional residents (estimated at from $104,000 to $106,000 in Tables 46 and 42, respectively, in Chapter VII); and if we take account of shifts in local tax burdens, the increase in local tax levies on sources other than power amounting to about $419,000

[18] A comment is in order on the discrepancy between the total gains ($1,193,-400), the locus of which we have identified consistent with our approach, and the difference ($1,489,500) between the annual operating cost of the federally financed and operated hydroelectric feature as compared with its counterpart undertaken as a private venture. The largest part ($131,600) of the total discrepancy is accounted for by use of the difference between the operating costs of an Ohio Valley thermal plant as an alternative to the federally developed Northwest hydroelectric plant, rather than the private Northwest plant. The next largest portion of the discrepancy ($127,700) is accounted for by the deduction from the railways' share of the gains of the estimated marginal costs associated with the increase in transportation services required for a Northwest aluminum reduction mill over that required for an Ohio Valley Plant. Since this portion defies allocation among co-operating factors, it was purposely omitted from consideration. Finally, a smaller part of the total is accounted for by the discrepancy between total BPA sales and the portion which could be accounted for readily in Table 48. This discrepancy left approximately 3 per cent of the total sales unaccounted for, and resulted in ommission of approximately $50,000 of the total difference in annual operating costs. A remaining discrepancy, amounting to less than 1 per cent, can be explained by errors caused by rounding.

(Table 38) would be required. These deductions produce an estimated net regional gain of approximately $130,000.[19] However, the estimated gains to households in other regions in the country stemming from the $540,000 difference in power bills, does not entirely compensate for the increase in federal tax liabilities of residents in these regions ($743,000 to $746,000 as estimated in Tables 46 and 42, respectively). On balance, therefore, there is some net income transfer to the Northwest in connection with the federally developed hydroelectric site.

If dynamic growth effects could be worked into the framework of analysis, there is little question that, over time, capital inflows into the region would be fostered to exploit complementary investment opportunities, followed by net in-migration, and other similar phenomena associated with regional economic growth. At least, this appears to be a tenable hypothesis and to a significant extent is one of the objectives (higher criteria) which have been used to justify the expenditure of federal funds for "the development of the West." [20]

Aside from the interregional income redistributive effects, there will be income transfers among members of society so long as the incidence of taxes among individuals is not proportional to the gains from the expenditures of such taxes. Furthermore, although owners of capital services are broadly diffused, there will be some income redistribution among owners to the extent that firms—whose venture capital is supplied by different individuals—participate to an unequal extent in the gains from federal hydroelectric development. This will also be true of owners of other factor services which are supplied to various firms that would participate to different degrees under alternative approaches to the development of hydroelectric sites.

---

[19] If data permitted a geographic breakdown to include only the relevant power marketing territory in lieu of the Census region which includes Washington, Oregon, and California, the net gain to households in the marketing territory probably would be greater, since about 90 per cent of the increased federal tax liabilities would fall on regional residents outside the marketing territory—Washington and California in this illustration.

[20] For a discussion of the objectives which serve as the justification for federal water resources development programs in the West, see Irving Fox, "Issues in Federal Water Resources Policy," *Law and Contemporary Problems*, Duke University, Summer 1957.

Thus, while the ultimate effect of a federally developed hydro-electric site in the Northwest results in some income transfer to the region, a host of additional redistributive consequences among members of society also attends the federal development of hydro-electric projects.[21]

Successive Rounds of Gains Under Local Development

Consider now the distribution of gains on the assumption the project's reimbursable feature is developed as a local undertaking. We shall first seek to identify the locus of gains on the assumption that the co-operator is a local public body—in this instance a municipality.

GAINS FROM LOCAL PUBLIC DEVELOPMENT

Our analysis of the differences in accounting costs (Table 38) indicated that annual operating costs for the project's reimbursable feature under local public direction would be about $1.2 million less than if the undertaking were a local private venture. The share of the gains from this difference in annual operating costs would depend, to a certain extent, on the distribution of electrical output of the local public body. Table 47 showed the distribution of the output of municipal systems in the Northwest as 57.3 per cent to final-demand uses and 36.6 per cent to derived-demand uses. This accounts for about 94 per cent of the total sales; the remainder, for miscellaneous uses, was omitted in the tabulation. If only the distribution of output among these two major categories of use is considered, the total gains with whose locus we are concerned amount to about $1.1 million.

We assume that the distribution of this gain is proportionate to the share of the output that each class of customer purchases. That

---

[21] Of course, these general conclusions are not restricted to federal water resources development policies, but apply to all governmental policies. Different regions and individuals will benefit as a result of other policies in various areas of governmental concern. This multiplicity of policies lends weight to the position that the effects of governmental action inspired by efficiency considerations will be more or less randomly distributed, and hence lead, over time, to an increase of welfare for almost everyone.

is, domestic-residential consumption would share in the gains to the extent of 57.3 per cent, or $672,000; and commercial-industrial users would participate in 36.6 per cent of the gains, or $429,200.

As in the case involving the marketing operations of the public distributors reselling federally developed power, we also assume that the locus of the gains associated with distribution of power to final-demand uses will remain with the households in the region. The regional locus of gains associated with the distribution of project output to derived-demand uses will be governed by the same considerations—and hence we employ the same basic assumptions—as for public distributors' marketing operations that involved the retailing of federally developed sources of energy. The marketing of project output by a local public body may involve some sales to the electro-process industries, especially if the project is substantially larger than that assumed for our hypothetical Willamette River site.[22] In that case, the analysis of the locus of gains would be comparable to that underlying Table 54. Since this contingency would not be in prospect in connection with our hypothetical Willamette Basin site, we do not repeat it here—in spite of the fact that it might be applicable to other hydroelectric developments in the Northwest.

Employing the assumptions similar to those used to identify the locus of gains in connection with public distributors of federally developed power, the appropriate magnitudes in this case are those shown in Table 56.

If the reimbursable project feature were developed by a municipality with a distribution of project output similar to the average among municipalities in the Pacific Northwest, most gains would center in the region in which the project is located. Of the total

---

[22] In the case of the Willamette River site, under federal development we assumed that a portion of the projects's output would be made available, in combination with output from other federally developed sources, to the electro-process industries. In the case of a relatively small development such as the Cougar Dam on the Willamette, the amount of output would not meet the needs of the city of Eugene as well as the requirements of an electro-process operation. On the other hand, there are plans for co-operative development of the Priest Rapids site on the Columbia, and the redevelopment of the Rock Island Dam by local public utility districts (Grant County and Chelan County respectively), which contemplate the distribution of some portion of the energy to electro-process firms.

TABLE 56. *Regional Locus of Gains from Local Public Development of Reimbursable Project Feature*

	Pacific Coast	Other regions
From derived-demand uses:		
55 per cent before-tax returns to capital:		
After-tax rewards to venture capital	$ 11,800	$106,300
Reduction in general tax liabilities [a]	14,800	103,300
12 per cent as labor's share	51,500	—
33 per cent as consumers' share	94,300	47,200
Total	$172,400	$256,800
From final-demand uses	$672,000	—
Regional locus of total gains	$844,400	$256,800

[a] Using weights derived from tax Model A.

difference in power bills between the local public and private operations of our illustration, about $844,000, or 77 per cent, would accrue to the region.[23] Since households in other regions would experience gains approximately a quarter of a million, against which increased federal tax liabilities exceeding $600,000 would obtain, there would be a significant net income transfer to the region accompanying local public development of the hydroelectric resource.[24]

[23] If the net regional gain is sought, however, it would be necessary to deduct from this figure the increase in federal tax liabilities of regional residents (estimated to be approximately $86,000 to $88,000 depending on the tax model assumed) and the increase in local tax levies against sources other than power (approximately $246,000 as indicated by data in Table 38).

[24] Development of some of the larger hydroelectric sites—such as Priest Rapids, Wanapum, Rocky Reach, and Wells—by local public bodies is likely to have additional income redistributive consequences within the power systems. This is likely to result from the competition which the federal system would face when power from these developments becomes available. The local public bodies could use part of the secondary energy to replace purchases from BPA as well as attempt to sell part of the secondary to BPA's existing industrial customers. As inducement, the utilities could offer the industrial customer an additional block of firm power which BPA would not be in a position to do. Such competition would be important to BPA and its customers, as secondary power revenues average about 20 per cent of the total. Under federal development, this competition would not exist. While these redistributive consequences eventually may be significant, they are difficult to evaluate quantitatively, and thus we only note them in passing.

GAINS FROM LOCAL PRIVATE DEVELOPMENT

Look, finally, at the distribution of gains on the assumption that the project's reimbursable feature is undertaken as a private venture. At first thought, there appear to be no gains whose distribution commands our attention, for the annual operating costs of the private electric utility would exceed corresponding costs for a federal or nonfederal public venture. We did not treat as losses to anyone the increased power bills consumers of privately developed power would be constrained to pay.[25] We therefore are not permitted in this case to argue that those whose tax liabilities would be reduced by virtue of the equivalent increased public revenues obtained from the private utility would be the gainers.

Our analysis of the distribution of gains from private financing of the reimbursable feature would be complete, except for the fact that the private utility may take advantage of the accelerated tax write-off privilege. Since private electric utilities in the Northwest have participated in the accelerated amortization program in the recent past, and additional requests for comparable treatment are pending,[26] it is useful to analyze the regional locus of gains associated with this policy.

In Chapter VII, we discovered that certification of 70 per cent of a $23 million investment in facilities for rapid amortization increases tax liabilities of the general taxpayers by about $250,000 annually, and we alluded to the regional incidence of the shifted tax liabilities. Moreover, we determined that the shift in tax burden did not represent a gain to the power consumers of the private electric utilities, but rather to the owners of the equity shares in the utility enterprise.

The distribution of common stock ownership by regions (given

[25] Our approach has been to treat the difference in annual operating costs between public and private development as a gain to consumers of public power, and the unmet portion of the opportunity costs and shifted tax liabilities as losses to others. We could have inverted the approach to consider the annual difference in operating costs between public and private development as losses to consumers of private power and the reduced federal tax liabilities, consequent on private development, as gains to the general public. Since we chose the former approach, however, we cannot now consider the reduction in general federal tax liabilities as gains to others.

[26] Pacific Power and Light Company, *Annual Report, 1955*, p. 10.

in Table 51) indicates the distribution of the gains from accelerated amortization. In order to facilitate the showing of net income transfers interregionally, we also use data (from Table 41) showing the distribution of increased general tax liabilities by regions, associated with the need to cover out of public revenues the costs of the rapid amortization program. We assume that the internal rate of return for funds invested in the expansion of facilities is such that the annual gains to common stock owners would be equal to the $250,000 estimated as the increased cost to the general public of this amortization policy. Applying both the per cent distribution of gains by regions and the per cent distribution of the increased tax burdens by regions, as weights for allocating the costs and gains, we can derive the annual net income transfers among regions corresponding to the tax amortization policy in this instance. This is shown in the last column in Table 57.

Because of the preponderance of stock ownership in the New England and Middle Atlantic states, these regions are the gainers from the tax amortization policy—even though the Middle Atlantic states contribute heavily in meeting tax requirements. The Pacific Coast region, in which the project is located, would also enjoy some net gain. All other regions would lose in the income transfer, with

TABLE 57. *Percentage Distribution of Gains and Costs of Accelerated Amortization by Regions, and Net Annual Income Transfers*

Regions	Distribution of gains by regions (per cent)	Distribution of increased general tax liabilities [a] (per cent)	Net annual income transfers among regions [b] ($ thousand)
New England	32.92	7.05	+64,520
Middle Atlantic	29.97	24.35	+14,016
South Atlantic	3.87	9.96	−15,189
East South Central ...	1.70	3.42	− 4,290
East North Central ...	10.47	25.53	−37,560
West North Central ...	4.32	7.86	− 8,829
West South Central ...	0.45	6.40	−14,839
Mountain	2.55	2.89	− 848
Pacific Coast	13.08	12.49	+ 1,471

[a] Using weights derived from tax Model A.
[b] Discrepancy in net of transfers caused by rounding.

the South Atlantic, East North Central, and the West South Central states experiencing quite large net losses.

These conclusions are based on use of our tax Model A. So far as the interregional distribution of costs and gains and net income transfers are concerned, use of tax Model B would not result in very great differences. This is not to deny that there would be significantly different income redistributive consequences among income classes and, of course, individuals within each region, depending on the tax model assumed to apply. But the regional incidence of increased tax liabilities is quite similar, irrespective of the tax model used.

Income Redistributive Consequences of Difference in Incidence of Costs and Gains

In this and the preceding chapter, we have been concerned essentially with the two aspects of the income redistributive consequences attending different approaches to the development of a reimbursable project feature.

In Chapter VII, we first looked at the differences in the accounting costs which would arise under alternative approaches to the development of a hypothetical Willamette Basin site. We attempted to estimate the unmet portion of the opportunity cost and the amount of shifted tax liabilities in connection with federal development, and to identify the incidence of these income transfers by income class and by regions. Similarly, in the case of local public development, we took that portion of the difference in annual operating costs between the local public and local private operation of identical facilities which would be enjoyed by virtue of the local public bodies' immunity from federal taxation and identified the incidence of the resulting increased general tax liabilities of others. In the case of the private electric utility, we took that portion of the increased general tax liability that would be occasioned by the use of accelerated amortization to determine the regional incidence of the costs.

In this chapter, we have tried to identify those who gain under the alternative approaches to the development of the project's reimbursable hydroelectric feature. On the basis of these crude but suggestive estimates, we can comment on the regional income redistribution inherent in the several alternative approaches.

Under federal development, approximately 70 per cent of the cost of hydroelectric development and the shifted tax burden of supporting public services would be borne by the residents of the Pacific Coast region. Of this total, power consumers would directly meet 94 per cent through the rates which they paid for power; residents of the region would contribute the remainder through increased federal tax liabilities. On the other side of the ledger, about 55 per cent of the difference in the annual operating costs between federal and private development would appear ultimately as gains to households in the region; the remainder would accrue ultimately to households in other regions of the nation. On balance, after all shifts in federal and local tax burdens are accounted for, the residents of the region in which federal hydroelectric development takes place would enjoy a net income gain; residents in other regions of the nation would suffer some net income loss. This suggests a net income transfer from other regions to the one in which the project is undertaken.

Moreover, to the extent that federally developed power would provide a more abundant supply of energy at lower rates than would have been provided in its absence, mobile resources would be attracted into the region and contribute to a more rapid rate of growth. The income redistributive consequence of this and similar dynamic phenomena, however, defy our analytic techniques. Since we can only speculate as to the ultimate dynamic consequences, we simply note this facet of the problem in passing.

Under local public development, in the absence of a scale of development which would provide energy for electric-process industries, the income redistribution in favor of the locality would appear to be somewhat greater. Most gains from lower annual operating costs as compared with private development would accrue to residents of the region. In our illustration, after allowance is made for increases in federal tax liabilities on regional residents, and an assumed increase in local tax levies on sources other than power, approximately a half million dollars annually would appear as a regional net gain. On the other side of the coin, the relatively lower extraregional gains would fall short of compensating for the shifted federal tax liabilities onto households in other regions of the nation; increased tax liabilities would exceed gains by approximately a third of a million.[27]

Under private development, we concluded that all of the costs of the hydroelectric development would be borne by the power consumers in the region. Moreover, since annual operating costs under private development were the highest, there would be no gains under private development over those attending development by alternative approaches. In one particular, however, there would be some income redistributive consequences under private development which did not appear under public development. These income transfers relate to the income redistribution attending accelerated amortization under private development. While no gains to the region by way of lower power rates would result from use of rapid amortization, some gains would accrue to residents of the region through their ownership of equity shares in the private utility enterprise. On balance, annual gains to owners of equity shares residing in Pacific Coast states would amount to $32,600 in our example, exceeding slightly the increased tax burden ($31,200) to the general taxpayers in the region. Accordingly, a slight regional net income gain would result from this policy. Of course, to the extent that the incidence of increased federal tax liabilities is different from the distribution of the increased dividend receipts among individuals in the region, there is an intraregional income redistribution attending use of accelerated amortization.

[27] In both cases of treating the redistributive consequences under public development, whether local or federal, we have purposely avoided treating the income redistributive consequences associated with that part of the differences in public and private annual operating costs which is associated with the differences in money costs and annual depreciation accruals. For this reason, as well as others previously noted, we cannot provide a perfectly balanced system of costs and gains. Not only this reason, but also the fact that our illustrative example will not be typical of every conceivable case of federal development or partnership arrangement, suggest that the details of our results should not be generalized to all cases.

ix   Conclusions

and Policy Implications

We have attempted in this volume to clarify some of the complex issues which beset resource development efforts. Our study has been narrowed to two aspects of this many-faceted problem: analysis of the conditions required to achieve economic efficiency in water development; and analysis of the differences in the pattern of income distribution which attend different water resources policies.

Values in addition to economic efficiency are at stake in water resources development; we have given them only passing consideration. Since water development has been an instrument for attaining certain social goals, water programs include numerous intangibles. Among these are the protection of human life in the flood plains, the preservation of scenic areas because of their aesthetic appeal, the improvement of public health and welfare through provision of recreation facilities, the assurance of security from vagaries of weather through irrigation agriculture—these, and many others. In addition our society has used water resources projects as a means of providing employment and settlement opportunities, of fostering the growth of underdeveloped or depressed regions, and of promoting the widespread use of electric power. These goals are commonly accepted— although individuals attach varying weights to each.

Still other values are of a more controversial nature. For example, individuals differ greatly in the strength of their preferences for private institutions as instruments for natural resources development. On the one hand are those who feel that there are values in private initiative and management which should be preserved at almost any cost. On the other are those who have a deep and abiding belief that natural resources are a property of the entire community and only through public development can society's interest be protected.

Even a superficial examination of the national effort to conserve and develop our water resources reveals that the foregoing factors have been significant—and, at times, of overriding importance—in determining what project or program should be undertaken. Yet values which are susceptible of economic evaluation are also of great importance, because major aspects of national well-being can be measured in economic terms. With a full recognition of the significance of noneconomic considerations, we feel that our study contributes to information in this area in two important respects. First, we have clarified to a substantial degree the factors which must be taken into account to achieve economic efficiency, a relevant consideration in public decisions relating to water resources development. Second, where "higher criteria" are given major weight, the type of analysis which we have illustrated provides a means of determining what is the economic cost to society of realizing such intangible values.

The first part of this study reviewed the conditions that would have to prevail in the economy for the free play of market forces to achieve the maximum economic output consistent with preferences of consumers making up a free society. We noted, however, that the market was not sufficiently comprehensive in its scope to provide every variety of economic good. Various goods or services —such as national defense, police protection, and, in the water field, flood control, pollution abatement, etc.—are traditionally regarded as collective goods. If such services are to be provided, public funds must be employed, because private developmental costs cannot be recovered for what are essentially nonmarketable commodities or services. We noted also certain technical conditions which lead to natural monopoly, and therefore require intervention of public authority in the interest of the consumer. Finally, the presence of external economies and diseconomies requires the intervention of public authority to ensure that uncompensated costs and gains are somehow taken into account and worked into the scheme of efficient production and distribution. For example, the cost inflicted on the anadromous fishing industry by the construction of hydroelectric generating facilities (in the absence of public intervention to ensure safeguards for migratory fish) is a real cost, despite its failure to appear on the financial accounts of the electric generating operation. The gains to those whose water supply is improved by the repulsion of salinity through maintaining minimum channel depth for navigation purposes, is a real gain, even though it does not appear as an increase in financial returns to the river development enterprise. Unless some corrective adjustment is provided, the private cost-gain calculus based only on market transactions will understate costs in the first instance and understate real economic gains in the second.

If the market institution, which is so admirably suited to individualistic action, is not sufficiently comprehensive to minister to every variety of economic want, or serves others only in an economically inefficient manner, then complementary institutions for group decisions and collective action are required to meet adequately the needs of the members of a free society. Historically, various instrumentalities—from the conservancy district and municipality throughout the entire range to the federal level of government, on the one hand, and public assistance to private enterprise, on the other—have represented the forms of collective action through the political process. Examples of all of these are to be found in the water resources field.

But while public participation in the water field is required if efficiency is to be achieved, the degree and forms of participation pose another question. There is a strong sentiment in favor of the idea that some combination of public and private efforts can overcome the limitations of purely private development, while utilizing private institutions to the extent that they can be effective. Our effort has been to lay the basis for a better understanding of the range of possibilities for achieving efficient co-operative arrangements in the water resources field. And, since hydroelectricity is a marketable project service, we have dévoted our analysis to the development of multiple purpose projects which include hydroelectric power.

Our analysis of the market mechanism, illustrated by examples drawn from actual cases, identified certain conditions which would have to be met for efficient development of water resources under private auspices. In summary, these are: (1) The hydroelectric potential of the project must be small in relation to the intended developer's electrical system or market. (2) If the proposed development involves storage sites, the developer must be able to recover the costs of providing the extra storage required to increase power generation at downstream installations. (3) For maximum efficiency, hydraulic and electrical integration must be achieved through co-ordinated operation of the system of interrelated reservoir and generating units. Finally, (4) where opportunities exist for economically justified nonmarketable project benefits, use of public revenues to subsidize private undertakings would be required to ensure efficient development as a private venture. These points were all illustrated in our review of actual cases, salient points of which are presented below.

In the Hells Canyon case, one factor which posed obstacles to efficient development was the enormous hydroelectric potential in that reach of river relative to the size of market for any system other than the federal electric system in the Pacific Northwest. The Hells Canyon site, with the addition of approximately 900,000 kilowatts of prime power, would have about quadrupled the existing capacity of the Idaho Power Company, although it would have been only a fractional increment to the federal power system in that region. A two-dam development would have provided a greater economic return for a smaller total investment than the three-dam plan which the Federal Power Commission licensed for private development. However, the more efficient two-dam scheme would have resulted in the addition of larger blocks of power than from the three-dam proposal. This would have made it more difficult for the private utility to absorb the increase in output at a profit.

The size of hydroelectric potential relative to the market did not constitute a problem in the case of the Coosa River development. Here the potential was less than half as great as in the Hells Canyon, and the Alabama Power Company system several times as large as the Idaho Power Company system. Yet it is apparent that because of the scale required to achieve efficiency in developing some hydroelectric sites, each case must be analyzed in terms of this consideration. In the Hells Canyon case, Idaho Power Company could not market its surplus power in the Northwest power pool where the vast public power development has established rates which Idaho Power Company could not meet profitably. An efficient scale of development of this reach of river as a private venture could be undertaken only with the assistance of a public subsidy. For example, the federal government might have arranged to purchase power which was surplus to the Idaho Power system from the more efficient plan at rates which would compensate Idaho Power Company, and resell the energy at competitive rates in the Northwest power pool. The net effect of such action could be to assure economically efficient development under private management, financed in part by general tax revenues, with income redistributive consequences somewhat similar to those occurring under public development.

Another problem in achieving efficient development employing both public and private institutions involves the direct interdependence of power production at hydroelectric plants along a stream. Under existing law, which considers hydroelectric potential as public property, a private developer of upstream storage is not entitled to compensation for benefits provided federal power plants downstream. Accordingly, no incentive exists for a private developer to incur the additional costs essential to developing an economically justified amount of storage capacity, viewing the hydraulic system in its entirety, if the benefits from the added storage escape appropriation by him.

Our study of Hells Canyon showed that the added prime power at downstream plants owned by the federal government, which would have resulted from the more efficient scale of development, did not represent any incentive for a private developer to provide the added storage capacity required—or to operate the reservoirs consistent with maximizing system output. The added output would accrue to the installations of the federal government which, in terms of the existing legal framework, receives such benefits as a form of *quid pro quo* in exchange for granting a private party the privilege of developing a public asset. In the case of the proposed development of the Coosa River under private auspices, direct interdependence among power-producing plants along the stream constituted no problem, because the whole of the hydroelectric potential would be integrated physically and economically into a single system. Any benefits to downstream installations from regulation provided by upstream developments would accrue to the same enterprise unit and hence provide incentive for developing the most efficient amount of storage capacity for power generation. In the Coosa system, the only storage site developed by a fiscally independent party is one in the headwaters of the stream. This one is developed by the federal government, which can assess charges to recover costs for the benefits provided parties downstream.

Under many circumstances, however, some means for compensating the private developer of storage for useful downstream regulation would be needed to meet the conditions of efficient development of storage capacity under private auspices. To accomplish this change where the federal government owns and operates downstream facilities would require amendment of the Federal Power Act. In view of the long tradition that hydroelectric potential is public property and a private developer should render incidental benefits to the public for the privilege of developing a power site, such a change may not be considered appropriate or desirable in light of legal equity or higher criteria.

A closely related problem is that of realizing the benefits of integrated system operation. In our general analysis, we have presented data indicating that the value of output from co-ordinated operation of all the reservoirs of a system can be higher than the output resulting from operation of each reservoir as though it were a physically independent unit. Accordingly, when more than one management unit is involved in developing and operating a river system, institutional arrangements must be provided to ensure co-ordinated operation of reservoirs if efficiency objectives are to be realized. We have not investigated in any systematic fashion what arrangements can realize such unified management, short of integrating all facilities under a single management unit. In the Coosa River case, the degree of integration under single management approached the ideal for meeting the conditions essential to providing incentives for co-ordinated reservoir operations. In the Hells Canyon case, however, there appears to be little evidence to suggest that such unified management would be attained under present plans.

Finally, where nonmarketable project services—such as flood control, pollution abatement, and salinity repulsion—can be economically justified, efficiency criteria would require that these be provided to maximize the value of the returns from development of a site. However, unless the costs incurred for inclusion of these public purposes are publicly borne, the costs would be shifted to the customers of the utility. If the market for electrical services were competitive, consumers of electricity would select their most economical alternative supplier. But since the utility industry has a captive clientele, the effect of providing nonmarketable project services by the electric utility is to compel the power consumers to finance the public benefits. This involves considerations of both equity and efficiency. Should the consumer of utility services be compelled to purchase flood protection for the community as a condition of receiving electric service to meet his needs? Since utility services are provided under monopoly conditions, his choice is between doing without an essential service or paying through his power bill a special assessment to reimburse the cost of protection enjoyed in large part by a different clientele. On the efficiency side, except under very special circumstances, the addition of such a fee above the normal cost of providing power will adversely affect the efficiency with which all commodities which the utility customer purchases are exchanged in product markets.

In neither the Hells Canyon nor the Coosa cases is the record entirely clear as to who will ultimately bear the cost of providing the nonmarketable project services for which public bodies have been traditionally responsible. It would appear, however, that in the typical case the cost of such services must be borne out of public revenues, consistent with financing of other public services. Otherwise, economically justified, but nonreimbursable, project services would be either slighted in the planning of multiple purpose projects under private development, or provided by some sort of inefficient tie-in sale for a package including the marketable project service.

To summarize: If economic efficiency is to be realized through partnership arrangements, four basic problems inherent in the character of river basin development must be overcome. Our study indicates these lines along which solutions may be found:

1. Where the most efficient scale of development is too large to permit marketing the output within the territory the most eligible private developer is franchised to serve, special marketing arrangements may be required.
2. Developers of headwater storage may require compensation for

the extra cost required to provide stream regulation for fiscally independent parties downstream, whether public or private.

3. Where maximizing the value of a system's output requires a high degree of co-ordination in reservoir operations, institutional arrangements to permit this degree of integrated management must be provided.

4. Where nonmarketable project services are to be included in a multiple purpose project consistent with efficiency goals, the cost of such services must be publicly borne.

It is not the purpose of this study to suggest whether or not such changes in policy are appropriate, desirable, or practicable. Such changes are matters of high policy involving conflicts of interests and values. As such, in a democratic community, the ultimate decisions ought accurately to mirror an informed public opinion on these questions. We have attempted only to specify the necessary conditions to be met and suggest the policy issues implicit in achieving efficient multiple purpose development— whether under partnership or other arrangements—to provide a basis for informed opinion.

Our investigations also illuminate some of the factors which determine the relative capability of different echelons of government—local, state, and federal—to achieve efficient river basin development. Where large interstate river systems are involved, agencies of local government, such as conservancy districts, are confronted with problems somewhat analogous to those of a private company in all respects except one. That is the fact that such public entities have the powers of assessment to recover costs of providing nonmarketable services. Yet the size of the efficient scale of development in relation to the jurisdiction of the lower echelons of government also may render difficult the execution of the most efficient plan of development for a large river system. Finally, the state or locality may be confronted with the same problems as a private developer in achieving co-ordinated system operations.

It is true that, where an entire river system and the benefits which accrue directly from its development fall entirely within a state, the state or one of its agents should be capable of developing a stream for multiple purposes consistent with our efficiency objectives, provided it has sufficient access to developmental capital. In some states and many local jurisdictions, however, account must be taken of constitutional limitations on the purposes to which public revenues can be put. While these may be subject to change, such limitations constitute practical obstacles to development under local auspices.

We have demonstrated in the body of this study that market prices and revenues are not always adequate guides to investment—and, where they are not, public intervention is required to achieve efficiency objectives. Efficiency is not the automatic result of public intervention, however. A major advantage of public authority is the ability through its taxing power to raise revenue which is independent of the marketability of the commodities or services to be provided. This advantage has risks. Access to financial resources without the discipline of the market requires spelling out explicitly the economically efficient operating rules to safeguard the efficiency objectives which such public expenditure is expected to achieve. Moreover, if the gains in efficiency result in a distribution of benefits different from the incidence of the costs, equity considerations are involved.

In addressing the question of the cost associated with raising public revenues—limited to the cases where such funds would be raised by federal taxation—we have recognized that taxes involve a reduction of private investment and consumption which represents opportunities foregone as a result of taxes. Given the current economic conditions and the most realistic tax alternatives, we have estimated the social cost of tax-raised revenue to be on the order of 5 or 6 per cent. That is, if economic advantages were not to be sacrificed, annual average benefits at the margin for any project would have to exceed the annual operating, maintenance, and amortization charges on capital by an amount equivalent to 5 or 6 per cent on investment. Public revenue used for projects whose economic, as contrasted with financial, returns did not measure up to this rate would represent investment in applications providing a lower social return than that available from uses in alternative applications. If, however, projects promising benefits in excess of 5 to 6 per cent on investment were not undertaken, the rate of development of the nation's water resources would be less than that required to achieve conditions of general economic efficiency. The results would appear as a lower national income and product than potentially would be possible.

The estimated opportunity cost for public capital derived in this study, it must be recognized, relates to a particular set of economic conditions—to relatively full employment and to the particular kinds of tax changes which we believe are most likely to be made by the two major parties. Our estimate of opportunity costs is not relevant as an investment criterion when there is generalized unemployment and idle industrial capacity, as was characteristic of the depression of the thirties. Moreover, it should not be looked upon as a guide to the level of returns which should attach to investments undertaken under different economic conditions than those assumed in connection with this study. The social cost of investment is the opportunity foregone from committing productive resources at a given time to one use as against another. Once the resources have been irrevocably committed, different criteria for the efficient management of existing plant become appropriate in lieu of the investment criteria we have employed.

Our estimate of the opportunity cost, however, indicates that projects which were formulated, but not undertaken, at a time when economic expectations appeared consistent with generally lower returns to investment appear to be designed with excessive capital under present economic conditions—if efficiency criteria alone are to guide public policy. The plan of the U. S. Corps of Engineers for the Coosa River, for example, appears overly intensive; this is partly because the development was planned with too low an imputed social cost for public capital. Similarly, a set of two dams of lower capital intensity might be more efficient economically than the more capital intensive High Dam for the Hells Canyon Reach of the Snake River, in view of the rise in the level of opportunity costs over that which was anticipated at the time the High Dam project was formulated. The significance of this should not be misinterpreted. It does not follow that a smaller number of structures would be justified for the development of the Columbia or Coosa than originally planned. But it does suggest that the degree of development which is justified, as measured by its capital inputs, is less intensive and conceivably would be reduced at the margin, compared with a plan which could be justified at a rate equivalent to 2.5 per cent on investment.

While the analysis of efficiency consequences of alternative ways of undertaking multiple purpose projects has been a major concern of our study, we have considered a related issue. Whenever public funds are used for any undertaking—whether to subsidize achievement of an efficiency objective under private operation or to do so more directly as a public undertaking—there will be some income redistributive consequences, so long as those who benefit from the public policy are in some measure different from those who bear its costs. In our analysis of the co-operative arrangements proposed for the Willamette River sites we treated explicitly the income redistributive consequences of different approaches to development.

Under public development, power from otherwise identical facilities can be provided at lower rates than those possible under private development, partly because of access to capital on more favorable terms and the immunity from intergovernmental taxation enjoyed by public enterprise. To the extent that a fully adequate supply of power at such rates could be made available continuously, such supply conditions would be favorable to industrial development of the Pacific Northwest. A more rapid rate of economic development for the region would be in prospect, under these conditions, than if the power were developed under private auspices.

Approximately 40 per cent of this difference in cost to customers between publicly and privately developed hydroelectric sources would be borne by regional residents, either through increased state and local taxes or increased federal tax liabilities. But approximately 55 per cent of the gains from the differential power rates under public development would accrue to the regional residents, with approximately 45 per cent going to persons residing in other regions. Given this difference in the distribution of costs and gains, there would be a net income transfer to the Pacific Northwest associated with public development of hydroelectric sources.

If an objective of federal development of hydroelectricity in the Pacific Northwest is to stimulate more rapid economic development in that region, both the income transfer to the region and the lower power rates which tend to attract mobile capital would favor attainment of this goal. If economic development of the Northwest is an objective, however, a long-term commitment for a stable and dependable rate of development is required of the Congress and federal authorities so as not to defeat, by undependable conditions of power supply, the developmental objectives the federal government seeks to promote.

The burden of a policy to promote rapid development of a particular region will fall approximately the same among regions, irrespective of whether our assumed tax change favoring consumption or that favoring investment is applied. The incidence will be different among income groups, however, depending on which of the two tax models is used. If we assume that development of the Northwest hydroelectric sites as federal undertakings would forestall reductions assumed in our tax model favorable to low-income groups and consumption, approximately 54 per cent of the total difference in cost would be borne by families with incomes under $5,000 annually, and only about 8 per cent by those in the income group exceeding $15,000 annually. On the other hand, if development of hydroelectric sites as federal ventures would forestall a reduction appropriate to our high-income, investment model, about 20 per cent of the total difference in costs would be borne by groups with income under $5,000 annually, and close to 38 per cent of the total difference by those in an income bracket exceeding $15,000 annually.

Under private development of Northwest hydroelectric sites the cost of power to customers would be greater than if the power were supplied through public development. If private development is undertaken with the aid of accelerated amortization privileges, the cost of power to customers is not decreased. Those who gain from such a policy are those who own shares of stock in the private utility. From the customer's viewpoint, there would be practically no advantages associated with private development of hydroelectric sites; the gains from rapid amortization privileges would go mainly to eastern investors in the private utilities, rather than to consumers of electricity through lower power charges.

To the extent that development of the Northwest is justified in terms of equity considerations—of assistance to the newer, relatively underdeveloped regions of the country because of the economic advantages enjoyed by the more wealthy, more fully developed regions—federal development of Northwest hydroelectric sites is consistent with this objective. Private development undertaken with the aid of accelerated amortization privileges is inconsistent with this objective, since it does not result in any more attractive power rates for developmental purposes than rates prevailing in the absence of accelerated amortization.

A public policy with one social objective in mind could result in an income redistribution in addition to, or as a side effect of, the explicit policy objective. In that case, there would be additional equity considerations for policy-makers to weigh. For example, if the industrialization of an underdeveloped region were to come principally at the expense of low-income groups in older, economically more advanced regions, the equity consideration underlying the economic development in the underdeveloped region may be compromised by the incidence of the burdens associated with the policy. In the case of private development of hydroelectric sites with the aid of accelerated amortization privileges, when the distribution of equity shares in these utilities is skewed toward the upper-income, investor classes and held predominantly in the older, financially more mature centers in eastern United States, neither the developmental nor equity objective is served.

As a final note, this study may serve to emphasize that it is difficult, if not impossible, to generalize as to what constitutes the most efficient approach to the development of water resources. Our conclusions have varied significantly, depending upon the specific conditions in the individual cases. Moreover, it is desirable to re-emphasize that an efficiency solution to a water resource development problem need not necessarily be the socially desirable solution; the latter depends on what weights attach to each of the separate issues within the larger policy context. Nevertheless, efficiency is a significant value in our society; in decisions regarding multiple purpose development, the public interest requires that efficiency considerations be given due weight.

Index

absolute group wants, 54

accounting costs, 141, 200; defined, 200n; differences in, 207-11

Ackerman, Edward A., vi

agriculture (*see also* farm prices): investment, financing of (1955), 82; sources of capital for, 83

Alabama-Coosa river system: congressional authorization for development of, 173; data, insufficiency of, 181-82, 181n, 197; equity considerations in, 192, 196; federal projects authorized for construction, 180n; and Hells Canyon case, comparison and summary of problems, 268-71; physical features of, 172; problems of interdependence, solutions of, 180; public interest in development of, 172;

Alabama Power Company (integrated) development plan, 175-81:

and Allatoona project, headwater benefits from, 180, 180n, 195-96;

controlled surcharge storage, provisions for, 177, 178, 182-83, 186;

economic efficiency of, 183, 196, 197-98;

factor inputs and project output, relation between, 192n;

flood control costs, recouping of, 192-96, 198;

flood control provisions, 177-78, 182-83;

as a multiple purpose development plan, 178-80, Fig., 179;

navigation locks, provision for, 178, 182;

and nonmarketable services, 184-85, 196;

Alabama-Coosa river system, *cont.*

Alabama Power Co. plan, *cont.*

total structures, 176-77, 191n-192n, Table, 177;

Corps of Engineers development plan, 172-75, Table, 174:

capital intensity of, 274;

evolution of, 185-87;

navigation locks, cost of, 182, 182n;

as not economically justified, 191, 192n;

storage for flood control, provisions, 186, 186n;

efficiency of alternative plans, compared, 181-92:

benefit-cost ratio, under federal development, 188;

benefit-cost ratio, under private development, 189;

cost, estimated, compared, 183, 183n;

costs and gains, incremental, under federal and private plans, 187;

data available for analysis, 182-83, Table, 184;

of federal development, alternate plans of, 187-88, 189-92, Tables, 188, 191;

federal and private plans, investment represented by, 191n-192n;

federal and private plans, paradox of different efficiencies under, 189-92;

generator capacity costs, compared, 192n;

installed generator capacity, compared, 183, 191n-192n;

private development, alternate plans of, 188-89, Table, 190;